THE KOREAS

A Global Studies Handbook

GLOBAL STUDIES: ASIA

THE KOREAS

A Global Studies Handbook

Mary E. Connor

A B C CLIO

Santa Barbara, California • Denver, Colorado • Oxford, England

Library of Congress Cataloging-in-Publication Data

Connor, Mary E.
    The Koreas : a global studies handbook / Mary E. Connor.
        p. cm. — (Global studies, Asia)
    ISBN 1-57607-277-0 (hardcover: alk.paper) —1-57607-728-4 (ebook)

    1. Korea (South) 2. Korea. I. Title. II. Series.
DS902 .C65 2002
951.9—dc21   2001008670

06 05 04 03 02   10 9 8 7 6 5 4 3 2

This book is also available on the World Wide Web as an e-book. Visit abc-clio.com for details.

ABC-CLIO, Inc.
130 Cremona Drive, P.O. Box 1911
Santa Barbara, California 93116-1911

This book is printed on acid-free paper.
Manufactured in the United States of America

For my husband, Gerry Fallon, and for America's Koreans

Contents

Series Editor's Foreword

It is imperative that as many Americans as possible develop a basic understanding of Asia. In an increasingly interconnected world, the fact that Asia contains almost 60 percent of all the planet's population is argument enough for increased knowledge of the continent on our parts. There are at least four other reasons, in addition to demography, that it is critical Americans become more familiar with Asia.

Americans of all ages, creeds, and colors are extensively involved economically with Asian countries. U.S.-Pacific two-way trade surpassed our trade with Europe in the 1970s. Japan, with the world's second largest economy, is also the second largest foreign investor in the United States.

American companies constitute the leading foreign investors in Japan.

The recent Asian economic crisis notwithstanding, since World War II East Asia has experienced the fastest rate of economic growth of all the world's regions. Recently, newly industrialized Southeast Asian countries such as Indonesia, Malaysia, and Thailand have joined the so-called Four Tigers, Hong Kong, the Republic of Korea, Singapore, and Taiwan, as leading areas for economic growth. In the past decade China has begun to realize its potential to be a world-influencing economic actor. Many Americans now depend upon Asians for their economic livelihoods and all of us consume products made in or by Asian companies.

It is impossible to be an informed American citizen without knowledge of Asia, a continent that directly impacts our national security.

America's war on terrorism is, as this foreword is composed, being conducted in an Asian country—Afghanistan. (What many Americans think of as the "Mideast" is, in actuality, Southwest Asia.) Both India and Pakistan now have nuclear weapons. The eventual reunification of the Korean Peninsula is fraught with the possibility of great promise or equally great peril. The question of U.S.-China relations is considered one of the world's major global geopolitical issues. Americans everywhere are affected by Asian political and military developments.

Asia and Asians have also become an important part of American culture.

Asian restaurants dot the American urban landscape. Buddhism is rapidly growing in the United States. Asian movies are becoming increasingly popular in the United States. Asian-Americans, while still a small percentage of the overall U.S. population, are one of the fastest growing ethnic groups in the United States. Many Asian-Americans exert considerable economic and political influence in this country. Asian sports, pop music, and cinema stars are becoming household names in America. Even Chinese language characters are becoming visible in the United States on everything from baseball caps to t-shirts to license plates. Followers of the ongoing debate on American educational reform will constantly encounter references to Asian student achievement.

Americans should also better understand Asia for its own sake. Anyone who considers themselves an educated person needs a basic understanding of Asia. The continent has a long, complex, and rich history. Asia is the birthplace of all the world's major religions including Christianity and Judaism.

Asian civilizations are some of the world's oldest. Asian arts and literature rank as some of humankind's most impressive achievements.

Our objectives in developing the Global Studies: Asia series are to assist a wide variety of citizens to both gain a basic understanding of Asian countries and to enable readers to be better positioned for more in-depth work. We envision the series being appropriate for libraries, educators, high school, introductory college and university students, business people, would-be tourists, and anyone who is curious about an Asian country or countries. Although there is some variation in the handbooks—the diversity of the countries requires slight variations in treatment—each volume includes narrative chapters on history and geography, economics, institutions, and society and contemporary issues. Readers should obtain a sound general understanding of the particular Asian country about which they read.

Each handbook also contains an extensive reference section. Since our guess is that many of the readers of this series will actually be traveling to Asia or interacting with Asians in this country, introductions to language, food, and etiquette are included. The reference section of each handbook also contains extensive information—including Web sites when relevant—about business and economic, cultural, educational, exchange, government, and tourist organizations. The reference sections conclude with capsule biographies of famous people, places, and events and a comprehensive annotated bibliography for further study.

—*Lucien Ellington*
Series Editor

Preface

The Koreas: A Global Studies Handbook is an attempt to meet the need for a general introduction to Korea with a focus on the economic, political, social, and cultural developments since the Korean War. What has been available is often too detailed for the general reader, especially the young. It is my hope that the book will serve those who are new to a study of Korea as well as those who have some knowledge of the nation's long and dramatic history; its distinctive culture; and the courage, perseverance, and accomplishments of its people. For those who wish to travel to Korea, the reference section, together with the narrative section, provides helpful information.

My intellectual odyssey with Korea began in 1993. By that time I had taught history (United States, European, and China and Japan) for twenty-two years on the secondary level. I had the good fortune to meet Dr. Jon Covell, Fulbright scholar, art historian, author of five books on Korea, and a woman whose passion for that culture was passed on to me. In one of our first conversations about Asia she said: "You know, Korea is the most interesting of the Asian cultures." I became captivated by Korea and incorporated its history and culture into my curriculum.

Since I began to discover more about Korea on my own, I have had the pleasure of communicating with many Koreans in the United States and abroad. Inevitably my passion for their country delights and at times amazes them. As a result of numerous speaking engagements and the publication of articles on teaching about Asia, I received a Korea Society Fellowship to study and travel in Korea. Since this fellowship, that country has become the center of my world. I am surprised that Americans know so little about it.

Many of the Koreans who migrated to the United States want to forget the hardships of the past and create a more secure life for their families. The word *han*, living with great and sustained sorrow, expresses the anguish that most Koreans lived with during the tumult of the twentieth century. From 1910 to 1945 the peninsula was under the harsh rule of the Japanese. Liberation came with the end of World War II, but the hopes of the indomitable Korean people were almost shattered by what followed: political division, occupation, and civil war. At the end of the war in 1953, Korea remained

Author at the demilitarized zone (DMZ), the area that divides the Korean peninsula into North and South Korea. Situated thirty miles northwest of Seoul, Panmunjom is the only location along the DMZ where visitors are permitted. (Courtesy of Mary Connor)

divided, heavily fortified, and occupied again, but this time by two rival superpowers: the United States and the Soviet Union. Both North and South were devastated by the war and ranked among the poorest nations of the world. After the U.S. Congress adopted the Immigration Act of 1965, it was possible for many Koreans to come to the United States. They decided to leave their homeland, fearing there might be yet another war.

In light of its turbulent history, strategic location, and the continual state of tension on the peninsula, Korea has often flashed across newspaper headlines and television screens during the past fifty years, only to disappear from view when the immediate crisis has passed. The periodic attention of the world means that few people in most countries have any historical context for understanding a particular event or its significance for the stability of East Asia. Since the attack on the World Trade Center and the Pentagon on September 11, 2001, Americans have suddenly become more interested in international affairs and our place in them.

Whether the reader of *The Koreas: A Global Studies Handbook* is a student, educator, businessperson, tourist, or someone who is simply curious, it will become clear just how closely involved the history of the United States is with that of Korea. The two nations have been linked since 1882 when Commodore Robert Shufeldt opened the country to the West by a treaty that was designed to enlarge trading opportunities. Although most people are aware that the United States provided the major support to defend South Korea when North Korea invaded in 1950, they are not aware that it has supplied more foreign aid to South Korea than to almost any other country. Thirty-seven thousand U.S. troops remain, and Korea is the most heavily fortified region in the world. Few people realize that while U.S. students demonstrated against the Vietnam War, three hundred thousand young South Koreans fought in it. In 1994 the United States almost went to war with North Korea because the CIA thought that North Korea had converted power-generating fuel rods at its nuclear reactor in Yongbyon to weapon-grade plutonium. Former president Jimmy Carter, as a private citizen, walked across the border with his wife, met with the leader of North Korea, and war was forestalled. In the twenty-first century the United States continues to be closely connected to Korea. The principal argument of President George W. Bush to develop a U.S. missile defense system is North Korea's nuclear weapons development program.

I have many people to thank for assisting me in writing this book. I am deeply grateful to Lucien Ellington, the series editor, for asking me to write *The Koreas* and for his encouragement along the way. My husband, Gerry Fallon, made the completion of this book a reality because of his patience, advice, encouragement, and invaluable computer assistance.

I wish to express gratitude to Yong Jin Choi and the Korea Society for my Summer Korean Studies Fellowship to study and travel in Korea. I also want to thank the Korea Foundation and the Freeman Foundation for providing the financial assistance that made this fellowship a reality. As I neared completion of the book, two staff members of the Korean Cultural Center in Los Angeles provided invaluable assistance. I wish to thank Richard McBride for his knowledge and expertise. He spent a considerable amount of time going through the entire manuscript and offering ideas to improve it. He also played a major role in developing the language section. Sejung Kim, the librarian, generously gave her time and provided me with resource materials, photographs, and encouragement. I am also very grateful to Occidental College for allowing me to use its library.

And finally, I should comment on the Korean spelling in this book. Our alphabet does not have sufficient symbols to translate the entire Korean sound system. It is not possible to convey the exact Korean pronunciation by means of the English alphabet. Different systems of romanization have been devised over the years; however, Western authors have preferred the McCune-Reischauer system that was adopted in 1984. For the most part, I have kept to this system.

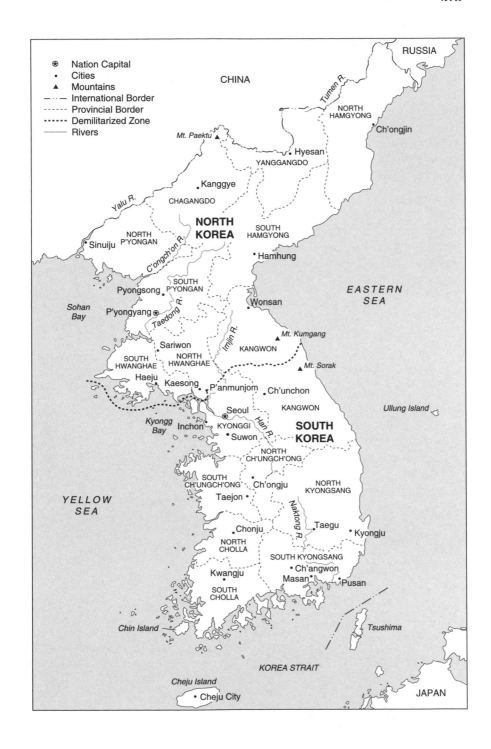

PART ONE
NARRATIVE SECTION

CHAPTER ONE
Geography and History

Korea is situated in the northeastern corner of Asia, bounded to the north by two giant neighbors: China and Russia. One hundred and twenty miles off the eastern coast lie the islands of Japan. Although Korea may appear small on a map of the Asian continent, the peninsula (85,563 square miles) is half the size of California and not much smaller than the combined areas of England, Scotland, and Wales. It is considerably smaller than Japan (145,370 square miles). The population is about 69 million, more than double that of California and less than half that of Japan. Since 1948, the land has been divided into the Republic of Korea (South Korea) and the Democratic People's Republic of Korea (North Korea).

In spite of powerful neighbors, major periods of foreign occupation (by China, Mongolia, Japan, and, after World War II, the United States and the Soviet Union), and division, the Koreans have remained a distinct people. They have an evident identity long preserved by geographic isolation and resistance, warfare and negotiation. In spite of the turbulent events of the twentieth century, which have included a thirty-five-year military occupation, one of the most brutal civil wars in history, and poverty ranking among the worst in the world, Koreans have not abandoned their traditional traits of warmth and generosity. Those who travel to South Korea often remark that the people are among the friendliest anywhere.

Notwithstanding the utter devastation of the Korean War, subsequent rapid economic growth was spectacular. Between 1953 and 1995, the Republic of Korea (ROK) progressed from being one of the poorest nations to becoming the world's eleventh largest economy, a development called the Miracle on the Han; however, it is the earthly, talented, and hardworking people who created the industrialized economy we see today. Another noteworthy advance since the 1980s has been the transformation from political instability and autocratic rule toward political tranquillity and democratization.

The communist regime of North Korea has also brought about many radical economic, social, and cultural changes but has continued to exercise totalitarian control for fifty years. In the process the

3

Democratic People's Republic of Korea (DPRK) has created a vastly different society than that of the South. The decline and eventual collapse of the Soviet Union and the world communist movement had a powerful impact on North Korea, as did the transition of China to what it calls a socialist market economy. The North rejected market reforms and sought to bargain its way out of difficulties with a nuclear weapons program and a buildup of conventional forces as its principal method of negotiation. Thus it has raised fears throughout the world about the dangers of nuclear warfare and has renewed political debate within the United States regarding national security.

These two distinct Koreas have recently grabbed the world's attention. In June 2000, leaders of North and South Korea met for the first time since the division in 1945. There is now hope to satisfy the yearning of the Korean people for resolution of their differences and for paving the way to reunification.

In the following pages, readers will be provided not only with a fundamental understanding of Korean geography and history but a clear sense of North and South Korea today and the ultimate place of a unified Korea in the world. It is hoped that this introduction will foster further inquiry into a most interesting culture.

THE PHYSICAL AND HUMAN GEOGRAPHY

This exquisitely beautiful land has four distinct seasons. Spring is warm and long, summer hot and humid, autumn cool, and winter cold. The weather in both parts of the peninsula is similar but colder and drier in northern winters. Summer brings the normal high temperature range between 80 and 90 degrees Fahrenheit for most of the country except the northern interior. Autumn, with its crisp air, blue sky, and glorious fall colors, is the season most widely loved.

Most of the country is mountainous; the eastern range is rugged and meets the ocean suddenly, making the eastern coast a very scenic one. Few peaks in the mountain range exceed 4,000 feet; however, the highest and most sacred place on the entire peninsula is Mount Paektu (9,000 feet), which straddles the Korean-Chinese border. For most of the land's history, the mountains and the sea have made it more difficult for invading armies to occupy the peninsula.

There are numerous small streams, long rivers, and flat, fertile plains. Only 22 percent of the land in South Korea is suitable for cultivation. In North Korea only 14 percent is arable. On the plains, green rice fields produce the bulk of the rice crop that feeds the

Rice fields near Kyongju, the ancient capital of the Silla kingdom (Courtesy of Mary Connor)

nation. The coastline is long compared to Korea's total land area because there is so much indentation. Approximately 3,400 islands lie off the coast. The largest of these is Cheju Island, with an area of 706 square miles.

With its north-south elongation, Korea separates the West Sea (the Yellow Sea) from the East Sea (the Sea of Japan). The land boundary between Korea and China is largely formed by two rivers: the Yalu River and the Tumen River, the last ten miles of which serve as a boundary with Russia. The peninsula, contiguous to China and Russia and adjacent to Japan by a short distance across the Korea Strait, has allowed Koreans to make contact with various civilizations. Thousands of years ago, the continental culture introduced Chinese characters, pottery, and Confucianism. These cultural influences were transformed and then transmitted to Japan.

The length of the peninsula is approximately 625 miles from the northern border to the southern tip. The area of the South, which is about the size of the state of Indiana, is smaller than that of the North (about the size of Mississippi). Considering its territorial size, the region has a relatively large number of rivers and streams. These waterways played crucial roles in shaping the people's way of life and the nation's industry. Cities such as Seoul and P'yongyang developed along major rivers as ports. With the arrival of railroads and automobiles, the importance of rivers declined. In the southern part of the peninsula, the Naktong and the Han are the two major waterways. The Han flows through Seoul, the capital of South Korea. The two longest rivers in North Korea are the Yalu and Tumen Rivers, which flow from Mount Paektu. Most rivers are used

extensively for irrigation. Because of the seasonal variations in precipitation, rivers are shallow most of the year except for the summer rainy season. This discrepancy gives rise to a great deal of variation in hydroelectric generation, as well as in water supply for
irrigation. Coastal and inland plains provide fertile farmland and
excellent locations for cities.

The Korean people, unlike Americans, are racially and linguisti-
cally homogeneous. Except for approximately 20,000 Chinese, no
sizable indigenous minorities exist. Although early cultural contacts
with China and Japan were extensive, the native population
remained conscious of ethnic differences and cultural distinctions.
Assimilation did not occur. Half a million Koreans live in Central
Asia, and two million more reside in the vast area of Manchuria. In
physical terms, they resemble the other peoples of Manchuria and
Mongolia. They have the almond-shaped eyes, black hair, and relatively high cheekbones. Like other Mongolians, babies are born with
blue spots on the lower part of their backs. Despite these similarities
to other Asian groups, Koreans have maintained their cultural as well
as ethnic identity.

According to U.S. State Department (July 2000) estimates, the
population of South Korea is 47.5 million and of North Korea 21.7
million. Birthrates are down in both nations. The annual growth rate
in the South is .93 percent with a life expectancy of 75 years. In the
North, the rate is an estimated 1.35 percent with a life expectancy of
70.74 years. Population density is much greater in the South, where
2 million people migrated following World War II.

During the transformation of a typical agricultural society into an
industrial one, significant migration from rural areas has occurred in
both North and South Korea. Neither territory now has an agrarian
sector larger than 27 percent of the population. Agriculture is 6 percent of the gross domestic product (GDP) of South Korea and 25 percent in the North. The South's urban population accounted for only
28 percent of the total in 1960. Today nearly 90 percent of the population lives in urban areas. Metropolitan growth and urbanization
have been most pronounced in the cities of Seoul and Pusan. In the
North 62 percent of the population lives in cities.

Employment opportunities, together with the best public and private institutions ranging from financial and commercial to educational and cultural entities, have led to the rapid growth of cities in
South Korea. This has led to the excessive concentration of people in
the capital, Seoul (11 million), and in the principal seaport, Pusan

(3.9 million), where people seem to live on top of each other. Other principal cities are Taegu, the center of the silk industry, Inch'on, the major port on the Yellow Sea, and Kyongju, the ancient capital. Air and water pollution in large cities is a significant problem.

In Seoul, high-rise apartment buildings are stacked close to each other and numbered in bold figures to simplify the process of locating a residence. Traffic jams and air pollution are inevitable; however, the subway system is efficient, inexpensive, and safe; and the streets are clean and free of litter.

The largest city in North Korea is the capital, P'yongyang, which has a population of approximately 2.7 million. It is described by some experts as one of the most efficient, best-run cities in Asia. The people live in modern high-rise buildings. The streets are clean and boulevards are lined with trees. Billboards with propaganda ("The respected father-comrade Kim Il Sung will live forever in the hearts of the people") appear everywhere. Air pollution is not a problem because of the reliance on hydroelectric power rather than fossil fuels, both for industry and the heating of urban residences. Pollution is also limited by the absence of private automobiles, restrictions on the use of gas-powered vehicles, and oil shortages. The lack of available consumer goods is evident. Smaller cities are not so pleasing to the eye with sterile buildings resembling Soviet proletarian architecture.

It is anticipated that further urbanization will continue in both Koreas, but that the rate will moderate. Public policy will be directed to balancing regional development. In South Korea the reduction of urban and rural disparities in socioeconomic conditions will be essential in alleviating the urbanization trend.

Most of the rural population in the South is involved with agriculture and lives in the lowlands of the western and southern coasts and along major river valleys. Clustered villages are common except in mountainous regions and on reclaimed land on the western coast. In these villages farming activities, such as transplanting rice from seabeds and harvesting and threshing rice, are often carried out through the cooperative efforts of the villagers. Principal agricultural products include rice, root crops, barley, vegetables, and fruit; pigs, chickens, milk, and eggs; and fish. Farm labor shortages have arisen primarily because of the excessive rural to urban migrations of young people.

South Korea was traditionally the peninsula's agricultural zone, and following the 1945 division of the country, the South was left with little industry and few resources but abundant manpower. Because of the rapid economic advances since the 1960s, the composition of the economy in terms of the GDP is 6 percent agriculture, 43 percent industry, and 51 percent services. Mining and manufacturing are major components of the economy. Leading industries are textiles, clothing, footwear, food processing, electronics, electrical equipment, shipbuilding, steel, motor vehicles, petrochemicals, and industrial machinery. Exports in 1999 were $143.7 billion.

In North Korea more than 90 percent of the command economy is socialized; agricultural land is collectivized. Farm villages are spartan, clean, and exemplify villages of the past. Principal agricultural products are rice, corn, potatoes, soybeans, pulse legumes, cattle, pigs, pork, and eggs. Farming is mechanized, but the country is not self-sufficient in food production. A shortage of arable land, several years of poor harvests, systemic inefficiencies, a cumbersome distribution system, and extensive floods in 1995 and 1996 followed by a severe drought in 1997 resulted in critical food shortages.

The partition of the Korean Peninsula after World War II left the North with most of the industry and abundant mineral resources but little agricultural land and few skilled workers. The country has succeeded in becoming industrialized and, up until recent years, overcame agricultural problems. State-owned industry produced 95 percent of the manufactured goods. Control of economic affairs is unusually tight even for a communist country because of the small size and homogeneity of the society and the strict rule of Kim Il Sung and his son, Kim Jong Il.

Some of the DPRK's major industries include military hardware, machine building, electric power, mining (coal, iron ore, magnetite, graphite, copper, zinc, lead, and precious metals), petrochemicals, steel, cement, textiles, and food processing. In recent years it has been a major exporter of military weapons. Military expenditures are estimated to be 25 percent of the GDP. The Soviet Union and China aided North Korea's development, but the theory of self-reliance was the government's guiding principle. It remains far behind South Korea in economic development and living standards. Estimated per capita income in the South is $8,581 and in the North $1,000.

Although much has changed on the peninsula in recent years, one thing that will never change is its geography. Korea sits at the vital center of Northeast Asia, one of the world's most strategically important and dynamic regions. What Koreans do in the years ahead will have an impact on their neighbors and on the international scene.

EARLY KOREA

Various tools from the Paleolithic Age uncovered in all parts of Korea indicate that human beings have inhabited the area for half a million years. It is not clear when their ancestors began to inhabit the peninsula, but most scholars agree that present-day Koreans are not the ethnic descendants of those Paleolithic people. Contemporary Koreans descended from Neolithic groups who entered the peninsula from areas north of Manchuria, probably in several successive migrations between 5500 and 2000 B.C.E.

The Koreans are Tungusic peoples, cousins of the Mongols, and their ethnic origin may be traced from those who lived in and around the Altaic Mountains in Central Asia. Some of the strongest evidence for this origin is the fact that modern Korean is part of the language family of northeast Asia called Altaic.

The early tribal peoples had a fishing, hunting, and gathering culture. They produced comb-pattern pottery similar to that found in northern Europe and Siberia and later, after the emergence of agriculture, built large aboveground tomb chambers of stone blocks, often mounded over with earth. Evidence of rectangular huts and burial sites in the form of dolmen and stone cysts is widespread. The early Koreans believed in animism and thought all natural objects had spirits. Artifacts were closely connected to their religious practices.

Their Bronze Age began about the ninth or eighth century and lasted until the fourth century B.C.E. People lived in dwellings of rectangular design in shallow pits on high ground above the flatlands where they grew their food. Agriculture during this age included rice cultivation. Clans came into contact, and advances in smelting bronze furnished powerful weapons for the conquest of different clans and contributed to the rise of larger units of tribal society and even walled towns. Early artwork in the form of wall paintings reflects strong influences of Siberian and Manchurian traditions. Korean bronze daggers spread to the island of Kyushu in Japan and greatly influenced the formation of the Japanese bronze culture.

Korea is one of the oldest countries in the world. The standard account of the origins of Ancient Choson is contained in the legend of the first great ruler, Tan'gun, who was born of a union between the son of the divine creator and a female bear that had achieved human form. Tan'gun made the walled city of P'yongyang the capital in 2333 B.C.E., called his country Choson (Land of the Morning Calm), and ruled for fifteen hundred years. No evidence has been found that supports whatever facts may lie beneath this myth, but over the centuries the legend has contributed to the Korean sense of identity as a distinct and proud race.

The walled-town state of Old Choson in time combined with others to form a single large confederation, the head of which came to be designated as its king. The use of iron hoes, plowshares, and sickles brought significant social changes. Food production increased, particularly benefiting the ruling elite. Artifacts from this period also include bronze and iron daggers and spears. Families still lived in pit dwellings, but the use of *ondol* devices (heating of flues under the floor) appeared.

Records indicate that the Chinese Han dynasty conquered Choson by 108 B.C.E. Although the new rulers allowed some political independence, the native population was forced to do whatever labor was demanded of them. Archaeological remains from this period reveal an absorption of cultural influences from the Han and a remarkable degree of refinement and luxury; most likely, the people eagerly cultivated the technological advancements and artistry that came with Han occupation. With the fall of that dynasty in 220 C.E., the military retreated, and the country was on its own. Despite a 300-year occupation, an ethnic identity persisted among the descendants of the Choson culture, in part because of geography and the radical difference between the Altaic and Chinese languages.

THE THREE KINGDOMS

With the end of Han dominance the Three Kingdoms gradually arose: Koguryo [pronounced ko-goo-rio] (37 B.C.E.–668 C.E.) in the north, Paekche [pronounced peck-chay] (18 B.C.E.–660 C.E.) in the southwest, and Silla [pronounced shil-la] (57 B.C.E.–935 C.E.) in the southeast. Each of the Three Kingdoms left records of the influence of Confucianism on government and society.

Throughout the lifetimes of the Three Kingdoms and afterwards Korea maintained a close relationship with China. The relationship was maintained through what was called tributary diplomacy, the formal recognition that China's power was superior. Tribute was a gesture of friendship and involved commercial trade and cultural exchanges. It did not mean that the Three Kingdoms were colonies of China.

The Koguryo tribes lived in the mountainous region north of the Yalu River and maintained an aristocratic society of mounted warriors who demanded tribute from surrounding agricultural peoples. During the fourth century C.E. Koguryo grew in strength and spread over the northern two-thirds of the peninsula. Meanwhile another centrally organized state, Paekche, appeared in the valley of the Han River. At the end of the fourth century an independent kingdom named Silla appeared. From the fourth to the second half of the seventh century C.E., most of the peninsula was divided among these three states. Each kingdom eagerly sought cultural innovations from China yet retained distinct cultural elements unique to it. The Three Kingdoms also engaged in continuous warfare with each other.

Koguryo's proximity to China promoted continuous new influences. In 372 C.E. a monk introduced Buddhism. Ultimately this religion became the spiritual foundation of the nation. About the same time a university was organized to teach the Confucian classics. Additional Chinese influences included a law code, a complex style of bureaucratic government, a tax system, and corvée labor (the obligation of a vassal to work without pay). The artistic skills of Koguryo people can be seen in royal tombs that contain some of the finest wall paintings of the fourth and fifth centuries. When Koguryo was defeated in the seventh century, it was incorporated into a state called Parhae in eastern Manchuria and northern Korea and rose to its zenith of power and cultural achievement in the early ninth century. Although Parhae is not considered one of the three early kingdoms, Koreans consider this state to be an integral part of their history.

Paekche, the second of the kingdoms, is not as well known in terms of its government and culture. Shortly after Buddhism was introduced to Koguryo, it arrived in Paekche through connections across the Yellow Sea. Beautiful tiles and other artifacts suggest that Chinese-style arts and crafts were becoming highly developed, but many objects, such as funerary urns, reveal characteristics that are unique to Korea. Several tombs of the kings of Paekche have been discovered, and artifacts demonstrate the impressive artistic ability and architectural skills of Paekche workers. In the sixth century Korea became a conduit for transmitting culture to Japan. The people of Paekche sailed to Japan and introduced Chinese characters, Buddhism, music, and art. A Kudaragi tree, planted by the Paekche Koreans, is still standing at the Horyu temple near Nara. The painted murals of the temple are attributed to a Koguryo monk. Long drum-shaped tombs are similar to Japanese tombs of the same time period.

The stone pagoda of the Punhwang Temple was built during the reign of Queen Sondak (r. 632–647) and is the only one surviving from the preunified Silla period. Originally the pagoda had nine stories but only three remain. (Courtesy of Mary Connor)

In the fourth century Paekche and Koguryo began nearly three centuries of war with one another.

Silla, the third native kingdom to emerge, was initially more backward, less influenced by Chinese culture, and its arts retained nomadic traditions. Silla ultimately became the longest dynasty in Korean history, lasting from 57 B.C.E. to 935 C.E. Silla is also noteworthy for the position that women held in government and society. Although Confucianism had started making inroads into Silla, its teaching of inequality between men and women does not seem to have had an impact. Two women occupied the throne of Silla and one occupied the throne of Unified Silla in the ninth century. However, they were the exceptions. They came to the throne because of their relatively strong social position.

In the kingdom's early years, the people of Silla had to struggle to survive against the threat of Paekche and Japanese land pirates from Kaya, a small kingdom in southern Korea. Their tribal and aristocratic social structure ultimately sustained them. By the sixth century the Chinese title *wang* (king) had been adopted, and Buddhism was accepted as the state religion. Identifying the king with the new religion worked to consolidate authority, but the aristocrats retained power in the government on the basis of hereditary bone ranks, meaning bloodline. The top bone ranks monopolized the bureaucracy. Bone ranks also conferred various privileges in everyday life including the size of the home, the color of dress, and the trappings of horses. The aristocracy also dominated the military. The *Hwarang* (Flowery Princes) were not peasant bands of warriors as in China, but the young sons of aristocrats who followed a very strict code of conduct combining Confucian doctrines (loyalty, filial piety, righteousness), Daoist ethics (patience, simplicity, contentment, and harmony), and Buddhist teachings of compassion.

Distinctive elements of Silla culture may be found in magnificent decorations, such as gold crowns, bracelets, and ear pendants, that have been found in the tombs of the royalty and nobility. All of these artifacts reveal a high level of artistry and testify to the wealth of the aristocracy. Earthenware technology was transmitted to Japan and became the basis for stoneware of the Japanese Kofun period. Ch'omsongdae, one of the oldest astronomical observatories in the world (constructed between 632 and 647 C.E.), can be seen today in Kyongju and attests to the ingenuity of these early ancestors.

The rise of the Tang dynasty during the seventh century gave Silla an opportunity to extend its kingdom. An alliance between Silla and the Tang dynasty was arranged, and their combined forces defeated both Paekche and Koguryo. The Tang had expected to conquer Silla as the Han dynasty had done; however, the defeated people of Koguryo and Paekche allied with Silla against the Tang forces, and Silla emerged as a unified state. In Kyongju are burial mounds of those who accomplished this great feat. Silla's unification in 668 C.E. did not include the entire peninsula, but this omission did not diminish the importance of its independence. Because Silla became independent from Tang political domination, the territory and people of Unified Silla were able to lay the groundwork for a long-lasting national culture. The historical significance of the unification of Silla cannot be overemphasized. Unified Silla laid the foundation for the historical development of the Korean people.

UNIFIED SILLA (668–935 C.E.)

Unified Silla survived for nearly three centuries and for a time, along with Tang China, was probably more advanced than any area of

Kwaenung Tomb, the tomb of King Wonsong of Unified Silla, is in the area of Kyongju. (Courtesy of Mary Connor)

Europe except for the Byzantine Empire. Freed from the worries of constant domestic conflicts and external invasions, it achieved rapid development in the arts, religion, commerce, education, printing techniques, and other fields. Trade with Tang China and Japan flourished. In fact, Silla ships came to dominate the maritime lanes in East Asia. The government was a powerful state system under a single monarch. Educational institutions were well established and technology highly advanced. Present-day Kyongju, then the capital of Silla, became the center of learning and creativity and grew into a large city with approximately 1 million people.

Monks traveled to China and India to study Mahayana Buddhism and Son (Zen), which at that time had more appeal than Confucianism. Chinese political institutions did influence the development of government; however, hereditary bone rank continued to determine government positions. Slavery was prevalent and contributed significantly to the growing affluence of the hereditary aristocracy.

Travelers today still witness the achievements of the golden age of Silla. The craftsmanship and aesthetics of that period are thought to surpass all others throughout the whole of Korean history. The objective of the artisans was to create a beauty of idealized harmony combined with refined artistic craftsmanship. Massive stone pagodas may be found throughout the South. Unlike Chinese and Japanese pagodas, which were built with bricks or wood, Silla's stone pagodas reveal incomparable technical superiority and harmonious beauty. Buddhist statues are considered as fine as those produced in Tang China. The famed Pulguk temple near Kyongju stands as a monument to Silla's ability to create a sense of harmony through superior artistry. The great Buddhist images of the Pulguk-sa and the large stone Buddha and bas-reliefs of the Sokkuram grotto convey a sense of spirituality even for the non-Buddhist and are among the finest works of Buddhist art in the Tang style. The Emille Bell, beautifully resonant and exquisitely wrought, is the largest surviving bronze bell and is exhibited at the National Museum in Kyongju.

As religion and scholarship advanced, printing techniques were improved to print Buddhist and Confucian texts. When the Sakyamuni Pagoda (completed in 751 C.E.) from Pulguk-sa was dismantled in 1966 for repairs, the *Pure Light Dharani Sutra* and seventy cultural relics were found in the pagoda. One of the texts is regarded as the oldest text printed with wooden blocks in the world.

One limitation on cultural development in Silla, as in early Japan, was the lack of a writing system suitable for transcribing the native language. Since Chinese characters were the only writing the early Koreans and Japanese knew, they were forced to write in an alien language. A method and set of rules were developed to represent a word either with a Chinese character having its sound or with one sharing its meaning. What developed was a full-fledged writing system called *idu,* and later, a more sophisticated system called *hyangch'al* was developed.

Silla began to decline by the middle of the eighth century. Wealthy families challenged one another, the bone ranks system brought little unity, and the youthful Hwarang warriors degenerated. The borrowed Chinese political institutions had not evolved into a government based on merit and so became increasingly costly and inefficient. After the king was assassinated in 780, political turmoil was chronic, and succession by violent means was the norm for the next 150 years. By the end of the ninth century peasant uprisings swept the country. In 918 General Wang Kon seized control, moved the capital to Kaesong, and reunified Korea. Kyongju faded into obscurity. Not until the twentieth century were the magnificent achievements of Unified Silla rediscovered. If the treasures of Kyongju had been known over the centuries, they most likely would have been stolen, destroyed, and lost forever.

THE KORYO DYNASTY (918–1392)

Early Koryo

In 918 General Wang Kon founded a new unified dynasty that was to last over four and one half centuries. He named it Koryo, an abbreviation of Koguryo and the origin of the name Korea. Wang Kon implemented a policy of northern expansion, abolished the bone rank system, and put in place a Chinese form of centralized government. Kaesong (located north of the mouth of the Han River) became the national capital. Wang Kon showed his diplomatic skills by treating his conquered subjects with compassion; he gave the former Silla king an important government position and large landholdings. He also married a woman from the Silla royal family and gave other grants of land to Silla and Paekche officials who pledged loyalty to him. The nobility became part of the Koryo bureaucracy; consequently, a tradition of aristocratic continuity was established that would continue to be part of the Korean political tradition into the twentieth century.

The Koryo state incorporated elements of Confucianism. In 958 a civil service exam was set up on the Chinese model, schools were opened to teach the Confucian texts, and the central army was made powerful and permanent. Regional capitals were established in P'yongyang, Kyongju, and Seoul. By the eleventh century, in spite of threats from Khitan armies to the north, Koryo had established a unified government over the entire peninsula to the boundary of the Yalu River.

In spite of the adoption of the Confucian political ideals, Koryo deference to aristocrats created a significant departure from Confucianism. Few commoners had opportunities in the government because of class prejudices and petty restrictions. The sons of high aristocrats could hold important posts without taking the qualifying examinations. Military officers advanced by reason of family ancestry. Nobles received their own tax-free lands from the government in accordance with their rank; consequently, the tax base to support the government was reduced. The nobility chose not to live on their estates, left them in the hands of local aristocrats, and congregated in Kaesong. Most people were commoners or base people: slaves, government workers, specialized artisans (such as those in porcelain factories), and peasants. The merchant class virtually disappeared. Most of the national wealth was located in the capital in the hands of the royal court and the aristocracy.

Buddhism, at its height in the tenth and eleventh century in Koryo, played a major role in social life and acted as a principal force in cultural achievements. Since it was believed that personal and national well-being could be assured through faith and pious acts, hundreds of temples throughout Korea, and over fifty in the capital alone, were constructed. Many royal princes and aristocrats entered the clergy. Monasteries were exempted from taxes, grew affluent by sizable contributions from the wealthy, held large estates, and some even conducted banking practices. Sons of the elite entered the clergy. Buddhist teachers served as advisors to government officials. One of the greatest achievements was the publication of the entire Buddhist Tripitaka on woodblocks in 1087. These were later destroyed by the Mongols; however, 81,000 new blocks were completed in 1251 and can be seen at Haein-sa, one of Korea's most beautiful temples. These wood-block carvings are the finest examples of some twenty Tripitaka carvings created in East Asia. By 1234, if not earlier, Koryo had also invented movable metal type, two centuries before Gutenberg. Koryo's use of this printing method is the earliest in the history of the world.

The Buddhist art of the Koryo matched the artistic excellence of Silla, but landscape painting and porcelain became increasingly important. Celadons with delicate colors (especially jade green), graceful curves, elegant shapes, and exquisite inlaid designs of flowers or animals rank among the finest accomplishments in earthenware in the world and are considered the crowning glory of Koryo's artistic achievements.

Koryo made notable literary accomplishments during this period. A private Confucian school was founded in 1055, and Kim Pusik, a great scholar-statesman, compiled in 1145 the *History of the Three Kingdoms,* the oldest surviving history of Korea. A great concern was the establishment of libraries, the acquisition of books, and book duplication by a wood-block technique. Chinese music, as well as traditional Korean music (*hyangak*), flourished. The former was employed in Confucian ceremonies, the latter continued to be the music of the people. Many new instruments were either imported or invented. The hourglass-shaped drum, the *changgo,* became the most popular instrument in Korea.

Later Koryo

Centralized rule, which had been patterned after China, began to show signs of decay in the second half of the eleventh century. Weak

The Tongsipcha-gak (East Cross Tower) is a watchtower in Seoul built at the place where the outer wall of Kyongbok-kung (Kyongbok Palace) bends northward to the East Palace Gate. Kyongbok-kung, built in 1394–1395, was burned down during the Hideyoshi invasions (1592–1598). It is not known exactly how much was actually destroyed, but it was rebuilt in 1868 by Taewon'gun, King Kojong's father. (Courtesy of Mary Connor)

kings, aristocratic access to government taxes, incessant conflicts among noble families, military coups, peasant rebellions, and slave uprisings contributed to instability. Aristocrats held to the principle that civilian rulers were superior to the military; so officers experienced political and economic hardships. In 1196 an officer, Ch'oe Ch'unghon, rose to power, killed those who challenged his authority, established dictatorial rule, and brought stability for over half a century. This military rule brought a new landed elite to the top and an end to the hereditary status system. Most likely the presence of Mongolian and Manchurian armies to the north meant that a centralized force was needed for protection.

In the early thirteenth century Genghis Khan, whose genius for leadership and power had united the normally independent Mongol tribes, was about to conquer half the known world. In 1215 he captured Peking, and the rulers of northern China were defeated. In 1231 the Mongols with vastly superior forces invaded the peninsula, seized the capital of Kaesong, and demanded a huge tribute. Peasants and the lowborn classes resisted and were mercilessly slaughtered. Over 200,000 people were taken captive, countless people were left dead, and an entire region was reduced to ashes because the invaders torched the fields. Kings were forced to marry Mongolian princesses, the governmental structure was changed to signify subservience, and military garrisons and officials were stationed all over the peninsula. By 1271 the military leadership surrendered and was forced to accept Yuan suzerainty. The peasants were burdened with the responsibility of tribute obligations, and many were forced to build ships and furnish supplies for Mongolian expeditions against Japan. Tribute included gold, silver, horses, ginseng, hawks, artisans, women, and eunuchs. Intolerable suffering left deep scars. The royal family maintained a relatively powerless facade under the direct control of the Yuan.

Because of the vastness of the Mongolian Empire, Korea was now more open to cultural and technological influences. The cotton plant was introduced and replaced hemp, which led to a marked improvement in clothing. Other innovations included a calendar, gunpowder, and astronomical and mathematical knowledge.

The firm hand of the Mongols served to sustain the Koryo dynasty for about a century, but beneath the surface the foundations of government were crumbling. Farmland continued to flow from public domain to the estates of the nobility. Large numbers of formerly tax-paying commoners were reduced to slaves. Extended periods of invasions, repeated attacks by Japanese pirates, and reduced financial support led to increased reliance on Mongol power. As internal dissension and paralysis of Mongol leaders spread in the fourteenth century, Koryo attempted to reassert control; but rival factions supporting the Mongols and the Ming dynasty emerged. General Yi Songgye, ordered to support a mobilization against a Ming invasion, thought the plan unwise and resisted because he did not believe the smaller kingdom could hold out against the much larger force. Yi and his army attacked the capital instead. Seizing the throne in 1392, he brought the 474-year Koryo dynasty to an end.

THE CHOSON DYNASTY (1392–1910)

The Early Period: 1392 to the Seventeenth Century

Yi Songgye (more commonly called T'aejo r.1392–1398) founded Korea's longest dynasty, which lasted until this century. The new kingdom was renamed Choson. The capital was moved from Kaesong to Seoul, which became the political, economic, and cultural center of Korea and has remained so ever since. To protect the new capital, T'aejo ordered the construction of a great ten-mile wall with massive gates, parts of which remains today. The Namdaemun Gate, once Seoul's principal city gate, continues to be very impressive although surrounded by tall office buildings and vehicular congestion.

T'aejo continued the traditional relationship with China. At least four missions per year visited the Chinese capital. The purpose of each mission was political, but the missions also allowed for cultural borrowing and economic exchange. Articles exported included horses, ginseng, furs, and ramie cloth. In return, Korea received silk, medicines, books, and porcelain. During the next five centuries Korea gave virtually unquestioned loyalty to Chinese political institutions and readily accepted cultural influences.

In spite of the fact that T'aejo was a devout Buddhist, he directed the dynasty to adopt neo-Confucianism. Although Confucianism had influenced Korea for centuries, the new approach was to create an ideal society in harmony with the particular attitudes and concerns of the Choson dynasty. The establishment of Confucian schools became a high priority. For the first 150 years Choson experienced peace and prosperity under the guidance of enlightened kings. T'aejo and his successors built a strong foundation for the dynasty; they restructured society through the bureaucracy, strengthened national defense, and promoted the economy and culture of the kingdom. National boundaries were established along the Yalu and Tumen Rivers.

T'aejo's son, T'aejong (r.1400–1418), dedicated himself to the completion of reforms that had begun under his father's rule.

Courtyard and pond at the Ch'angdok-kung (palace) in Seoul. In 1405 King T'aejong, the third ruler of the Choson dynasty, built the palace to serve as a royal villa. After 1615 the seat of the government was moved to this location, and kings ruled Korea from this palace for about 300 years. (Courtesy of Mary Connor)

Sejong (r.1418–1450) became Korea's greatest monarch by bringing stability and prosperity to his nation. In addition to mastering Confucian learning, he was able to successfully negotiate with the *yangban* (office-holding aristocrats) scholars. His rule was known for progressive government, a phonetic script, economic development, scientific discovery, and technological innovation. He showed great concern for the peasants, providing tax reform and relief in times of drought and flood. Scholars were instructed to draw upon the knowledge of elderly peasants to publish a book on agriculture; this book became the classic book on Korean agriculture.

During the Choson dynasty Korea became a model Confucian society and emphasized the importance of education, social stability, filial piety, and good government based on a hierarchical social order of the elite selected through competitive civil service examinations. Another dimension of neo-Confucian principles related to male and female relationships. Women were raised to understand that they were inferior and should be submissive to men at all times; they should be obedient to their fathers, then later to their husbands and

Traditional thatch cottages (Hahoe Folk Village). The Korean people lived in thatched cottages for centuries. Hahoe is a genuine folk village with roots that can be traced back over 600 years. (Courtesy of Mary Connor)

in-laws, and when widowed, to their sons. These ideas combined the practice of ancestor worship with the custom of the eldest male becoming spiritual head of the family.

Neo-Confucianism had a strong impact. Prior to this time, Buddhist and Confucian beliefs had coexisted, but now there were restrictions against the practice of Buddhism and limitations on the number of monasteries. Neo-Confucianism condemned the reclusive lives of Buddhist monks and rejected the Daoist search for immortality. Although individuals other than the yangban were allowed to sit for civil service examinations, the hereditary elite continued to serve as the majority of the high officials in government. A scholar during the time of King Sejong formulated the idea that rulers had a mandate from heaven as in China. Ethical conduct was essential for preserving their rule. Bad conduct destroyed the right to rule, and the overthrow of a government was justified. This notion predated John Locke's theory of the right of revolution by three hundred years.

The influence of Confucianism contributed to the stability of society and perpetuated for centuries the continuation of a very rigid class structure. Of the total population, 10 percent was of the yangban class, the upper-class landowners whose goal was education in the Confucian classics and government or military service. They married within their class and lived apart from the rest of society. Over 50 percent of the population was known as *yangmin* (good people). They were the farmers, merchants, fishermen, and craftsmen. The next class was the *chonmin* (the lowborn). These people belonged to certain disdained hereditary professions, such as butchery, or were shamans, entertainers, or slaves. It is estimated that more than one-third of the population was enslaved in a system that existed into the twentieth century.

Confucianism also influenced the growth of the Chinese examination system that had been used during the Koryo dynasty, but in the Choson dynasty it was the principal means of attaining high government office. Most villages started their own schools to prepare young men for the challenges of a classical education. Examinations for the military paralleled those for government. This system produced officials based on academic achievement as opposed to social status, military success, or wealth and made professional service the most certain route to acquisition of wealth. This system initially produced an effective bureaucracy; however, in time it too deteriorated and finally ended with the overthrow of the Choson dynasty by the Japanese in 1910.

Confucianism also had an impact on economic development. Its beliefs helped to perpetuate a static agrarian society and promoted contempt for the development of commerce, an activity seen as self-serving and socially divisive. A road system was maintained, but trade within the country and with the outside world (except for China and Japan) remained limited. In spite of the continuous flow of goods and ideas from China, Korea remained culturally distinct. In social structure, economic development, character traits, language, homes, dress, and food, it was in no danger of being culturally absorbed. Items exported to Japan included rice, cotton, hemp and ramie cloth, and porcelain ware. The Buddhist Tripitaka, Confucian writings, histories, temple bells, and Buddhist images were also exported to Japan. In exchange the Japanese exported minerals not available in Korea and luxury items for the yangban class.

Despite the conservative tendencies of Confucianism, there were significant technological advances in early Choson. A rain gauge was invented in 1442, and accurate records of precipitation were maintained some two hundred years before Europe began such practices. Movable type was more prevalent in Korea in the fifteenth century than any other place in the world. King Sejong and the Academy of Scholars made one of the greatest cultural innovations: a writing system. Known today as *han'gul,* it allowed people to write in characters appropriate to their spoken language. The educated classes preferred Chinese characters and continued using them in important documents. Women and the lower class used han'gul. It was not until the end of Japanese occupation that han'gul was in wide use. Today it is considered to be the most scientific system of writing in the world.

The influence of Confucianism may also be seen in the arts. Chinese-style landscapes, shrines, and Chinese music were characteristic of Choson. Enormous palaces, such as the Ch'angdok-kung in Seoul, were constructed and reflected the ambition of kings. In Seoul today one can see a few buildings that were part of the palace built by the first Choson king. During this dynasty green celadons gave way to white porcelain, and brown ware appeared in the sixteenth century.

Despite the influence of the early enlightened monarchs, there were signs of difficulties that ultimately weakened the Choson dynasty. Although the government closely resembled a Confucian state, the kings had limited power and for the most part were not highly respected by the yangban. To garner their support, the monarchs doled out generous grants of nontaxable land. For the peasants this meant increasingly burdensome taxes. Since yangban were forbidden to participate in trade, their principal objective was to serve in the bureaucracy. Extreme competition for government posts led to the growth of hereditary groupings where they could no longer marry or associate with rival families. Geographic rivalries between yangban resulted in systematic purges of hundreds of officials, even executions. Feuds among the nobility had existed in China for hundreds of years, but it was a much greater problem in Korea, probably because its kings did not have the power of a Chinese emperor.

As these intense factions were growing, Toyotomi Hideyoshi was crushing his rivals and reunifying Japan. In 1592 he launched an invasion against Korea in what was to be a step toward challenging the Ming dynasty and creating an empire. Because the Choson dynasty had been relatively free from foreign threats and the yangban aristocrats were accustomed to peace, they were ill prepared for a major invasion. Within a month the Japanese captured Seoul and nearly the entire peninsula. However, Admiral Yi Sunsin rescued the nation. For a year he had strengthened his naval forces, building warships and training the crews. He constructed turtle boats with a protective covering (probably the first use of iron plate) to ward off enemy arrows and shells. Spikes and canons were placed around each ship. With the assistance of these formidable warships, Admiral

Replica of Admiral Sunsin's turtle boat, Korean War Museum, Seoul (Courtesy of Mary Connor)

Yi stopped Japanese advances and severed connections to their supply routes. Meanwhile, yangban, peasant farmers, and slaves united into guerrilla armies, and Ming forces arrived to support their tributary state. Peace negotiations were then attempted but failed. The Japanese launched another attack in 1597, but Admiral Yi and his fleet won a resounding victory. Before the year was over, Hideyoshi died and the Japanese completely withdrew.

This invasion has been emphasized in Korean literature and still contributes to bitterness against the Japanese. The invasion was disastrous. Nearly all the provinces suffered pillage and slaughter. The population decreased, and famine and disease became widespread. Buildings, works of art, and historical records were destroyed by fire. The government was weakened, agricultural production decreased, and the tax yield declined enormously.

Korea had barely recovered from the invasions when the Manchus invaded from the north, seized land, and overthrew the Ming dynasty. Generally, this invasion was less destructive than those of the Japanese, except for the northwest where the Manchu forces wrought almost total devastation. In 1637 Choson was forced to accept the suzerainty of the newly formed Qing. The Koreans considered the Manchus to be barbarians, and for China to be ruled by them seemed the end of civilization. Hostility toward the Qing, as with the Japanese, lasted for a long time.

A Nation in Transition: The Seventeenth, Eighteenth, and Nineteenth Centuries

The invasions by the Japanese and the Manchus were a turning point in Korean history. Devastated by what the outside world had wrought, monarchs adopted a policy of isolation. They remained weak, and the government lacked sufficient funding. To alleviate some of its financial difficulties, the government minted more coins. Tax reforms were also implemented. Upward social mobility, almost unknown before the war, began to take place. To raise revenue, the government allowed rich peasants and merchants to acquire yangban status by buying it; meanwhile, many of the original yangban lost their lands, status, and political power.

Although the economy remained essentially agricultural, a mercantile economy was beginning to develop, and it significantly influenced the class structure. In the past the government had restricted trade; now merchants were freer from government restrictions and began to be more active within and outside the country. This growth of wealth now brought status to a class of people that had been previously treated with disdain and, at the same time, contributed to the decline of the yangban. Over time some merchants in urban areas amassed fortunes through the control of trade and handcraft pro-

Monument to Hendrick Hamel, Cheju Island, South Korea. In 1653 a Dutch ship was wrecked near Cheju Island on the southwestern coast. Hamel and his crew were rescued but held as spies for thirteen years. He escaped, returned to Holland, and published the first book on Korea in 1668, thereby introducing the country to Europe. (Courtesy of Mary Connor)

duction, while many small merchants became bankrupt. In rural areas some peasants became rich; many poor peasants had to give up their farms and became part of a growing number of landless vagrants. Social distinctions also began to fade between commoners and slaves. Many slaves received freedom in exchange for military service or simply bought their own freedom.

In spite of a policy of isolation, outside forces continued to have a significant impact. Koreans on tribute missions made contact with Jesuit scholars and brought back books on new scientific discoveries, maps, telescopes, and alarm clocks. Around the same time, a Dutch ship was wrecked near Cheju Island. Though the sailors were rescued, the Dutchmen were held as spies for an extended period of time. One of them, Henrick Hamel, escaped and returned to Holland to write a book on Korea. Because of these contacts with foreigners, Koreans began to have greater curiosity about the West, and Europeans acquired some knowledge about Korea.

Prior to the seventeenth century, a group of Confucian scholars suggested reforms and started the *Sirhak* (Practical Learning) Movement. They rejected neo-Confucianism and recommended practical solutions to the problems of their time. Because of the dramatic influences of Western science and Chinese scholarship, these scholars continued to explore ways to resolve problems of the common people through land reform and promotion of social equality. The Japanese invasions and antagonism against the Qing dynasty ultimately fueled revolutionary ideas of cultural and political independence from China. The Sirhak movement, which also promoted revolutionary ideas of the rights of man and social equality, continued to grow during the eighteenth and early nineteenth centuries and contributed to the publication of books on political, economic, health, and educational reform. The movement also influenced the growth of historical writing, fiction, poetry, and genre painting. The greatest change in the field of literature came with the great number of works written in han'gul. Ultimately the spirit of the Sirhak movement was to play a significant role in the reform movements of the late nineteenth century.

After the yangban became weak, a popular folk culture grew rapidly. Greater realism and individualism were evident in the arts. Genre painting of ordinary events of everyday life became very popular. Folk music, including songs, dance, and mask plays, was performed. Shamanist beliefs were also evident in the musical and dramatic performances. A new form of dramatic narrative music (*p'ansori*) and musical drama (*changguk*) developed, enriching the lives of the Korean people.

Catholicism ultimately became a major force for change. When contacts were initially made with Jesuit missionaries in the early seventeenth century, Catholicism (known as *Western Learning*) had little impact. When a Sirhak scholar was baptized by a Catholic priest in Peking, the number of converts began to increase. What attracted many to Catholicism was the belief in the equality of the children of God. For women in particular, Catholicism had great appeal. When the government learned that Christianity disagreed with Confucian tenets, such as ancestor worship, persecutions and executions followed; however, missionaries continued to spread their religion. The anti-Catholic policy was relaxed in 1849 but resumed in the 1860s with a vengeance and made Christian martyrs out of approximately 8,000 people, including several missionaries.

In the 1860s a new religion was established in reaction to Catholicism, government corruption, social injustice, and peasant poverty. It was called *Tonghak* (Eastern Learning). Frequent natural calamities were contributing factors to this movement: floods, famine, and epidemics occurred repeatedly and engendered major peasant uprisings. Ch'oe Cheu, the founder of Tonghak, combined concepts from Daoism, Buddhism, neo-Confucianism, Catholicism, and Shamanism. Ch'oe also advocated political, social, and economic reforms to alleviate the suffering of the poor. Throughout the land, desperate peasants fell under his influence. Alarmed by Tonghak's growing popularity, the government decapitated its founder in 1864 on charges of subversion. Nevertheless, the movement continued to grow under the leadership of Ch'oe's successor.

In spite of these intellectual, social, and economic developments, the government resisted desperately needed reforms because powerful yangban officials feared change. National policy served their interests, not the welfare of the people. Their policies were doomed to fail. Yet the dynasty managed to remain in power until even greater challenges, the threat of Japan and Western nations, emerged in the late nineteenth and early twentieth centuries.

THE OPENING OF KOREA, ATTEMPTS AT REFORM, AND NATIONAL PERIL

The Korean people encountered additional problems in the nineteenth century as a result of the industrialization, nationalism, and imperialism of major world powers. Western nations, such as Great Britain, France, Russia, and the United States, and a modernized Japan actively pursued policies enacted to secure wealth in Asian markets.

The West referred to Korea as the "hermit kingdom" because it had for centuries essentially rejected all outside contact. Rejection of the West had been based on a general disdain for foreigners combined with the belief that Confucianism was the only valid belief; thus any civilization that thought differently should be kept out. Relations with the Western barbarians would mean abandonment of those values upon which all of civilization rested. Until the nineteenth century, foreign relations consisted of an annual tribute mission to Peking and limited contact with Japan. In the nineteenth century the West and Japan forced Korea to end its long entrenched policies of isolation. Once opened to the world, it encountered a variety of challenges: exploitation, war, and the potential loss of national sovereignty.

During the late nineteenth century, European nations and the United States made continuous demands for commercial ties. Ernest Oppert, a German and naturalized U.S. citizen, tried twice on his own to open trade with Korea but was refused. The French, in retaliation for the executions of French priests in 1866, invaded and had a brief war on Kanghwa Island. In 1871, in response to the threats from foreign powers, the staunchly isolationist Taewon'gun, regent to the future King Kojong, declared that the official policy was one of isolation; however, Japan became decidedly more warlike and aggressive. In 1876 Japanese warships invaded and demanded diplomatic and commercial relations. The Japanese said that if Korea refused, there would be war. Forced by what is now known as gunboat diplomacy, the government signed the Kanghwa Treaty, the first unequal treaty with an imperialist power. Within it was a clause that said Korea was a sovereign nation, paving the way for Japanese aggression without interference from China. Additional provisions opened ports with the stipulation that Japanese residents would be subject to Japanese laws in Japanese courts, business and trade would be conducted without interference, and business in the ports would take place under extraterritorial privileges. Korea gained no such privileges in Japan.

In 1866 an American ship, the *General Sherman,* sailed boldly up the Taedong River to P'yongyang to force the government to accept commercial relations with the United States. When told that any foreign commerce was a violation of the law, the *General Sherman* continued up the river. When a hostile crowd gathered, the frightened crew fired their muskets. Local residents and soldiers set the ship afire and killed all twenty-four crew members on board. As a result of this incident U.S. Secretary of State William Seward decided to punish the Koreans and to open their ports by force. When five U.S. warships entered Korean waters, they were met by canons and newly strengthened fortifications. U.S. Marines were able to capture some forts, but the government refused to negotiate.

In 1873 King Kojong decided to deal more effectively with the outside world by promoting reforms in foreign trade, arms production, and foreign-language education. He pursued a more open and flexible foreign policy than his regent Taewon'gun had followed. His hope was to establish diplomatic ties with the United States, a potential ally in helping fend off growing threats from Japan and Russia. Officials in China, now believing that Korea needed to end its policies of seclusion to survive, offered to mediate a treaty between the United States and Korea. Consequently, in 1882 Commodore Robert Shufeldt of the United States signed the Korean-American Treaty of Amity and Commerce in Inch'on. The treaty gave extraterritorial rights to U.S. citizens, fixed tariffs, and established port concessions and consular representation. When the terms of the treaty were explained to King Kojong, he was led to believe that the United States would guarantee the country's sovereign independence. This treaty was followed by similar agreements with Britain, Germany, Italy, Russia, France, and Austria-Hungary. All treaties were unequal in that they favored Western interests over national ones.

After the conclusion of these treaties, the government of Korea sent missions to Japan and the United States to learn more about these countries and to promote friendly relations. When the members returned, they brought back progressive ideas: modernization of the government, economic development, educational reform, social equality, and independence from China. Despite the efforts of these would-be reformers, conservatives in government allowed only a few revisions, such as improved military training, the opening of a palace school staffed with American teachers, and the establishment of modern farming and a modern postal system.

With the influx of Protestant missionaries, Christianity spread and modern schools were established. In 1885 Presbyterians established a school for boys, and a year later, Methodists established the first modern school for girls. Protestant missionaries also established hospitals and gave lectures on agriculture, commerce, and industry. Their teachings fostered concepts of freedom and equality. In the late nineteenth century nationalists also established schools, one of which is now Korea University.

Although King Kojong promoted reforms to strengthen the nation, he was weak-willed and easily manipulated by his wife, Queen Min. The queen, together with conservative Confucian officials, saw potential political threats in reform. In 1882 the Chinese sent troops to Korea and crushed an anti-queen movement planned by progressives and the former regent, Taewon'gun. The Chinese put Queen Min in charge, and thousands of Chinese troops were now stationed in Seoul. Two years later the queen was overthrown in a successful, but short-lived, coup supported by the Japanese. Within a few days, 1,500 Chinese soldiers overwhelmed a small contingent of Japanese troops. The coup leaders fled for their lives to Japan. Queen Min was again in charge with her conservative pro-Chinese supporters. Hopes for a modernized, independent Korea vanished.

In addition to severe domestic problems, Korea became increasingly the center of rivalry among England, Russia, China, and Japan. The monarchy began to lean toward an anti-Qing, pro-Russian policy to curtail Chinese and Japanese involvement in Korea. As Russia advanced toward the Korean peninsula, Britain took over a strategic Korean island without the consent of the government. As rival powers positioned themselves around Korea, the conniving Queen Min and her supporters took more and more control over a government that was infamous for its incompetence, corruption, and debauchery. The Japanese began to take greater interest in the Korean rice and soybean market to meet the demands of the rapid growth of Japan's population. At the same time Japan increased its position in Korea's foreign trade and monopolized business in many port cities and elsewhere. Because of the challenges within and outside Korea, popular uprisings against the Min government began to break out in the 1890s, and banditry was everywhere.

THE TONGHAK STRUGGLE, WAR, AND THE KABO REFORMS

Although Tonghak, or Eastern Learning, was a religious movement, it did respond to governmental corruption, foreign exploitation, and the desperate conditions of the peasants. Massive demonstrations took place in 1892 and 1893. In 1894, Chon Pongjun, the leader of Tonghak, galvanized public discontent and ultimately began the largest peasant insurrection in Korean history. When initial protests led nowhere, the peasants resorted to violence. The government responded with mass executions. After another uprising, the Tonghak army defeated government forces. Meanwhile, King Kojong appealed to China to put down the rebellions. These uprisings now allowed Japan an opportunity to further involve itself in the national affairs of Korea.

In the summer of 1894, the Japanese attacked Chinese soldiers and warships in the area of Seoul, setting off the Sino-Japanese War. One victory followed another, demonstrating that Japan was now a formidable power. The Tonghaks organized an army to drive out the invaders; however, they suffered thousands of casualties. When their leader, Chon Pongjun, was captured and executed in Seoul, the rebellion ended. The Japanese won a quick victory. After centuries of strong political and cultural ties, China was forced to accept Korea's independence. Japan now tightened controls over the country.

After the war, the Japanese hoped to modernize Korea and bring it into its sphere of influence. Japan demanded that the government carry out internal reforms, expel pro-Chinese officials, and appoint pro-Japanese officials in their places. This led to what is called the Kabo Reforms of the 1894–1896 period. The officials who undertook the Kabo Reforms had all studied or lived in Japan or the United States. With encouragement, these officials began reforms that they felt would help the nation survive the challenges brought by the great powers. A council was created that acted independently of the king and queen and consisted of people who had supported progressive reforms. It abolished the Chinese-style bureaucracy, reformed local government, opened opportunities for talented people to serve in the government, introduced a modern court system, eliminated class distinctions, and freed slaves. An incidental result of the reforms led to Japan's even more dominant role in making Korea a major market for their goods.

As Japan tightened its grip, Queen Min secretly began to make overtures for Russian support to challenge the Island Empire. In 1895, as part of an effort to maintain power, Japanese officials organized and carried out the murder of the queen. She was stabbed, doused with kerosene, and set afire to destroy the evidence. The king and the crown prince dressed themselves as court ladies, rode in sedan chairs, and fled to the Russian legation where they stayed for a year. The country was run by the king under Russian supervision, and all reforms came to an end.

During King Kojong's residence at the Russian legation, he was apparently not a prisoner, but merely feared returning to his palace. In 1897, after hearing about growing unrest, he returned to his palace and declared himself emperor in the belief that he would have the power and the status of his counterparts in China and Japan. The nation's fate was now between Russia and Japan, who had already formulated some agreements regarding Korea. At one point Russian and Japanese representatives contemplated dividing the peninsula between them, but they could not agree on the terms. Later, when Russia and Japan demanded concessions, the king relented. Kojong gave timber rights to Russia and commercial banking rights along with over two hundred business concessions to Japan. Gold mines, railroads, and electric power systems were granted to the United States.

THE INDEPENDENCE MOVEMENT, MODERNIZATION, WAR, AND ANNEXATION

As Korea became a pawn in a world power struggle, many individuals and groups emerged to challenge the state of affairs. Now a more broadly based social movement than the Tonghak began to criticize the government's ineffective policies and fought aggressively for independence from foreign powers, particularly Japan. A group of reform-minded people in Seoul organized a political party called the Independence Club in 1896. The members, many of whom had formerly served in the government, demanded that Emperor Kojong implement the changes prescribed by the Kabo Reforms.

Several members of the Independence Club, including Syngman Rhee, who would later be South Korea's first president, became prominent leaders. The club proposed the construction of Independence Gate, Independence Hall (now considered one of the finest museums in Korea), and Independence Park and received a favorable response. Additional Independence Club goals included protection of the country's independence from foreign aggression, revocation of all economic concessions, and adoption of a foreign policy that favored none of the rival powers trying to advance their interests on the peninsula. The club also sought to establish modern schools, develop industry, and create a defense system. Another objective was to support the growth of the democratic process.

As a result of the efforts of the Independence Club and the commitment of many dedicated people, modern schools were founded and many Korean-language magazines and newspapers began to be published. The use of han'gul increased as did literacy. Literary figures emerged and promoted a new cultural movement based on national independence and equality. Medical care improved, telegraph and telephone systems were established, and streetcar and railroad lines were installed. New banking institutions and Western architecture appeared. Korea appeared to be on its way to modernization.

The Independence Club frequently presented its grievances to the government. The club called for dismissal of corrupt officials and the end of granting concessions to foreign powers. The public became increasingly open in support of change; for example, merchants closed shops and women began to protest. Growing increasingly resentful of the direct challenges to their authority, government officials began to arrest club leaders. In 1898, when Kojong ordered an end to the club, all opportunities for independence and modernization simply collapsed. Consequently, the emperor destroyed the only group capable of reinvigorating the Choson dynasty.

With the growing power and rivalry of Russia and Japan, Korea was also threatened at her borders. The Russians had obtained rights from China to build the trans-Siberian railroad through Manchuria and to lease some Chinese ports. When the Chinese attempted to expel foreigners during the Boxer Rebellion in 1900, Russia moved troops into Manchuria and waited for an opportunity to invade. In 1902 an alarmed Japan negotiated a treaty with Britain, which agreed to Japan's aggressive policies. In return, Japan promised that it would check Russia's southern advances in the Far East.

In 1903 the Russian-Japanese rivalry reached a critical point when Japan gave an ultimatum to Russia to withdraw troops from Manchuria. When it refused, Japan declared war in 1904 and quickly won on both land and sea. In 1905 U.S. President Theodore Roosevelt negotiated the Portsmouth Treaty in which Russia acknowledged Japan's rights in Korea. For this, Roosevelt received the Nobel Peace Prize. Since the United States had recently established the Philippines as a U.S. territory following the Spanish-American War (1898), Roosevelt agreed to another treaty, the Taft-Katsura Agreement, to give Japan a free hand in Korea in exchange for the promise that it would not interfere in the Philippines. As long as Japanese imperialism was directed toward Korea and Manchuria and away from American and British possessions, it had the support of the Western powers.

With this support Japan moved quickly to establish a Korean protectorate. After publicly protesting the Protectorate Treaty, Kojong appealed without success to the United States and other world powers to support independence. The Japanese forced him to abdicate in 1907, and his mentally retarded son, Sunjong, became emperor of Korea and the puppet of Japan. More than 140,000 patriots joined guerrilla armies to resist the Japanese. Thousands of them died in their struggle, but even after annexation, Korean emigrants in Manchuria continued to resist. By 1909 the powerful Japanese military had ended most resistance. A powerless Emperor Sunjong signed the Treaty of Annexation in 1910. The Choson dynasty, which had ruled Korea for 500 years, ceased to exist.

THE COLONIAL PERIOD (1910–1945)

The First Phase of Japanese Rule, 1910–1919

Annexation inaugurated a thirty-five-year period of Japanese occupation that has left a bitter legacy. The experience heightened animosities that had existed ever since the Hideyoshi invasions of the late sixteenth century; however, no previous events could have ever prepared people for the catastrophic economic, political, and social changes that were to come. Colonial rule affected every aspect of life. What happened between 1910 and 1945 is crucial for understanding the post–World War II attitudes toward the Japanese. The impact of foreign domination stimulated nationalism, influenced cultural development, and created class and ideological conflicts that persist today.

The colonizers were convinced that control over Korea was vital to their strategic and economic well-being. Although they felt they knew how to rule, they really lacked the ability to govern other people, in part because of their long antiforeign tradition. To justify the takeover, the Japanese convinced themselves that despite the fact that Koreans were the same race, they were inferior people. During the first years citizens were controlled by a draconian police system that deprived them of basic freedoms. Japan moved quickly to pacify the country. All newspapers were suspended, political parties were abolished, and public gatherings were disallowed. Japan's close proximity made it easier to dominate all facets of life.

Authority was invested in the governor-general, who was appointed by the emperor. He controlled the military and civil police force, made all laws, oversaw the judicial system, and had fiscal independence and total control of all appointments. All officials, including teachers, were required to carry a sword as a symbol of authority. The colonial bureaucracy grew rapidly, with Japanese officials dominating, especially in the upper and middle levels. Hiring practices eliminated educated and experienced Koreans from governmental service. Japanese officials received more pay. In the past local governments had been left alone, but now the most insignificant matters became official concerns. Koreans were bound by the laws of Japan, whereas Japanese were guaranteed citizen rights.

The police had the power to judge, sentence, and execute even for minor offenses. They wore military uniforms, carried swords, and were allowed to intrude into every aspect of life. They were the controlling agency in politics, education, religion, morals, health and public welfare, and tax collection. Even the large Korean contingent in the police force supplied the governor-general with information that set Korean against Korean.

The first decade of Japanese rule has been called the dark period because of the extensive repression of political and cultural life. The right of assembly was abolished. Police kept watch on intellectual, religious, and political leaders. In 1912 alone, there were over 50,000 arrests. The occupiers created an educational system to train a labor force to serve the homeland's economic development and to educate Koreans in Japanese customs, culture, and language. The government established controls over curriculum and textbooks for public schools. Japanese-imposed regulations impacted private schools to the extent that many of them ceased to exist. Schools were segregated between Korean and Japanese children, and the latter experienced better instruction and facilities. Education was limited for most native children; only 5 percent received more than primary education. The goal of education was to make Korean children loyal, useful, and obedient subjects of the emperor. Japanese was spoken, and Korean was taught as a second language. National history was rewritten from a Japanese perspective. Despite educational discrimination, literacy increased, and with it opposition to colonial rule grew. Because the Japanese limited access to colleges and universities, many bright Korean students traveled to Japan for higher education. There they were exposed to radical political ideas unavailable to students at home and ultimately established close contacts with a generation of political activists from around the world.

Another significant development during the first stage of the colonial period related to land laws. A Land Survey Bureau was created that required all owners to prove their land titles. Inequities in landholding had been a problem for centuries. The policies strengthened and codified the position of wealthy landowners and contributed to the deterioration of rural life. Large landowners had no difficulty reporting their holdings; however, many small landowners were unfamiliar with reporting regulations and lost their land. Tenancy rates increased to 80 percent in some areas. The widening gap between those who held land and those who did not caused tremendous social tension. In addition to the policies of the Land Survey Bureau, the governor-general seized land that had belonged to the royal family and became the largest landowner in Korea.

The colonists also consolidated their positions in communications, public services, and economic activities throughout the peninsula. Railroads were particularly vital to Japan for strategic and economic reasons. The governor-general took control of mining, forestry, and fisheries. Japan was now free to exploit Korea's gold, silver, iron, tungsten, and coal. A law was passed requiring approval for the formation of public or private corporations. Few Koreans received approval, making the number of Korean businesses insignificant compared to that of the occupiers. Japanese banks dominated the economy, and Korean businesses were dependent on them.

The oppressive rule that accompanied the first phase of colonial rule contributed to a growing number of Koreans abroad, in places such as Manchuria and Russia, who expressed opposition to colonial rule. Some became contract laborers in Hawaii, others settled in California. Many of the new activists were students who became radicalized by foreign contacts and by their own experiences of ethnic discrimination. After 1914 the major powers were consumed by World War I. Although Koreans tried to get the attention of other nations, there was little interest in responding to their appeals.

The Second Phase of Colonial Rule, 1919–1931

The United States emerged as a world power after World War I. President Woodrow Wilson raised the hopes of colonized peoples around the globe with his commitment to self-determination of peoples, national autonomy, and world peace. While most radical political leaders were in exile or in jail, Christian and Buddhist leaders in Korea now began to plan a national movement for independence. They wanted a nationwide demonstration on March 1, 1919. It was to be a nonviolent expression of their desire to be free and independent from Japan. Thirty-three nationalists signed the Declaration of Independence. The death of the former emperor, Kojong, in January and subsequent rumors that the Japanese were involved in his death further inflamed anti-Japanese sentiments. Widespread demonstrations broke out in Seoul and elsewhere during the following months. The Japanese were caught by surprise and the police responded with thousands of arrests, beatings, and the destruction of homes, churches, and even entire villages. A seventeen-year-old girl named Yu Kwansun was tortured by the police and died in prison.

The demonstrations failed to bring independence. What the March First Movement did accomplish was to unify the people in a dramatic new way. The Japanese became more sensitive to world opinion. As a result there were some alterations in Japanese policies, and the slogan "Harmony between Japan and Korea" was adopted, but there was no letup on the domination of Korea.

The Japanese developed "Cultural Policy Reforms" in hopes of improving world opinion of their colonial rule. These new policies included plans for greater efficiency of administration and police

Independence Monument, Seoul, Korea. On March 1, 1919, the Korean people began a nationwide demonstration expressing their desire to be free and independent of Japan. The words of their Declaration of Independence are inscribed on this memorial. (Courtesy of Mary Connor)

controls. The Japanese plotted ways to manipulate Koreans into supporting them. Whipping for minor offenses ended, but repression increased for militant nationalists and revolutionaries. Some minor adjustments were made to bring salaries more in line with those of Japanese civil servants. Promises were made to bring equality of education to the schools. Korean newspapers could be published again; however, they were subject to very strict censorship. The police no longer wore uniforms, but the size of the Japanese force was increased significantly. The objective was to create an army of informers so that no demonstration could catch the leaders by surprise as had the March First Movement. Another dimension of their program was to increase rice production; but most of the rice was exported to Japan. Korean per capita rice consumption dropped throughout colonial occupation.

Although these reforms now seem somewhat insignificant, the period following the March First Movement was a time of hope. Newspapers were published, and groups were formed throughout the colony. Koreans realized that direct confrontations with the Japanese would be met with force, so they developed a gradual approach to independence. Some worked for the creation of a true Korean university, while others focused on economic development of native businesses. Societies developed that fostered a national consciousness in literature, history, drama, music, and film. These activities were largely limited to the well-educated elite and did not have broad interest or the support of the people.

Many nationalists were forced to flee their homeland and join others in Shanghai and elsewhere. In 1919, nationalists in Shanghai established the Provisional Government of the Republic of Korea in exile and elected Dr. Syngman Rhee its first president. Other nationalists were attracted to communism because of the Russian Revolution and the emergence of a Soviet Union as champion of oppressed peoples everywhere. Exiles were free to read and discuss radical ideas and join groups supporting Marxist-Leninist ideology and national liberation. Ultimately, the differing ideologies seriously divided the movement. Not only was it divided, but no group was able to garner mass national support. In the twenty-first century both North and South Korea continue to be influenced significantly by the class and ideological conflicts that developed during and after the period of colonial rule.

The Third Phase of Japanese Occupation and World War II, 1931–1945

For a variety of reasons Japan's policies changed in the 1930s. As international trade shrank because of the worldwide depression, the Japanese realized that its new industrial economy was overextended beyond what the small empire could support. Chinese nationalist forces appeared to threaten its interests on the continent. In response to these developments, Japan seized Manchuria in 1931, made it a puppet state, utilized its rich natural resources, and developed its industry. In Japan itself the military took over the government. Korea was now to serve as the base for Japan's Asian plan. Newly instituted policies emphasized rural self-sufficiency and increased industrial production. As industry expanded, thousands of peasants took factory jobs.

Some resistance to the Japanese continued. Korean communists in the north organized underground peasant brigades that attacked their landlords and the police. Labor strikes were frequent. Some small guerrilla units managed to survive into the 1930s. One of the units was led by Kim Il Sung.

By 1934 the Japanese began to be bolder, forcing the Koreans into the cultural and political life of its empire with the objective of eliminating the differences between them. Educational policies included a new curriculum that emphasized Japanese language instruction, ethics, and history. All children now attended school together. These new policies also included a pledge to the emperor, attendance at Shinto ceremonies, and the elimination of the study and use of the Korean language altogether. Koreans particularly objected to forced attendance at Shinto ceremonies.

When war broke out between Japan and China in 1937, the governor-general began to shut down all Korean organizations. By 1940 virtually all Korean-language newspapers were closed. The Japanese created mass organizations to bring everybody into the war effort. They also reduced the number of Koreans in government and relegated those who remained to inferior positions. The colonial police recruited lower-class individuals for government service, creating great resentment among the general population and turning Koreans against one another.

In 1939 the oppressors struck at the most cherished source of family identity by forcing Koreans to adopt Japanese names. In a nation where reverence for ancestors and family lineage had been a way of life for thousands of years, this policy could only create a deep and lasting resentment on the part of the people. The Japanese believed that the very survival of the empire depended on their subjects acting and thinking like Japanese citizens. Their assimilation policies were doomed to fail because they included the belief that the Japanese and the Koreans could become one even though the Koreans were discriminated against for their ethnicity.

There were Koreans who attempted to succeed in the colonial system by collaborating. Ambitious, educated men had very few chances to succeed unless they did work within the system. Rejection of the system would limit opportunities for a good job and lead to poverty, jail, or exile. Some of these collaborators profited enormously from the war effort. Many thought that by cooperating with Japan, Korea would become modernized.

After the United States entered the war in the Pacific, there were even greater hardships for the Korean people. They worked in mines and factories in Manchuria and Japan, guarded prison camps, built military facilities, and served the troops in various capacities. The Japanese organized the entire colony into Neighborhood Patriotic Organizations, which were responsible for providing labor, collecting money for the war effort, security, and rationing. People were forced to donate gold and silver jewelry and brass and other metals to the war effort. School hours were reduced so children could work as factory laborers or in the fields. Some men had been serving in Japanese forces since 1910, but the final years of the war brought such a terrible shortage of manpower that great numbers were forced into the military. One of the most shameful developments was the so-called Comfort Corps, made up of between 100,000 and 200,000 young Korean women who were forced to serve the sexual needs of Japanese troops. Thousands of Korean men served in the military, and approximately 4 million, or 16 percent of the population, lived outside the country or worked in factories and mines in Manchuria, northern Korea, and Japan.

The independence movement continued to grow through the involvement of exiled leaders, but divisions between nationalists and communists grew stronger throughout the 1930s. During the 1940s in China, the major Korean noncommunist resistance forces came together to form the Korean Restoration Army, which ultimately reached 3,000 members. This army worked with Chiang Kai'shek's Nationalist Peoples Party (KMT), developing close contacts with supporters of Chinese nationalists and with U.S. military advisors. At the same time, the majority of Korean communists was working with its Chinese counterparts and gained invaluable military and organizational skills. Korean communist guerrillas in Manchuria went into hiding in the Soviet Union. Among them was Kim Il Sung, who survived the Japanese extermination campaigns of the late 1930s. The Japanese had considered him to be one of the most effective and dangerous of the guerrillas. Overseas, Syngman Rhee worked tirelessly to become the leader of the government in exile. As the war was coming to a close, nationalists at home and abroad would vie for the leadership of an independent Korea.

When the emperor of Japan surrendered unofficially on August 15, 1945, it was a day of jubilation for Koreans. Flags that had been hidden by the Korean people now were unfurled on the streets and the people celebrated freedom and national independence. It seemed that for the first time since early in the twentieth century, Koreans could shape their own destiny. However, Korea was soon to be divided after being unified for nearly thirteen hundred years.

LIBERATION, DIVISION, AND THE BEGINNINGS OF THE COLD WAR (1945–1950)

In 1943, Franklin Delano Roosevelt, Winston Churchill, and Chiang Kai'shek issued the Cairo Agreement, which stated that "in due course Korea shall become free and independent." Joseph Stalin indicated support of this agreement in July 1945 by signing the Potsdam Declaration. In August, the Soviet Union, in accordance with the Yalta Agreement of February 1945, declared war on Japan and poured troops into Korea while U.S. troops were still fighting in Okinawa. Americans could not move quickly enough to stop Soviet occupation of the entire peninsula. Immediately after the second atomic bomb was dropped on Nagasaki, U.S. officials proposed the division of Korea at the thirty-eighth parallel in an attempt to prevent a complete takeover by the Soviets. In their haste, U.S. officials acted unilaterally. Their proposal involved a temporary division: the Soviet Union would establish a military zone north of the thirty-eighth parallel, and the United States would occupy a military zone to the south. Much to the surprise of U.S. military authorities, Stalin immediately accepted the proposal. American forces began to arrive in South Korea the following month.

For an accurate assessment of the events following liberation, the legacy of Japanese occupation should be considered. Japan's colonial policies had a revolutionary impact on Korean politics and society. In 1945 Korea was a mix of old and new classes, political groups, and conflicting ideologies. About 80 percent of the population still lived on the land, but an assortment of businesspeople, white-collar workers, factory laborers, and landless peasants who had been uprooted from their villages during the war were returning home. The colonial period had created nationalists with different ideologies and experiences who had remained within Korea or lived abroad. Rival groups had their own political agendas and supported different figures.

Two political factions developed in the liberation period. On the right were those who had collaborated enthusiastically with the Japanese and those who felt they had no choice but to collaborate in order to survive, support their families, and maintain their status in society. Others on the right were Koreans with limited education or no property who had comprised 40 percent of the colonial police force. On the left was a broad spectrum of society—students, intellectuals, peasants, laborers—politicized by the colonial experience. They decried the inequities between classes that had prevailed for centuries and were attracted to the promises of Marxism and Leninism to bring equality and justice to the poor and oppressed. Those attracted to communism desired a redistribution of wealth with an emphasis upon land reform. Intense feelings existed between those who had collaborated and those who had not, between conservatives and the radical left, and between nationalists and communists.

Meanwhile tensions that had existed between the United States and the Soviet Union since the Russian Revolution increased during the war because of opposing strategies, conflicting ideologies, and plain misunderstanding. The U.S. War Department had anticipated a prolonged conflict in the Pacific and sought the support of the Soviet Union against Japan. Once the atomic bomb was developed, the United States knew the war would soon be over and wanted to keep the USSR out of Japan. When the atomic bombs were dropped on August 6 and 9, the Soviet Union declared war on Japan, fulfilled her obligations from the Yalta Agreement, renewed age-old interests in Korea, and sent thousands of troops into areas that had been under Japanese dominion: Manchuria and Korea.

Immediately after the unconditional surrender, a temporary peace-keeping organization, the Committee for the Preparation of Korean Independence (CPKI), was formed in August 1945 to assist in the transition, maintain order, and formulate plans for a new national government. By September there were committees in all of the major cities and in the smallest villages throughout all thirteen provinces. Several hundred delegates met in Seoul, announced the formation of the Korean People's Republic (KPR), and established a schedule for future national elections.

Scholars debate the political character of the KPR. The traditional American and South Korean view is that the KPR was a leftist organization with the objective of making Korea a communist state. Revisionist historians stress that the KPR was primarily a leftist organization but desired a coalition government, as shown by the inclusion of right-leaning nationalists, such as Syngman Rhee. The platform of the KPR was indeed revolutionary; it called for the confiscation of land from the Japanese and all who had collaborated with them. Peasants would be given land, major industries nationalized, an eight-hour day established, child labor prohibited, and a minimum wage determined. All men and women were to have the right to vote except those who had been collaborators. There was also to be freedom of speech, press, and religion. It seemed at the time that the KPR was a reflection of the popular will of the majority of the people.

Japanese authorities in Seoul informed U.S. leaders that local communists and independence supporters were plotting to subvert the peace process and warned of violence. Consequently, when the U.S. forces arrived in September, top officers were suspicious that the KPR was part of a Soviet communist conspiracy. Throughout the fall of 1945, Koreans dismantled the colonial administration at every level and expelled collaborators from positions of power. Communists played a significant part in the process, but they were not necessarily the leaders; there was always active participation by the local population.

General John Hodge, the leader of the U.S. occupation forces, under orders from Washington, refused to recognize the KPR or any Korean government. He set up the United States Army Military Government in Korea (USAMGIK) and began to reestablish the colonial administrative government by appointing people who had served as collaborators. U.S. leaders were unaware of the stigma associated with collaboration and felt it necessary to quickly create a government free of leftist influences. Many Koreans appointed to the new government were upper class, propertied, anticommunist, well educated, and English-speaking. Hodge began to carry out policies to end all KPR committees south of the thirty-eighth parallel.

The Soviet occupation forces treated the KPR very differently. In the North collaborators were thrown out of office and the colonial bureaucratic government destroyed. Large industries were nationalized. Japanese land was confiscated, and the majority of landlords lost most of their property. The objectives of the KPR were carried out with little violence because many northern landlords had already fled south.

In the final months of 1945, the foreign ministers of the Allies met in Moscow to establish an international solution to the Korean situation. The diplomats agreed to authorize the formation of a joint U.S.–USSR commission to establish a government in consultation with its leaders to end the Allied occupation. The new administration would be put under a five-year trusteeship of the Allies. Koreans in both the Soviet and U.S. occupied zones reacted violently to the plan and carried out nationwide demonstrations. Many factors contributed to the response, but the main reason for protest was the right-left polarization of national politics that came with Soviet and U.S. occupation. In early 1946, Soviet pressure on Korean communists led to support of the Moscow Agreement; however, violence between nationalists and communists continued to occur throughout the peninsula.

Most of the turmoil existed south of the thirty-eighth parallel. As a result of the trusteeship decision and subsequent U.S. political and economic policies, people grew increasingly hostile to U.S. military rule. Strikes, mass demonstrations, and bloodshed followed. From the U.S. point of view, events in Korea seemed to mirror fears at home. Labor strikes in both countries were perceived as communist inspired.

Another important reason for the polarization of politics on the peninsula was the honor bestowed by the Americans and the Soviets on their favorite patriots who returned from years in exile. The Soviets gave their support to General Kim Il Sung, a young but famous and charismatic anti-Japanese guerrilla fighter, who had established close contacts with communists in China and Russia while in exile. In February 1946 a provisional government, the Interim People's Committee, was inaugurated with Kim in control. He soon moved toward a dictatorship by eliminating nationalist and religious organizations, nationalizing businesses, and organizing an army. During this time some 2 million Koreans fled to the South.

Almost simultaneously with the growth of autocratic government in the North, the USAMGIK supported the development of a rightist, anticommunist government in the South. In October 1945 Dr. Syngman Rhee, a seventy-year-old patriot, who had been active in the independence movement, returned to his homeland with much fanfare. Educated in the United States, he had established close ties with governmental figures in Washington and with nationalist leader Chiang Kai'shek. An outspoken anticommunist, Rhee immediately condemned the Soviet Union, Korean communists, and the KPR.

Because of his personal dislike for Rhee together with pressure from the U.S. State Department, General Hodge tried to form a coalition government acceptable to the Soviets. The plan was to exclude the extremes of the right (Syngman Rhee) and left (Kim Il Sung) and form a trusteeship determined by the Moscow Agreement. Unfortunately, Koreans were too polarized to accept a coalition government. Relations had also deteriorated between the United States and the Soviet Union because of the continued Soviet occupation of Eastern Europe and the implementation of President Harry Truman's policy of containment.

Considering the international tensions of the time, it is understandable that two separate governments emerged on the peninsula. The final step of this unfolding tragedy came in May 1947 when the United States appealed to the newly created United Nations to

The East Gate and Seoul residences in the early 1950s. This photograph was taken by U.S. Army Corporal Alfred (Bud) Hallam, who was killed during the Korean War. (Courtesy of Mary Connor/Alfred Hallam)

resolve the Korea question. In November, despite protests from the Soviets, the United Nations General Assembly voted to send a commission to Korea to conduct national elections, establish a government, and end Allied occupation.

Most people wanted an immediate end to occupation and supported the UN plan. The Soviet Union disputed the UN's authority to conduct elections and rejected the resolution. Dr. Syngman Rhee and his supporters advocated elections in the South. Many opposed these elections for the obvious reason that they would lead to the permanent division of the peninsula. Members of the UN commission were determined to carry out elections, and on May 10, 1948, the first democratic elections were held in the South. Two months later a constitution was adopted, and on August 15 the Republic of Korea (ROK) was established with Syngman Rhee as its first president. The ROK claimed that it was the only legitimate government on the peninsula. The United States and many other democratic nations promptly recognized the new government. In August, the North Korean communists had their own elections that were approved by the Soviet Union. A constitution was adopted for a separate state called the Democratic

People's Republic of Korea (DPRK), and Kim Il Sung was elected premier. Northern leaders claimed theirs was the only legitimate government on the peninsula and that P'yongyang was to be the temporary capital. In late 1948 the Soviets withdrew their troops but left behind a sizable amount of modern military equipment and advisors to train Kim Il Sung's forces. The Americans left South Korea the following year, leaving poorly trained and inadequately supplied forces to defend independence with the assistance of U.S. military advisors. Fighting began less than two years later.

THE KOREAN WAR (1950–1953)

There has been much debate over the causes of the Korean War. The end of the Cold War era and recent research in Soviet archives has given further perspectives on the complexities of the war's origins. There is no doubt that the northern troops actually crossed the thirty-eighth parallel on June 25, 1950. This event, however, has to be viewed within the context of important international developments and the polarization that existed on the peninsula. U.S. policy makers were strongly influenced by the lessons of the 1930s. They knew that "appeasement" of dictators simply encouraged them to escalate their demands, whereas decisive action to stop aggression would force them to withdraw. The Cold War was about to become very hot.

With the end of World War II, the tenuous alliance between the Western powers and the Soviet Union deteriorated, and ideological competition ushered in economic and political instability throughout the world. The Soviet Union occupied Eastern Europe and successfully tested an atomic bomb, ending the U.S. nuclear monopoly. To stop Russian expansion and the threat of communism, the United States adopted the Truman Doctrine, the Marshall Plan, and the containment policy. To protect national security and maintain peace, the United States entered its first peacetime military alliance by joining the North Atlantic Treaty Organization. In 1949 Mao Zedong's army won the Chinese civil war, brought communism to the most populous country in the world, and proclaimed the People's Republic of China. Critics of the Truman administration claimed that the United States. had "lost China." Senator Joseph McCarthy, in February of 1950, further heightened U.S. security concerns by charging that the State Department was thoroughly infested with communists.

Meanwhile, there was continuous leftist guerrilla warfare throughout much of South Korea. Skirmishes between North and South Korean forces at the thirty-eighth parallel became frequent. Rhee and his generals spoke often of military operations to take over the North. Between 1945 and 1950 Kim Il Sung repeatedly asked Joseph Stalin for permission to invade the South. In 1950 when he again asked for Soviet support in unifying the country and promised a quick victory, the Soviet leader reluctantly gave his permission as long as Mao Zedong would support the invasion. Mao agreed and released over 60,000 battle-hardened Koreans from the People's Liberation Army for duty in North Korea.

Early Sunday, on June 25, 1950, North Korean troops opened fire and launched a well-planned attack against South Korea. Equipped with Soviet tanks and fighter planes, the North Korean army crossed the thirty-eighth parallel and, within three days, captured Seoul and overran most of the peninsula in a short period of time. While the war began as a civil war, it became the first major power conflict since World War II, and it brought the Korean peninsula to the center of global attention. It was feared at the time to represent the beginnings of a third world war.

Without a formal declaration of war, President Harry Truman tried to halt the invasion with U.S. air and naval forces, but the combined South Korean and U.S. forces could not stop the advances of the superior forces of the North Korean army. Within a short time it had captured all but the area around the port city of Pusan.

Realizing the grave danger to the Republic of Korea, Truman requested the assistance of the United Nations to support it. Stalin was apparently still lukewarm about Kim Il Sung's war against South Korea. Because the Soviet Union was boycotting the United Nations Security Council to protest the United Nation's refusal to grant the People's Republic of China membership, its representative was not present to veto the UN resolution to defend South Korea. After the Security Council voted, General Douglas MacArthur was named commander of the UN forces (90 percent of them American).

The U.S. Army, Navy, Air Force, and Marines arrived in Korea and, together with troops from Great Britain, France, Canada, and Australia, launched a counterattack. MacArthur carried off a daring amphibious landing at Inch'on, several hundred miles behind North Korean lines. Eighteen thousand American marines landed on September 15, 1950, and quickly moved inland. The UN forces liberated Seoul and pushed the DPRK troops back to the thirty-eighth parallel. Even before Inch'on, Truman had redefined the objectives of the

United States in fighting the war. He now believed that the whole peninsula should be liberated from communism and reunified by force.

In September Truman authorized United Nations forces to cross the thirty-eighth parallel. Together with the ROK they marched north, captured the capital, P'yongyang, and continued to move well into the North in pursuit of fleeing troops. U.S. aircraft also bombed bridges along the Yalu River, the border with China. Mao warned that he would not permit the continued attacks on transportation links with Korea. Although the collapse of their communist ally seemed imminent in mid-October, tens of thousands of Chinese soldiers poured into Korea from Manchuria and drove the UN forces back again. On January 4, 1951, Seoul fell a second time, but by March UN forces succeeded in recapturing the capital city. The front then stabilized around the thirty-eighth parallel.

The United States and the Soviet Union welcomed negotiations, but MacArthur had other ideas. The general wanted to extend the war into China, liberate it from communism, and restore Chiang Kai'shek to power. In April, fed up with MacArthur's insubordination and backed by the joint chiefs of staff, Truman fired him.

Armistice talks began in July 1951, but the fighting and dying continued for two more years. The most controversial issue in the negotiations was the fate of the prisoners of war (POWs). The United States maintained it would only return those North Korean and Chinese prisoners who wished to go home. The DPRK objected. Both sides were involved with brainwashing prisoners to resist repatriation.

As the POW issue continued to prolong negotiations, U.S. officials made vague public statements about the use of atomic weapons. U.S. bombers devastated dams, rice fields, factories, airfields, and bridges. Casualties on both sides mounted. Finally, after two years of negotiations and the ultimate involvement of twenty-one countries, a truce was signed at Panmunjom on July 27, 1953, and a four-mile-wide demilitarized zone (DMZ) was established across the peninsula. China ultimately withdrew its forces in 1958, but the United States continues to maintain approximately 37,000 troops.

When the war finally ended, the two Koreas, for all they had suffered, would control essentially the same territory they held when the war erupted. It devastated both halves of a nation that had only begun to recover from four decades of Japanese occupation and the shock of division. Around 3 million people, approximately one-tenth of the entire population, were killed, wounded, or missing. Another 5 million became refugees. It is estimated that 900,000 Chinese and

A view of the Joint Security Area at the demilitarized zone (DMZ). The armistice was signed in one of these buildings at the end of the Korean War in 1953. (Courtesy of Mary Connor)

520,000 North Koreans were killed or wounded, as were about 400,000 UN command troops, nearly two-thirds of them South Koreans. U.S. casualties were 54,000 dead and another 103,000 wounded. ROK property losses were put at $2 billion, the equivalent of its gross national product for 1949; DPRK losses were estimated at only slightly less. Forty-eight years after the war an estimated 10 million people remained separated from their families by the thirty-eighth parallel. North and South Korea are technically still at war.

DIVIDED KOREA: THE SOUTH KOREAN EXPERIENCE (1953–2000)

The First and Second Republics, 1948–1961

For South Korea, the next several decades would bring radical changes in government and tremendous economic growth. The war left the country with massive economic, social, and political problems, including thousands of war widows, orphans, unemployed people, discharged soldiers, and laid-off workers. President Syngman

Rhee, unable to see that he had outlived his usefulness, became increasingly domineering and autocratic. With the support of the Liberal Party, he revised the constitution, gave unlimited tenure to his office, and suppressed the opposition Democratic Party. Assassination had eliminated a number of his potential rivals. The spark that brought his administration to an end was the effort to rig the election of 1960.

Aware of their own unpopularity, Rhee and his supporters used every means to ensure victory for the Liberal Party. Demonstrations erupted, especially among students. Protests broke out, leading to police violence and the death of a student. Nearly all of the students in Seoul poured into the streets and were fired upon as they neared the presidential palace. Martial law was declared, and troops dispersed the crowds. Rhee had no choice but to step down. The students led the people into the first successful democratic revolution in the country's history.

The Second Republic (1960–1961), a liberal democratic regime with Premier Chang Myon at its helm, lasted only eight months. The new government was unable to improve economic conditions, demonstrate competent leadership, or control the growing communist influence. In May 1961 Major General Park Chung Hee and young army officers overthrew the administration. For the first time since the fourteenth century the military was at the center of politics. Park was to be the key figure in a new arrangement of power that would last nearly two decades.

The Third and Fourth Republics, 1963–1979

Park Chung Hee and army officers quickly put Seoul under military occupation, and social stability was restored. The government promised that it would take a strong stand against communist infiltrators, develop stronger relations with the United States, establish a self-supporting economy, unify the nation, and hold elections the following year to establish a new civilian government. The election was held in 1963, and Park, who had resigned from the army, was elected president of the Third Republic. And there began a long era of authoritarian rule. Park was reelected to a second term (1967), and in his reelection for a third term (1971), he defeated Kim Dae-jung.

Under President Park's leadership, the human and natural resources of the country were effectively organized for the first time in modern history. The economy began to grow rapidly, per capita

income soared, and exports rose by over 30 percent a year. Successful as he was in rescuing a backward economy, Park so consolidated
his power and manipulated the constitution to remain in office indefinitely.

Park's foreign policy included normalization of relations with
Japan in 1965 and the first formal dialogue with North Korea. His
agreement to the normalization and to sending troops to aid the
United States in Vietnam during President Lyndon Johnson's administration led to massive demonstrations on the part of opposition parties and students. Major changes on the international scene destabi-
lized his administration: the Nixon Doctrine, the retreat of the United
States from Vietnam, the Arab oil embargo, Nixon's policy of détente
with China, and the withdrawal of 20,000 U.S. troops from South
Korea. A slowdown in the economy together with the international
situation led Park and his advisors to silence dissent. In 1972 he
declared martial law, suspended the constitution, and dissolved the
National Assembly and all political parties. By the end of that year he
was the head of the Fourth Republic and had transformed the presidency into a dictatorship.

Park held power for seven more years. He survived one assassination attempt, but another killed his wife, who was a popular public
figure. This event generated public sympathy. However, as economic
problems continued into the late 1970s and the credibility of Park's
administration began to suffer from an influence-peddling scandal,
public discontent grew, and he became increasingly isolated from his
own supporters. Finally, on October 26, 1979, the director of the
Korean CIA assassinated him. The prime minister immediately
became acting president.

The Fifth Republic, 1980–1988

During the next several months the country was in turmoil. In
December 1979 General Chun Doo Hwan carried out a coup, became
president of the Fifth Republic, declared martial law, and ruthlessly
suppressed popular demonstrations. In the midst of this political crisis, the bloody Kwangju Uprising of students and citizens occurred,
resulting in possibly 2,000 casualties and causing antigovernment
sentiment that lasted for years.

In 1981 President Chun promised that he would build what he
called a Great Korea in a new era. Although it was essentially the same
as the Third and Fourth Republics in its autocratic rule, the Fifth

Republic made two significant achievements: the first-ever surplus in the international balance of payments and a peaceful transfer of power at the end of his seven-year term. However, during the Fifth Republic, students became more radical, leftist, and anti-American than ever before. Another critical development that led to massive demonstrations was the brutal murder by the police of a Seoul National University student. Riots came to a head in June 1987 and broke out in major cities throughout Korea. Chun was forced to concede to a Democratization Manifesto (Declaration of Democratization and Reforms) by ex-general Roh Tae Woo, the chair of the Democratic Justice Party. A new constitution, calling for direct presidential elections, was subsequently adopted, and President Roh's Sixth Republic was inaugurated in February 1988.

The Sixth Republic, 1988–1993

Roh Tae Woo, a childhood friend of Chun Doo Hwan, had served in both the Korean and Vietnam Wars, and over the years, rose through the ranks to become a general in 1979. Roh was a member of the Chun-led junta that ordered the brutal suppression of demonstrators in Kwangju in May 1980. After Chun became president, Roh resigned from the military and served in several posts in Chun's administration. As head of the Seoul Olympic Committee from 1983–1986, he oversaw South Korea's preparations for the 1988 Summer Olympic Games held in Seoul.

By June of 1987 Chun had chosen Roh to be the candidate of the Democratic Justice Party in the upcoming presidential elections. Under the country's existing constitution, Roh was practically guaranteed to win the presidency, and this prospect ignited widespread popular unrest. In response, Roh proposed a broad program of democratic reforms, which led to the approval of a new constitution in October 1987. One of the main provisions was the direct election of the president by popular vote. He won the election in December because both major opposition candidates, Kim Young Sam and Kim Dae-jung, split the opposition vote. Roh began his five-year term as president in February 1988.

As president, he committed himself to democratization. In 1990 the Democratic Justice Party merged with two opposition parties to form the Democratic Liberal Party. In foreign affairs Roh cultivated new ties with the former Soviet Union, China, and many Eastern European countries. He obtained South Korea's admission into the United

Korean War Museum, Seoul. The museum, one of the best in Korea, traces the history of war from the Three Kingdoms period to the Korean War. (Courtesy of Mary Connor)

Nations and signed an agreement in 1991 calling for nonaggression between the two Koreas. In February 1993 Kim Young Sam, whose anticorruption reforms targeted Roh and Chun, succeeded him.

In 1995 Roh publicly apologized for having illegally amassed $650,000 in secret political donations. He was tried, found guilty of corruption charges, fined, and sentenced to prison for seventeen years. In 1997 he received pardon from outgoing president Kim Young Sam and president-elect Kim Dae-jung.

Civilian Government, Kim Young Sam, 1993–1998

On February 25, 1993, Kim Young Sam, who won the 1992 presidential election, was sworn in as the first civilian president of Korea. He defeated Kim Dae-jung and another leading candidate. Active in politics since 1954, Kim Young Sam was expelled from the National Assembly for his opposition to Park, leading to riots and mass demonstrations. During Chun's presidency Kim was placed under house arrest and banned from any political activity. In 1983, his house arrest was lifted and he returned to political activity in 1985.

Once in power, Kim established civilian control over the military and tried to make the government more responsive to the electorate. He pursued reforms to eliminate political corruption and abuses of power and allowed two of his presidential predecessors, Roh Tae Woo and Chun Doo Hwan, to be prosecuted and convicted of various crimes committed when in power. The economy continued to grow at a rapid rate during his presidency, and with wages rising rapidly, the standard of living reached that of other industrialized nations.

Kim was constitutionally barred from seeking a second term. His popularity declined rapidly in the last year of his five-year term as a result of corruption within his administration and the increasingly precarious state of the South Korean economy, which was caught in the financial crisis sweeping through Southeast and East Asia in late 1997. The longtime opposition leader Kim Dae-jung succeeded him as president.

Kim Dae-jung, 1998–

Kim Dae-jung's election, the first true opposition party victory in a presidential election, came at an extraordinarily difficult time, with a new round of corruption scandals and the worst economic crisis in decades to hit Korea and other parts of East and Southeast Asia. The new president was faced with the enormous challenges of restoring economic stability while promoting greater democracy, developing positive relations with the major powers, and establishing an active policy, now widely spoken of as the Sunshine Policy, of cooperation with North Korea.

Kim has been a major advocate of greater and more substantial democracy in political life, and he fulfilled his idea of participatory democracy shortly after coming to office by creating a committee consisting of labor, management, and government to address the economic crisis. One of his first acts was to grant immediate pardons to Chun and Roh, who had been his bitter enemies.

Since coming to office, Kim has improved relations with Japan, China, and Russia. In 1998 the prime minister of Japan, Obuchi Keizo, signed a joint declaration with South Korea, which included the first written apology from Japan for its harsh colonial rule. In 2002 Japan and South Korea will cohost the World Cup, a sign of reduced tensions in the perennially difficult relationship between the two nations. Relations with the United States have been very positive. In 2000, some tensions between the two countries developed over the news of a U.S. massacre of civilians at No Gun Ri during the war and the continued presence of 37,000 troops on South Korean soil.

The Kim administration has advocated a policy of engagement

with North Korea more actively than any previous ROK government. Between June 13 and 15, 2000, Kim Dae-jung met in P'yongyang with Kim Jong Il, the leader of the DPRK, the first meeting of the heads of North and South since the peninsula was divided in 1945. While the leaders did not deal with the North's weapons programs, its development and foreign sales of advanced missiles, or its demand that the United States withdraw its troops from the South, they did make some very important agreements. They agreed to allow visits between some of the 1.2 million family members separated since the Korean War. They also agreed to resolve other human rights problems; narrow the gap between the two economies; and speed cultural, athletic, medical, and environmental cooperation and exchanges.

After the summit, Kim Dae-jung received the Nobel Peace Prize for his efforts of reconciliation. He was revered as a hero at home and widely respected throughout the world. In spite of his remarkable achievements, he still had many challenges ahead: restructuring the *chaebol* (large conglomerates), ending political corruption, extending human rights, and paving the way for eventual reunification. Kim's problems grew in the final months of 2001 as the global economy weakened, exports dropped, and his Sunshine Policy grew more unpopular. In September the National Assembly passed a motion against the National Unification Minister. The vote signified the belief on the part of the opposition that the policies toward North Korea allowed too many concessions without demanding conciliatory gestures in return. Despite this vote, analysts said that Kim Dae-jung was not likely to abandon his engagement policy.

DIVIDED KOREA: THE NORTH KOREAN EXPERIENCE (1953–2001)

The Democratic People's Republic of Korea is a mystifying nation that resists easy description. The closed nature of North Korean society makes it impossible to explore the nature of its socialist system through direct examination of the experiences of ordinary citizens. Although a lack of reliable information inhibits assessment of economic, political, and social developments since 1953, much can be learned from examining the leadership and policies of Kim Il Sung. The Great Leader was chief-of-state from 1948 until his death in 1994 when his son, Kim Jong Il, became the Dear Leader.

The division of the country in 1945 left each Korea with half an economy. Prior to that time most of the natural resources and approximately 85 percent of heavy industry were located in the North, while 75 percent of the country's light manufacturing and almost all the agricultural production were in the South. The Korean War left both sides economically and socially devastated.

During and after the war, Kim eliminated his enemies and rivals, and his supporters nurtured his personality cult, making him a superhuman being. His supporters also glorified the revolutionary spirit of his grandparents, parents, and other relatives. After 1953, Kim Il Sung created an austere, militarized, and highly regimented society. Although officially extolling *juche* (pronounced joo´ chay), or self-reliance, North Korea in reality relied heavily on Soviet and Chinese economic and military support. It did receive substantial economic aid from China and the Soviet Union but much less aid than what the South received from the United States and Japan.

Kim Il Sung began a three-year plan at the end of the war and a five-year plan that succeeded it; both stressed the reconstruction and development of major destroyed industries, sacrificing the needs of consumers. The emphasis on industrialization, combined with unprecedented aid from the Soviet bloc, pushed the growth rate to 25 percent annually for the decade following the war, and for two decades the North's growth outdistanced the South's. The achievements were so remarkable that some Western economists spoke of the "North Korean Miracle."

When the Soviet Union and China became unreliable allies in the 1960s, Kim Il Sung advocated national self-reliance; people needed to count on their own national leaders and resources to solve problems. Kim felt no hesitation in proclaiming that under juche, "man is the master of everything and decides everything." To prove that he had a greater commitment and ability than anyone else, he had history rewritten. The revision proclaimed Kim to be the originator of the Korean revolutionary movement, the founder of the People's Army, and the liberator of Korea from Japan. In order to perpetuate his legacy and prolong his revolutionary ideology, Kim Il Sung took steps to establish his dynasty. In the early 1970s he began to prepare his son, Kim Jong Il, to succeed him.

North Korea was also influenced by the policies of South Korean president Park Chung Hee who proclaimed in 1961 that anticommunism was the most important principle of his administration. Park worked to develop strong ties with the United States and Japan, sent troops to support the United States in Vietnam, and received greater military and economic aid in exchange. He also officially reestablished relations with Japan. Kim's response to these trends was to build up North Korea's military capabilities and to prepare for all-out war. Military spending rose from 4 percent to yearly averages ranging from 20 to 30 percent of the national budget. This represented a major drain on the country's resources and has affected the government's ability to meet its economic objectives.

During the 1970s, North Korea, noting the more rapid economic development in the South, attempted a large-scale modernization program through the importation of Western technology, principally in the heavy industrial sectors. Unable to finance its debt through exports that shrank steadily after the worldwide recession stemming from the oil crisis of the 1970s, the DPRK became the first communist country to default on its loans from free-market economies. In 1979, it was able to renegotiate much of its international debt, but in 1980 it defaulted again on most of its loans. Largely because of these debt problems, but also because of a prolonged drought and economic mismanagement, industrial growth slowed and per capita GNP was one-third of the South's by 1979.

North Korea's problems worsened in the 1980s and 1990s. Various initiatives were established to boost the country's economic situation. Trade was opened to the capitalist world. The government also tried mobilizing workers to work harder, better, and faster. Since the 1970s, the DPRK has been a major arms supplier to countries such as Libya, Iran, and Syria. The collapse of the Soviet Union forced it to aggressively pursue foreign investment, relations with capitalist firms, and new zones of free trade. In spite of the economic problems and the initiatives to deal with them, the country's basic economic structure and institutions have not changed.

In 1993, Kim's defense policy became a great concern for the United States when intelligence analysis estimated that North Korea was less than two years away from being able to strike South Korea and Japan with nuclear missiles. When the Atomic Energy Agency announced that North Korea was in violation of its obligations under the Nuclear Non-Proliferation Treaty, and the United Sates and its allies pushed for UN sanctions against P'yongyang, North Korea threatened that sanctions would be equivalent to a declaration of war. The crisis was eased in June 1994 when former U.S. president Jimmy Carter persuaded Kim to freeze the nuclear program to prevent international sanctions and to begin talks about ending North Korea's international isolation. Kim died three weeks after his meeting with Carter at age eighty-two.

Most experts predicted that the North Korean regime, struggling to reverse the country's economic decline, would not survive Kim's death. A year later devastating rains and floods left thousands homeless, and nearly half the country's farmland was ruined. Reports from defectors to the South claimed that people were starving.

Despite these disasters Kim Jong Il has assumed complete control of the country. He built strong links with the army as the only sure foundation for his rule at a time of endemic food shortage and low public morale. In 1998 he seemed to justify the worst Western images of him when he claimed he had merely test-fired a missile that North Korea launched over Japan. He is described as one of the world's most mysterious leaders, a calculating politician and a masterful manipulator who is aware of the complexities of international relations and smart enough to carve out new directions for his regime. China has pressured Kim to open up—mostly out of fear that North Korean intransigence could lead to a greater U.S. presence in Asia, something Beijing is eager to avoid.

Since 1994 the United States and South Korea have pursued a policy of engagement with North Korea to improve relations, to contain its nuclear program, and to offer the country a form of development assistance. The alternative to such a policy would be quarantine and confrontation. These options were ruled out in 1994 as posing too high a risk for the population of South Korea, which would suffer devastation as a result of any miscalculation. However, continued brinkmanship on the part of the North Korean leadership and its own checkered record in domestic policy has raised real doubts about its abilities. It is not certain whether it has the capacity or preparedness to change its ways sufficiently to deal with the root causes of the continued confrontation on the peninsula. The country's missile program must be restrained, and clandestine nuclear activities have to be watched. U.S. intelligence reports predict that there could be an intercontinental ballistic attack as early as 2005. Even though the United States is the most powerful military power on earth, it cannot necessarily protect itself from nuclear attack from a country such as North Korea. Resolution to the problem on the peninsula is critical for maintaining peace.

KOREA'S PLACE IN THE WORLD

North Korea's policies of self-reliance were a reaction to the prolonged sufferings of the twentieth century. After the extreme hardships of

Triumphal Arch, P'yongyang. This is a photograph of the Kim Jong Il and Kim Dae-jung motorcade upon arrival in P'yongyang, the capital of North Korea, in June 2000. (Photographed by Cheong Wa Dae, Presidential Residence of the Republic of Korea, Photographer's Press Pool)

colonialism, poverty, and civil war, juche appeared to be the means by which the nation could protect itself from the agony of the past. When the Cold War ended, this policy seemed out of place. The auspicious summit of June 2000 heralded new possibilities for the peninsula.

On August 15, 2000, the fifty-fifth anniversary of independence from Japan, two hundred families were reunited for the first time since the Korean War. Since these dramatic reunions, separated families are even more aware of the reality of their sharp ideological and economic differences. Despite these differences, five thousand years of history demonstrate that the Koreans are a determined people with a tradition of survival against difficult odds.

One hopes that the historic meeting between Kim Dae-jung and Kim Jong Il signals the end of the enmity between the Koreas. Although the twentieth century was replete with pain and horror, the meeting between the two Korean leaders could come to symbolize the hopes that the twenty-first century will be a century of reconciliation, reunification, and peace.

References

A Handbook of Korea. Seoul: Korean Overseas Information Service. 1993.

About Geography, "Geography and Map of North Korea," http://geography.about. com/ . . /geography/library/cia/blcnorthkorea.htm (cited August 13, 2000).

Breen, Michael. 1998. *The Koreans: Who They Are, What They Want, Where Their Future Lies.* New York: St. Martin's Press.

Choi, Yong Jin. 2000. (Personal communication). Director, Korean Studies Program. Korea Society.

Cumings, Bruce. 1997. *Korea's Place in the Sun: A Modern History.* New York: W. W. Norton.

Eckert, Carter et al. 1990. *Korea Old and New: A History.* Seoul: Ilchokak Publishers.

Hart-Landsberg, Martin. 1998. *Korea: Division, Reunification, and U.S. Foreign Policy.* New York: Monthly Review Press.

Kim, Yung-Chung, ed. 1976. *Women of Korea: A History from Ancient Times to 1945.* Seoul: Ewha Womans University Press.

Korea Information Service. 1999. *Facts about Korea.* Seoul: Korea Information Service.

Lee, Ki-baik. 1984. *A New History of Korea.* Seoul: Ilchokak Publishers.

Nahm, Andrew. 1987. *A Panorama of 5000 Years: A Korean History.* Seoul: Hollym.

Oberdorfer, Don. 1997. *The Two Koreas: A Contemporary History.* Reading, MA: Addison-Wesley.

Oh, Kongdan, ed. 2000. *Korea Briefing, 1997–1999: Challenges and Changes at the Turn of the Twentieth Century.* New York: M. E. Sharpe, Inc.

Reitman, Valerie. 2000. "Amid Tears, Koreans Cross 50-Year Divide," *Los Angeles Times,* 16 August.

Saccone, Richard. 1993. *Fifty Famous People Who Helped Shape Korea.* Seoul: Hollym Corporation.

Sohn, Yong Taik and Kwang Jae Jim, eds. 1998. *Facts and Fallacies about Korea.* Seoul: Korean Educational Development Institute.

Suh, Dae-Sook. 1988. *Kim Il Sung: The North Korean Leader.* New York: Columbia University Press.

The World Factbook, "North Korea," http://www.odei.gov/cia/publications/factbook/geos/kn.html (cited August 15, 2001).

U.S. Department of State, "Background Note: South Korea," http://www.state.gov/r/pa/bgn/index.cfin?docid=2800 (cited August 15, 2001).

CHAPTER TWO
Economic Development since 1945

SOUTH KOREA

Few countries in the world have matched South Korea's rapid progress in improving its national economic prosperity from 1962 to 1997. In slightly longer than one generation, a country with few natural resources was resurrected from profound poverty to world-class industrialization, trade, and wealth. Sometimes this success story is referred to as the Miracle on the Han. Whether or not it is due to divine intervention, the founders of the Republic of Korea in 1948 would have been astonished to learn that within fifty years this new nation was to become one the world's great economies. Despite the devastating downturn in most Asian economies in the late 1990s, the country showed promising signs of reform and renewed economic growth. Recent developments offer the even greater but more elusive dream of again being part of one Korea.

Panoramic photograph of Seoul. The capital of South Korea is a modern metropolis of 11 million people. The city is safe and clean, and its underground railways are convenient and inexpensive. Even though Seoul is a huge city, South Koreans are inevitably very gracious and helpful to foreign visitors. (Courtesy of Mary Connor)

Precolonial Influences through Japanese Occupation: 1876–1945

In the nineteenth century the West made forays into East Asia in order to benefit from new trade. Along with military muscle to force favorable treaty concessions, attempts were made to modernize the ancient cultures. Japan imitated the industry and military of Western powers and was eager to copy their dynamic expansionism as well. In 1876 Japan forced commercial relations on Korea. As a result of Japanese investments in electrical and communication facilities and railroad construction, Korea experienced rapid economic growth and a rise in per capita income. A small capitalist class emerged during this time as it collaborated with Japanese economic interests. However, in 1910 the hopes for a modern national economy were dashed when Korea became a colony of Japan.

Japanese needs and interests increasingly determined the country's development. The chief beneficiaries of economic expansion were Japan and its colonists. Harsh exploitation forced the population to assimilate, mobilize, and support Japan in war. Railroads, roads, rice mills, textile factories, hydroelectric plants, smelters, oil refineries, shipyards, and new cities were built to service the empire. The economy actually grew very rapidly, but the income of the average Korean remained low because most of the gains went to the Japanese. In 1930, the per capita income was $270, but by the last year of the war, it deteriorated to $251.

The Japanese owned the industrial sector, and the agricultural sector worked primarily to support them. By 1936 more than half of all farm output was shipped to Japan, residents were deported to work in Manchuria and Japan, and farmers were forced to become urban factory workers. During the war years most of the heavy industry was located in the North and the textile industry in the South. Three of the family-owned conglomerates, which have become characteristic of the Korean economy, were founded by men who began their careers during occupation: Yi Pyongch'ol (Samsung), Ku Inhoe (Lucky), and Chung Chu-Yong (Hyundai). These chaebol were patterned after the Japanese *zaibatsu* (money cliques).

Liberation, the Korean War, and the Early Republic: 1945–1960

With the surrender of the Japanese in 1945, colonial occupation ended. Although people rejoiced in their liberation, the sudden loss of Japanese capital, management skills, and technology was devastating. Furthermore, because of the conflicting social and economic systems of the victorious allies, particularly the Soviet Union and the United States, Koreans were now at odds with each other. Antagonism intensified between peasant and landlord and between those who resisted and those who collaborated.

The political division had a particularly destructive effect in the area controlled by the U.S. military forces because the North had most of the advantages when separate development began. Among natural resources, 90 percent of the iron and 98 percent of the bituminous coal industries were located there. The population of the South grew by 25 percent, causing severe food shortages as refugees fled the North and exiles were repatriated from Japan.

The vast majority of people were poor peasants, and a tiny landlord minority held whatever wealth remained. There were thousands of unemployed factory workers and a hundred times as many poor peasants. Six financial cliques, the chaebol, overwhelmingly dominated investment in the heavy industry Japan had developed. Korean managers were altogether excluded, and large-scale businesses very rarely had local ownership. Education, especially in technological training, was severely limited, so a native entrepreneurial class had little opportunity to emerge.

From 1945 to 1948 the United States Army Military Government in Korea (USAMGIK) established direct control over South Korea. As a result of the Cold War and its global containment policy, the United States utilized Japanese-trained police and favored conservative landowners and businesspeople to create an environment where a market economy could thrive. Without this backing, the undeveloped capitalist class would most likely have been swept away in the political turmoil following the war. Whatever market system there was functioned through aid and development programs. Land reform was initially very limited; only 16.5 percent of all farmers became full owners of the land they farmed. When the United States ended its post–World War II occupation, the per capita income was $86.

Syngman Rhee served as the first president of the newly created Republic of Korea from 1948–1960. Although reunification was his highest priority, he hoped to create a stable, viable economy at a time when imports were running at twenty times exports. As soon as Rhee came into power, the government adopted the Land Reform Act, which resulted in one of the most extensive and successful land reform measures in the world. Before this measure, ownership was extremely unequal. Now farm ownership was limited to three *chongbo* (about 7.35 acres), creating a much more equitable income distribution within the agricultural sector.

Two years after Rhee assumed the presidency, the United States, with the support of the United Nations, intervened to halt an invasion by the North Koreans and then later maintained thousands of troops and provided millions of dollars to build up the military forces of the ROK. By the end of the war, Korea was one of the poorest countries in the world. Three years of fighting had destroyed both halves of the country. Nearly 50 percent of the industrial capacity and a third of the housing in the South were destroyed along with much of the public infrastructure. Agriculture was very primitive, unmechanized, and subject to flood and drought. The war eliminated one-quarter of the entire wealth of the country. There were many thousands of war-widows and more than 100,000 orphans. Of the 279,000 unemployed, 72,000 were university graduates and 51,000 were discharged soldiers and laid-off workers.

To rehabilitate the war-ravaged economy, the Rhee administration's principal strategy was a policy of import substitution to limit dependency on foreign resources by increasing domestic production not only in agriculture but also mining and light industry. Consumer nondurables such as textiles and food were primarily financed by the United States in the form of aid and local military procurement, as were 90 percent of imports. The reason for this generosity was the U.S. desire to contain communism and to enable the South to become a self-supporting democracy. Economic health in the 1950s remained for all practical purposes under foreign control.

The forces behind import substitution were the highly centralized family-based industrial and business conglomerates. These chaebol included Samsung, Lucky-Goldstar, and Ssangyong. Rhee's goal was domestic production to satisfy consumer demand. He wanted an industrial economy, with young industries protected, particularly from Japan, which he hated. Either import controls or tariffs were enacted. Overvalued exchange rates for the dollar against the *hwan* (later renamed the *won*) maximized U.S. aid and reduced the cost of imported capital and intermediate goods.

In order to industrialize, Syngman Rhee became proficient at obtaining foreign aid. By the end of the 1950s he had obtained so much aid from the United States that it was the equivalent to five-sixths of all imports. However, this easy access to foreign aid, government-controlled foreign exchange, and bank credit led to corruption and favoritism. Cabinet officials and Rhee's political friends became rich. Business success involved getting government-supported restrictions on imports. Many businesspeople became wealthy as a direct result of these policies and were later accused of unethical transactions.

The U.S. government supported the Rhee administration, but it did not always agree with it. American policy makers felt that the president should adopt an austerity budget in order to control inflation and to attract private investors. Rhee disagreed. President Dwight Eisenhower complained about Rhee's "blackmail" and U.S. Secretary of State John Foster Dulles called him a "master of evasion." Consequently, the United States periodically threatened to reduce its aid program, but Rhee knew that the United States would not abandon him. His approach to industrialization ultimately led to soaring inflation, food shortages, and almost total economic collapse. Meanwhile, the economy of North Korea surpassed that of the South.

Rapid Economic Growth and the State as Entrepreneur: 1961–1971

There seemed to be little hope for Korea's economic future in 1953; however, within ten years of the war, it entered a period of sustained high growth. Between 1962 and 1971 the annual growth rate averaged 13.8 percent. By the early 1970s Korea was considered a newly industrialized economy. The force for change came with the presidency of Park Chung Hee (1961–1979), who was able to organize the human and natural resources of the nation for the first time. Park believed that he had to destroy for all time the vicious cycle of poverty and economic stagnation by reforming the economic structure. He was also determined to surpass North Korea in economic development.

To pursue these goals Park began to make deals with business owners who could have been prosecuted for their illegal activities during the Rhee administration. If they would support his policies of nation-building through industrialization and export promotion, they would escape punishment. In this way he gained their support, foreign trade flourished, and rapid industrialization took place. When his First Five-Year Economic Plan (1962) was implemented, the total value of Korean exports amounted to $55 million; by 1972 it was $1.7 billion.

Even though the per capita GNP was even lower ($80) in 1960 than it had been at the end of U.S. occupation in 1948, South Korea

Table 1. Indicators of Korean Economic Growth

	GNP Growth Rate %	Exports (millions US$)	Rate of Unemployment %
1960	1.1	33	11.7
1965	5.8	175	7.4
1970	7.6	882	4.5
1975	6.8	5,003	4.1
1980	-4.8	17,214	5.2
1985	5.4	26,442	4.0
1990	9.6	65,016	2.4
1991	9.1	71,870	2.3
1992	5.0	76,632	2.4
1993	5.8	82,236	2.8
1994	8.2	96,013	2.4
1995	9.3	123,242	2.0
1996	6.8	129,715	2.0
1997	5.0	136,164	2.6
1998	-6.7	132,313	6.8
1999	10.7	143,685	6.3
2000	9.0	172,270	4.1

Note: The statistical information from 1960 to 1995 is based on GNP. The statistics available after 1995 are based on GDP. The variations are relatively slight.
Sources: Information was obtained from Byung-Nak Song's *The Rise of the Korean Economy* and the Korean National Statistical Office.

had many of the essential ingredients for rapid industrialization: international political support, access to foreign capital and technology, a small class of entrepreneurs, and a large supply of educated and cost-competitive workers. Heavy investment by the public and private sectors in education contributed significantly to economic growth. The amount of total investment in public and private education was greater than that of all other developing countries.

According to Alice H. Amsden, Korea's growth was to become a classic example of a late industrialized nation and embodied all of the elements common to countries such as India, Japan, and Taiwan. Each of these economies involved a high degree of state intervention, growth of large diversified business groups, emergence of salaried managers responsible for utilizing borrowed technology, and implementation of shop-floor management to optimize the transfer of technology. The shop-floor technique focuses on borrowed technology in order to improve quality and total productivity together with an effort to lower prices in order to beat the competition.

The new president moved quickly to increase state control over economic activity. His regime favored a mixed economy because it understood the successful use of state enterprises and planning in North Korea. Park was also a great admirer of the economic accomplishments of Japan and its colonial government in Korea, neither of which was exclusively based on free-market policies.

Because people could not survive with what they produced from their own land, agricultural policies were established to expand rice production through land clearing and the conversion of dry fields into rice paddies, which now achieved the legal designation of absolute arable land never to be used for other purposes. As a result of these regulations, the areas of rice production increased between 1970 and 1980, in spite of the rapid expansion of urban areas.

Because Korea has always had limited resources, its economy had to grow principally through manufacturing. Three objectives were established. First, the government would emphasize industrial growth over increases in per capita income. Second, the economy would be industry-oriented rather than resource- or service-oriented. Third, exports must increase. With the creation of more manufactured goods for export, the ROK could acquire foreign exchange to import food and raw materials.

To force rapid industrial growth and promote exports, the state assumed an entrepreneurial role in determining new products, new production processes, and new markets. In fact it became a stockholder in corporations, most of which also had some private stockholders. It also undertook financial service activities by obtaining foreign capital and providing low-interest or negative-interest loans.

Park nationalized the banking system, which allowed the government to determine the allocation and cost of credit. By 1970, the state directly controlled 96.4 percent of the financial assets. Thus it controlled interest rates and exercised considerable influence over businesses by means of subsidies, preferential tariffs, and a monopoly on foreign exchange. The Economic Planning Board and the Ministry of Trade and Industry were created to monitor and regulate the investments, prices, and trade activities of each firm.

The expansion of industrial capacity was achieved through existing chaebol. Their rate of growth accelerated to the point that they became vertically integrated in the production and distribution of a huge array of goods and services; consequently, these large business combinations greatly reduced their dependence on small firms. At one point, monopolies or oligopolies supplied 87.8 percent of 2,257 major manufactured goods. When start-up companies developed new products or made large profits, they were bought up quickly by the chaebol. Among the fifty largest of them (ranked by sales in 1992), 70 percent were established during the period between 1945 and 1960.

What made this rapid expansion possible was the military, whose leaders met weekly with key economic planners to be briefed on the current state of the economy. Planning and control offices were established in every major ministry of the government. Park's approach to economic development contradicted the U.S. policy recommendations given to Rhee; however, the U.S. government did not object because it was willing to accept whatever was necessary to ensure the stability of its Cold War protégé, noncommunist South Korea.

Government plans to encourage business obviously produced spectacular results. It is estimated that exports were responsible for approximately 30 percent of manufacturing employment by 1966 and about 45 percent by 1980. Although these programs led to impressive economic growth, they immediately revealed disparities in income between agricultural and urban areas. As the urban-rural income gap increased, poor rural people flocked to cities for greater economic opportunities. By the late 1960s, overconcentration in the largest cities, especially Seoul, became a major social problem. By 1995, 86 percent of Koreans lived on 2.3 percent of the national land.

Government pressure to increase production and exports forced companies to rely on loans from banks, either state owned or controlled, in order to finance their expansion. The government encouraged them to borrow money and set interest rates at a low or negative level. So companies borrowed money, often more than they needed. Any surplus was frequently used for real estate speculation. Of course, by borrowing heavily from the banks, the businesses found themselves under tight governmental control.

The National Tax Office employed many incentives. Firms were exempt from indirect taxes on income earned through export sales. Constant surveillance brought about strict compliance. Tax fraud drew down penalties and criminal prosecution. Among other inducements, export firms were granted reduced rates on the purchase of land for new industrial sites. Government agencies also tampered with the exchange-rate system, adopted favorable monetary and fiscal policies, implemented a system of import privileges for exporting firms, and provided cash subsidies to successful trading companies.

The government virtually ordered goals for individual firms, and the managers were expected to maximize exports over profits. If they achieved these goals, they would receive special favors, such as loans, tax benefits, and licenses to import restricted and highly demanded commodities or permits to purchase government properties at under-the-market prices. In exchange for these favors, businesses were obligated to give kickbacks to Park's party, but these transactions were inevitably very lucrative.

Recognition of successful businesspeople by awarding medals and citations was another very effective method of motivating the business community, especially in Korea where people are particularly loyal and patriotic. The administration also used threats—tax inspections, loss of financial support, and legal punishment—to force the business community to comply with its objectives. In this competitive atmosphere, the ability to start new enterprises depended on obtaining low-interest loans and special favors. There was a need for small subcontracting firms to supply components and services; however, many young, ambitious men who wanted to respond to this need by establishing their own businesses found it nearly impossible to do so because of burdensome governmental regulations. It was not a level playing field.

In order to be competitive in the international market, workers, managers, and businesspeople had to be increasingly efficient, innovative, and productive. However, it was low labor costs that consistently provided the competitive edge in international markets. A number of factors made this possible: a low standard of living in the early stages of economic development, a well-educated workforce, low pay relative to business profits, poor working conditions, a fifty-four-hour workweek, workers' endurance in the face of hardships, and the refusal to allow workers to unionize.

Labor and business were obviously treated very differently by the Park regime. The government worked to control wages and restrict labor union activities. When workers demanded better pay and improved working conditions in the late 1960s and early 1970s, labor laws were revised by Park to make unionization more difficult. The procedures for collective bargaining involved so many obstacles that union activity was virtually impossible. The police and other security forces ruthlessly suppressed workers, resulting in brutal violence and imprisonment. Only recently has the government modified its harsh treatment.

Although the success of Park's ambitious economic objectives far exceeded world expectations and was considered the zenith of achievement, favoritism for monopolies, concentration on single industries, and repression of labor were the sources of future difficulties.

New Industries, Inflation, and Urban Problems, 1971–1979

Throughout the Park regime the government continued to manage the economy. In the 1970s it supervised a transition to heavy and chemical industrialization (HCI), such as shipbuilding, petrochemicals, heavy machinery, electronics, and automobiles. Park's hope was to make steel, not shoes or wigs, the symbol of the nation's economy. In developing the steel and iron industry, the ROK faced many challenges: lack of natural resources and the need for huge amounts of capital and high levels of technology. In spite of these difficulties, it managed to construct, in a relatively short period of time, one of the largest and most competitive steel industries in the world: the Pohang Iron and Steel Mill (1973). The demand for steel came mainly from the developing world, not the advanced countries. By 1979 Korea was a surplus producer and net exporter of steel.

In creating a steel industry, big business had the certainty of financial support from the government and access to the latest technology. The chaebol were given a monopoly or oligopoly of goods and services and received enormous favors. During this time the relationship between the government and business changed. Rather than the dominant, and at times antagonistic, position of the state during the 1960s, it now developed a more symbiotic relationship.

Why was Korea so successful in developing the steel industry? Aside from intimate business-government cooperation that included long-term, low-interest loans, it had disciplined and industrious managers. And laborers were working long hours at low wages to reduce construction costs. The country also had the latest technology, such as the electric furnace and basic iron furnace, which further reduced costs and increased productivity. By 1982 the cost of steel per ton was $421.1 in the United States, $246.9 in Japan, and $200.7 in Korea. Among the developing countries, its performance was unmatched.

Park was also personally committed to the development of the semiconductor industry. As with steel, electronics had been a key target since 1965. In addition to the extensive infrastructure and support facilities provided by the state, manufacturers were given extensive privileges. Among them were tax reduction, exemption from bureaucratic red tape, and low-rent state-built factories. Companies also obtained substantial investment from the Japanese semiconductor industry.

With continued government support and foreign investments, the semiconductor industry expanded rapidly. In 1969 Samsung, the largest domestic chaebol, moved toward joint ventures with Japan. In spite of opposition from the government, Samsung-Sanyo merged, and since that time, Samsung has remained the leader of the electronics industry. By 1973, the industry accounted for more than 5 percent of national exports. By 1990, Korea had become one of the world's largest producers of semiconductor integrated circuits, behind only Japan and the United States. Three chaebol (Hyundai, Goldstar, and Samsung) made substantial investments in new product development.

Government emphasis on growth over stability created rapid but sharply fluctuating growth. Wholesale and consumer prices rose significantly at times. This inflation hurt creditors, savers, those on fixed incomes, and the retired. Also, with the rapid expansion of industry, the amount of investment exceeded the amount of domestic savings.

Economic stability did become an issue when international events threatened it. In 1971 President Nixon decided to correct the U.S. balance of payments problem by devaluing the dollar and allowing it to "float" in international money markets. Along with those of other nations throughout the world, the Korean economy was disrupted. When high inflation occurred as a result of the first oil crisis in 1973, the economy experienced another severe blow. Fortunately, it was able to recycle earnings by bidding on Middle East construction projects. The profits were used to buy oil. That construction boom began around 1976. The oil crisis also made giant tankers a necessity, so the country started from scratch to create a shipbuilding industry.

Absolute poverty had declined from 40 percent to about 5 percent by the early 1960s, but there appeared to be growing inequity of income and wealth distribution. Between 1965 and 1985, the top 20 percent of the population received about 47 percent of the national income; however, overall wealth was more concentrated because of real estate holdings. The top 5 percent of the population had 31 percent, and the top 1 percent had 14 percent of the national wealth. The accumulation of wealth through real estate speculation and windfall profits became a major discontent of ordinary citizens.

Another concern was the amount of foreign borrowing. The need to import oil and industrial materials led to increased foreign debt. By the end of Park's rule in 1979, total foreign debt had risen to $20.5 billion or 34.1 percent of the GNP. Also, the debt-equity ratio of large firms, which had been forced to increase their production and export capacity, was high, even compared to that of other newly industrialized Asian countries. Unfortunately, government loan guarantees were approved on the basis of political connections rather than on sound economic principles.

Expansionist policies led to the excessive concentration of industries and population in large cities. Urban problems, such as shortage of housing, lack of educational facilities, and poor public services, had already been major domestic issues. In promoting business expansion, Park favored his home region of North Kyongsang Province. Little towns near his birthplace were transformed into industrial cities, while in southwest Cholla peasants in thatched-roof huts lived at near-subsistence levels. Uneven regional development, inefficient use of human resources, regional tensions, and political instability plagued the nation.

Between 1965 and 1970, rural household incomes fell 33 percent in relation to urban incomes. This growing disparity brought about the New Village Movement in 1971 in order to bring immediate improvements in the income and living conditions of rural people to encourage them to stay on the farm. A price-support system for rice raised rural household incomes to almost the same level as urban household incomes by 1975. Another plan to restrict the expansion of Seoul created a land shortage and forced up the price of real estate. This created a greater gap between wage earners and property owners. In 1976, the government implemented a population redistribution plan for the capital region.

The Role of the United States and Economic Development in Korea: 1946–1976

Between 1946 and 1976 the United States provided a total of $12.6 billion in economic and military assistance to South Korea; this was "more dollars per capita of aid than to any other foreign country except South Vietnam and Israel" (Eckert 1990, 396). The United States financed not only approximately 70 percent of the country's imports, but nearly 80 percent of the total capital formation in transportation, manufacturing, and electric power. The United States also revived the textile industry. Almost all of the American economic assistance before 1964 was provided on a grant basis; consequently, it was possible for the country to begin its export-led growth in the 1960s with limited debt. The $6.8 billion in military aid (not including the cost of the Korean War) contributed significantly by freeing domestic resources for development. The United States also granted the Republic special privileges in U.S. markets.

Korea also profited greatly from U.S. technology and technical expertise. Monetary aid helped to finance new technology and to create official research and development organizations, such as the Korea Development Institute (KDI) and the Korea Institute of Science and Technology (KIST). American aid funds were also allocated for specific projects to support development plans.

A major contribution to economic growth occurred with South Korea's support of the United States in the Vietnam War. When President Lyndon Johnson sought international support for the war, few nations responded positively. The ROK became the most important contributor to the war effort by supplying about 300,000 troops between 1965 and 1973. In return the United States agreed in the Brown Memorandum to provide the equipment, training, supplies, and salaries of all ROK forces employed in Vietnam. It also agreed to modernize the military forces; purchase South Korean supplies, equipment, and services needed for the Vietnam War; and hire local contractors to participate in U.S. construction projects in South Vietnam. The ROK economy flourished as never before. Rapid export-led growth had started by 1965, but the war boom lifted the economy to a new level, one similar to what happened in Japan during the Korean War. By 1970 U.S. payments to South Korea under the Brown Memorandum were almost $1 billion.

The economic effects of Vietnam spiraled. Many firms, Hanjin and Hyundai among them, obtained tremendous financial assistance through their participation in the war effort. The founder of Hanjin, Cho Chunghun, set up a transport company in South Vietnam and ultimately was given full responsibility for the port of Qui Nhon. Later Cho established an air and transport firm to carry South Korean products and workers to South Vietnam. Two years afterward he took over the nearly bankrupt Korean Air Lines and used his Vietnam trade to revitalize the company and to raise Hanjin into the ranks of a chaebol by the 1970s. Hyundai also had spectacular success as a result of its involvement in Vietnam. It became a major construction company for the U.S. army in Vietnam and later used its connections and expertise to expand into the construction business in the Middle East.

The Role of Japan in Economic Development: 1961–1979

Diplomatic ties with Japan were not reestablished until 1965, in part because of the bitterness of the Korean people and the dogged anti-Japanese position of President Syngman Rhee. However, educated citizens, fluent in Japanese because of the assimilation policies of occupation, read Japanese newspapers, magazines, and books for the latest information on economic trends and technological innovation. As Japan began to reemerge as an important international economic force in the late 1950s, it became a model of economic development. Soon after Rhee was overthrown in 1960, the U.S. State Department applied pressure on the government to normalize relations with Japan. Park Chung Hee, fluent in Japanese and deeply influenced by his military training under the Japanese, needed few incentives to formalize ties with Japan.

The Normalization Treaty of 1965 led to widespread Japanese involvement in Korea, and the economic impact was immediate. Prior to 1965 most of Korea's trade was with the United States; however, within slightly more than twelve months, Japan surpassed the United States as Korea's most important trading partner and continued to hold this position throughout the 1960s and 1970s. Since 1971, Japan's investment in South Korea has been more substantial than that of any other country.

Normalization came at a fortuitous time. The United States had cut back the aid Park desperately needed for economic development. The ROK–Japan Normalization Treaty included $300 million in grants, $200 million in public loans, and $300 million (later raised to $500 million) in commercial credit over a decade. In 1982 the Chun Doo Hwan regime signed a second loan agreement for $4 billion. Large amounts of private Japanese capital and technology also poured into South Korea and facilitated rapid economic development. The Japanese government continued its commitment and eventually helped to pay for the 1988 Summer Olympics in Seoul.

Korean bitterness toward the Japanese continued, but geographic location and language stimulated economic cooperation. Tokyo and Seoul are only two hours apart by air and are in the same time zone. Korean and Japanese grammar and syntax are similar in many respects, and mastery of each other's language is relatively easy. Both written languages use Chinese characters. The Japanese sound system is particularly easy for Koreans to master. In addition to mastering the Japanese language with relative ease, Koreans learned the Japanese ways of doing business and managing the economy.

Economic Stability, Social Equity, and Labor Militancy: 1979–1988

The economy of the ROK faced its first national economic crisis in 1979. Massive foreign debt grew to over $20 billion. The inflation rate shot up to 21.2 percent. Export earnings plummeted. The trade deficit reached $4,396 billion. Students joined workers in protests and strikes. When the demonstrators demanded his resignation, Park called out the police, who brutally silenced all protests. Within weeks, the head of the Korean Central Intelligence Agency (KCIA), who claimed that he was preventing the slaughter of innocent civilians, assassinated Park.

Parlaying his close friendship with Park and his appointment to investigate the assassination, Major General Chun Doo Hwan moved swiftly to solidify and increase his power. Beginning with a military coup on December 12, 1979, Chun seized control over the military. Within the next ten months he illegally assumed control over the KCIA, declared martial law, and strengthened the police force. He continued Park's top-down management style and promotion of exports, but he emphasized stability. The government lowered interest rates to reduce business costs. Concomitantly, pressure had to be put on businesses to keep prices down. The government also worked to keep foreign exchange rates within a narrow range and to keep wages under control. The administration attempted to harness inflation.

One of the additional problems to emerge was the fact that most of the newly established heavy industries were dependent on Japanese components, machinery, and technology. For example, South Korea had built one of the largest shipyards in the world, but only the hulls were produced domestically; all the machinery, engines, and instruments were imported from Japan.

In 1980 the GNP rate fell by 4.8 percent, and inflation reached 25.6 percent. Within the next twelve months, Korea was to become the third largest debtor nation in the world after Mexico and Brazil, and most of South Korea's debt was short-term. The Carter administration offered Chun $600 million in import credits. Encouraged by this degree of support from the United States, Chun eliminated all labor agitation. Japan also assisted with a $4 billion loan at preferential interest rates. In return Chun opened Korean markets to American and Japanese service industries, such as banks and insurance companies, and to American agricultural exports of rice, wheat, tobacco, and fruit.

By the mid-1980s exports of heavy industrial goods exploded, and the economy grew by more than 12 percent per year from 1985 through 1988. Inflation remained low and unemployment ranged from 2 to 4 percent. Company assets and the stock market began to be more important sources of capital than loans from the government, though those loans remained significant. The total value of the stock market increased 28-fold between 1980 and 1989. That value was only 9 percent of the GNP in 1985, but nearly 57 percent in 1988. By the early 1990s Korea was the ninth largest market in the world.

The Chun regime also set out immediately to end the concentration of power of the conglomerates. Nonetheless, the business community resisted Chun's reforms when they went against its interests. The Fair Trade and Monopoly Act was enacted in April 1981 to decrease the chaebol's economic concentration and price-fixing. Predictably, the provisions of the act were not effectively enforced. Two years after its enactment no fewer than 258 cases were cited of attempts to increase horizontal integration by the acquisition of independent firms. When ordered to take over troubled firms, the chaebol demanded tax subsidies and money as conditions of these forced mergers. The government accepted these stipulations; yet the consolidations did not necessarily materialize.

Restructuring was intended to stop overinvestment and duplicate investment and to reduce the fiscal burden on the public. However, by the 1980s the structure of business concentration could not be corrected because the economy depended so heavily upon the chaebol that it was very difficult to eliminate their activities without bringing harm to the economy. Although Chun did reduce inefficient competition, he created a new type of state-business alliance. He postponed essential reforms and in this continued a tradition that lasted until the Asian crisis in 1997.

The conglomerates were now in a position to take advantage of the global economic expansion. Foreign investors and consumers regained confidence in the South Korean economy and Chun's strategies to achieve rapid economic growth. In 1986 Korea achieved its first trade surplus of $4.2 billion. In only two more years the surplus reached $11.4 billion. These results were achieved by massive exports of cars, computers, microwaves, and consumer electronics, most of which were sold in the United States.

In spite of such outward signs of success, there were serious economic and social problems with the growth model. Newer production techniques included automation and computerization that eliminated jobs. A shift from labor- to capital-intensive organization was overdue. High on the agenda should have been the economic infrastructure, such as ports, roads, and railroads. The country would suffer the consequences in the last decade of the century.

Prior to the 1980s the state had used its power over credit and markets to manage investment and production. However, with the growth of the economy, the chaebol amassed more power, to the point that they could collectively dominate state policy. As revenues from exports boomed, they gained almost complete financial independence from the government. Meanwhile, they poured money into land and stock speculation instead of productive investments and contributed to the increased cost of housing and the general rate of inflation. Unfortunately, the government was not strong enough to force them to sell their real estate and use the capital for core enterprises and the development a stronger position in global markets.

In the mid-1980s, big companies began investing overseas. The labor-intensive industries, such as footwear and textiles, were having difficulties; consequently, management explored relocating to countries where labor costs were cheaper. At the same time, electronics firms were concerned that the protective tariffs developed nations placed on imported goods would hurt the industry. To avoid such import tariffs, they established plants in Europe and North America.

Another problem was nonperforming assets (NPAs). The government's attempt to solve this problem made the concentration of power in the chaebol even worse. The shipping industry provides a good example. By the early 1980s, Korea's overexpanded and overinvested shipping industry found itself in severe competition from foreign firms that got support and protection from their governments. When the second oil shock and a resulting global business slowdown occurred, cutthroat competition among national firms threatened the financial stability of many shippers. The government then stepped in and implemented mergers, leaving the remaining firms supposedly solvent. This program was intended primarily to help the creditor banks carrying the NPAs. However, to implement the mergers, more financial support had to be extended in the form of debt rescheduling and new loans.

To deal with the NPA problem, the government provided tax exemptions and deductions when the collateral of the NPAs was sold off. Tax privileges were also provided to institutions in financial difficulty and to the firms that were taking them over. The government then moved to provide financial privileges to the banks that took over the failing firms. The details of these transactions were not made public, even after the takeovers were completed. These maneuvers became a serious political issue. In most cases the firms taking over the insolvent companies were affiliates of the chaebol. As a result the NPA problem further worsened.

During this period the government announced that it was implementing liberalization and deregulation policies; however, the government's role with business did not decrease. Privatization of government-owned banks was minimal. These banks operated as arms of governmental policies and lent money to the well-established and favored groups. The financial resources of the banks were still concentrated in very limited sectors determined by the government. Interest remained artificially low.

South Korea's success in the export market created conflicts with the United States. Since the U.S. trade deficit increased significantly in the 1980s, South Korea was pressured to increase the value of the won and to open more of its markets to U.S. products. The government agreed and allowed the won to rise by 16 percent to the dollar in 1988. It also agreed to reduce trade barriers.

This success also threatened Japan. After the United States forced Japan to revalue the yen, Japan realized that South Korean automobiles and consumer electronics were now seriously threatening its position in U.S. markets. In response to this development, Japan delayed technology and components to South Korean producers. The importance of this development is conveyed by the fact that in 1986, when South Korea registered its first trade surplus of $4.2 billion, the country ran a trade deficit with Japan of $5.4 billion. Some 90 percent of imports from Japan were targeted for use in export industries.

Even more threatening to economic growth was the rise of labor militancy in the 1980s. Part of the strategy in developing heavy and chemical industries was the creation of massive industrial complexes with nearby housing for large communities of workers. In 1985 there were two major strikes: one against Daewoo Motors and the other against Daewoo Apparel. Daewoo Motors was the first significant strike against a chaebol. The second was notable because it led to sol-idarity strikes by other workers in the area and enjoyed the support of students and people who leaned toward socialism.

By 1987 widespread strikes broke out against the chaebol. They were supported not only by employees of the conglomerates but also by those in small and medium-sized manufacturing firms and by white-collar workers in numerous occupations such as health, finance, research, education, transportation, and tourism. The pri-mary objective of labor was to obtain union recognition and improve working conditions.

Strong controls had kept workers in line. The government allowed one union per company. Some companies disallowed unions. In small companies, management could intimidate workers so that the minimum number of employees necessary by law to form a union would not be met. Only 12 percent of the 17 million people in the workforce belonged to unions in 1987.

During a period of rapid industrialization workers saw no particu-lar improvement in pay or work conditions. In the 1980s Korea had the longest average workweek in the world. For persons employed in manufacturing in 1984, 73 percent of men and 62 percent of women worked at least fifty-four hours per week. The percentage of indus-trial accidents was higher than in Taiwan or Japan. Between 1964 and 1994, 39,000 workers were killed and 2.9 million were injured in work-related accidents.

Samsung, with its sophisticated management policies, for the most part was able to avoid labor violence; however, this was not the case with Hyundai. Chung Chu-Yong, the head of Hyundai, main-tained the view that workers had no rights to make demands in his company. In one instance, a prolonged strike at the shipyard cost the company millions of dollars and forced twenty suppliers into near bankruptcy. It finally ended when 9,000 riot troops were dispatched.

Another significant development in labor activity was the formation of workers' organizations that were initially regional, but became national in scope. Unions for workers in small and medium-sized indus-tries created the Korea Trade Union Congress (KTUC) and called for democracy, self-reliance, and national reunification. This development influenced the creation of the Conference of Large Factory Trade Unions, which included sixteen of the largest workplace unions. It agreed to pursue concerns relating to prices, housing, and taxation.

A federation was formed that included workers in hospitals, schools, the media, financial institutions, and printing businesses. As a result of these labor organizations, wages increased by nearly 25 percent in 1989. Labor militancy and international economic conditions helped cause exports to fall and the trade deficit to rise. The rate of exports fell from 28.4 percent in 1988 to 5.7 percent in 1989.

The World Stage: 1988–1992

For Korea 1988 was a year of great significance. Roh Tae Woo's inauguration on February 25 marked the first peaceful transformation of presidential power since 1948. A revised economic and social plan was introduced stating that political democracy brought with it a strong demand for a more equitable distribution of wealth. The planners believed it was time to accommodate farmers, fishermen, and industrial workers. The public blamed the concentration of power and wealth of the chaebol for a myriad of social and economic problems. In particular, the big four (Daewoo, Hyundai, Lucky-Goldstar, and Samsung), were denounced as greedy and unscrupulous. Responding to public pressure, President Roh's economic advisors attempted to limit the chaebol's lines of credit and their central role in exports and to shift subsidies to smaller businesses.

The year 1988 was also of great significance because the Summer Olympic Games came to Seoul, and the Republic was now able to give the world its first good look at modern Korea. Global television brought the opening ceremonies to more than 1 billion people, the largest television audience in history for any event up to that time. As the Roh government (1988–1993) saw it, the Twenty-fourth Olympiad was an international coming-out party and an opportunity to show the world that South Korea was no longer poverty-stricken, but a strong, modern, prosperous country. In preparation for this event, which would bring the largest influx of foreigners since the war, the government invested heavily in building roads, subways, and housing. In the minds of South Koreans, this event marked the triumph over the North.

By the mid-1980s Korean exports (color televisions, automobiles, and computers) became increasingly competitive with the United States and Japan. Realizing that Korea would need to diversify its export markets to avoid sanctions and restraints in concentrated markets, Roh Tae Woo tried hard to expand trade with socialist countries. Trade delegations were sent to Eastern Europe and the Soviet Union and later to China and Vietnam. Aside from the extraordinary achievements, by the mid- to late-1980s there was little change in

Cheju Island, the Yellow Sea, and magnificent resort hotel. Cheju Island, one of the most popular spots for Koreans and foreign travelers, is considered "the Hawaii of Korea." It includes geographic features similar to Hawaii, such as spectacular beaches, extinct volcanoes, waterfalls, and palm trees. (Courtesy of Mary Connor)

the strategies used to deal with labor and no success in coping with the powerful chaebol. Roh continued his predecessor's tough policies toward labor and unionization.

By 1988 the Republic of Korea had amazed the world by becoming one of the top five trade-surplus countries along with Japan, Germany, Taiwan, and Canada. The main trading partner was the United States. The surplus with the United States grew from $4.3 billion in 1985 to $8.7 billion in 1988. Approximately 35 percent of Korean exports were sent to the United States and 15 percent to Japan. In 1989, when the teachers defied the government and formed the National Teachers and Educational Workers Union, Roh ordered all teachers associated with the union fired. More than 1,600 lost their jobs in the union's first year. Hundreds were imprisoned for demonstrating for the right to form a union. Trade offices were subsequently established. Trade with China reached $10 billion by 1992. South Koreans became economic advisers to some of the former Soviet republics.

Even with the support of the public, the government was unable to enact effective legislation against the chaebol. For example, the government attempted unsuccessfully to pass a law that required what was called a real name bank account, a measure that might have forced substantial compliance with tax regulations. However, after a few years of struggle, bureaucrats and political leaders once again realized that the chaebol were too large to subdue. The government succumbed to pressure and allowed them easier access to credit and new tax incentives for corporate investment.

One way that the chaebol maintained their power was to install their own people into the government. One-third of the fathers-in-law of owners were high-ranking officials in all three branches of the government. For example, President Roh Tae Woo married two children into chaebol-owning families. He also appointed one of his relatives to be minister of commerce and industry and another minister of political affairs.

Although these practices created dangerous ties between business and government, they reflect the Korean management style, a Confucian tradition stressing the importance of family. In spite of the rapid changes that have taken place in recent years, the family remains the basic social organization and the model for behavior of entrepreneurs. Business founders are expected to provide not only for their own immediate families, but also for their close relatives, distant relatives, and members of the clan.

When Roh was put on trial in 1996, three years after his presidency, ordinary people were stunned by the enormity of the illegal funds that he had managed to accumulate from the business sector. The degree of corruption that appeared at a time when democratization was taking place demonstrated the powerful and resilient ties between the state and big business together with ancient tradition.

During the 1990s Korea's economy began to slow. World economic conditions caused a slowdown in export growth. Widespread strikes and rapid wage increases occurred at home. For most people the quality of life seemed to deteriorate. Inflation was higher than it had been for some time. Violent crime increased. Air pollution was prevalent in all urban areas. Seoul, with one-quarter of the Republic's population, was in a constant state of traffic gridlock.

Changes were also emerging in the labor market. Improved living standards created a demand for foreign labor to perform menial jobs that many people no longer wanted. In 1991 there was a 20 percent labor shortage among unskilled workers. Illegal workers, especially ethnic Koreans from Manchuria, began to enter the country. At the same time the highly educated had more difficulty obtaining desirable positions. Unemployment in 1991 was only 1.1 percent for those with less than a junior-high-school education, but more than three times as much for those with some college.

Ten percent of landowners held 66 percent of the land, and capital gains from real estate exceeded the GNP in 1989. Land prices increased by more than 100 percent between 1987 and 1991. Consequently, land and high housing costs again became major economic and social issues. The public was increasingly concerned about the economy. Roh's successor, Kim Young Sam, vowed to build a New Korea, fight corruption, revitalize the weakened economy, and restore national self-confidence.

Failed Reform and Increased Labor Agitation: 1992–1997

In 1992, for the first time in more than thirty years, a nonmilitary leader became president through direct election. Kim Young Sam defeated Kim Dae-jung and Chung Chu-Yong, the founder of Hyundai. His campaign platform incorporated goals that resonated with the middle class. His victory was a test of economic reform.

A sluggish economy, particularly in the first quarter of 1992, made revitalization his first priority. He knew that the current problems had to be approached differently than in the past. The institutions that had brought economic growth were now inhibiting it. The engine for the new advance was to be the innovative spirit of the Korean people. The first step included a number of short-term measures for recovery: a more flexible monetary policy, creation of a $1.75 billion fund to assist small and medium-sized companies, reduction of regulations in order to encourage private initiative, and the encouragement of foreign investment for technological development. The Five-Year Plan for the New Economy included budgetary, banking, and administrative reforms. Some of the specific plans eliminated tax evasion and tax exemption for preferred groups, ended regulations hostile to innovative economic activities, and increased public support for housing and the environment. Kim pledged to weaken the chaebol monopoly over economic life by allowing market forces to shape the labor situation, investment, and credit allocation decisions.

Economic conditions became more serious after Kim's first year in office. The GNP grew at a slower annual rate of only 3.3 percent in the first quarter and 4.2 percent in the second, and capital investment

Massive apartment structures, Seoul. The high cost of housing has been a major economic issue for city dwellers. (Courtesy of Mary Connor)

was down by 15 percent in the first six months. Chaebol leaders blamed Kim's antagonistic policies and bellicose rhetoric against North Korea for undermining business confidence and progress.

As the economy weakened and pressures mounted, Kim abandoned his plans for radical restructuring, justifying his actions in the name of market efficiency. He eliminated restrictions on chaebol borrowing, permitted them to purchase controlling shares in privatized state industries, and reduced government supervision and regulation of investment and production. As a result, the value of the top thirty chaebol rose from 13.5 percent of the GNP in 1992 to 16.2 percent in 1995. That year a government report showed that the top five chaebol—Hyundai, Samsung, Daewoo, LG (formerly Lucky-Goldstar), and Sunkyung—accounted for 55.7 percent of the combined assets of the thirty chaebol and 66 percent of their annual sales.

Kim also changed his mind on labor. Originally he promised that he would avoid involvement in disputes. After thousands of Hyundai autoworkers and ship workers went on strike, he sent out the riot police. Thousands were arrested. The administration would not allow the economy to suffer because of illegal labor activity. When Korea Telecommunications workers demonstrated for improved working conditions, the government arrested the union leaders. Kim warned that any act by a striking union member would be considered an attempt to overthrow the government. As soon as approximately one hundred teachers signed a statement calling for education reform and offered their recommendations, the government insisted their demands must be connected to union strategy and arrested some of the teachers.

Pro-chaebol and antilabor policies did produce growth but no long-term solutions. In 1994 exports grew by 17 percent and the GNP by 8.34 percent. In 1995 exports jumped another 32 percent and the GNP rose 9.3 percent. Nonetheless, imports surpassed exports and the trade deficit reached $20 billion by 1996. One of the principal reasons for this apparent anomaly is that manufacturing needed Japanese capital, technology, and components. Of the $29 billion of negative trade, $15 billion was with Japan.

There were several reasons for the continued growth of the trade deficit. In order to get into the Organization for Economic Cooperation and Development (OECD), Kim had to lower trade barriers, thereby allowing Japanese and U.S. producers to increase exports to the ROK. Meanwhile, regional overproduction, caused by other Asian countries trying to adopt South Korea's export strategy, resulted in increased competition and lower prices for major exports, such as computer memory chips, steel, and petrochemicals.

As the country continued to struggle with the economy, labor became increasingly militant. In 1995, the Conference of Large Factory Trade Unions and the Korea Congress of Independent Industrial Federations joined together with newly formed public sector unions to form the Korea Confederation of Trade Unions (KCTU). The government declared it illegal.

In 1996, workers in five public state-run corporations declared their intentions to organize a general strike over wages, working conditions, and the reinstatement of 200 fired workers. When the government refused to negotiate unless certain terms were met, the KCTU threatened to call a nationwide general strike. One day before the unions were to begin their strike, the government backed down and agreed to increase wages significantly and to reinstate the fired workers. Unsuccessful in their efforts to oust the Kim regime, diverse groups of militant activists joined together to develop new strategies.

To reestablish business confidence, Kim took actions that past dictators had taken. In December 1996 in a secret National Assembly meeting with no opposition party members present, two bills were passed. One gave power to the National Security Planning Agency (formerly the KCIA). The second strengthened labor laws to make it easier for companies to fire workers and end strikes.

The Economic Collapse: 1997

In the first six months of 1997 thousands of companies declared bankruptcy. These included Kia (one of the country's largest automobile manufacturers), Hanbo Steel and General Construction (part of the fourteenth largest chaebol), and Sammi Steel (part of the twenty-sixth largest chaebol). The inability of the government to deal with these problems, particularly the bankruptcy of Kia, the tenth largest conglomerate, served as a warning to domestic and foreign investors. The bankruptcies were a signal to the world not only of serious problems in the economy, but of the even graver economic problems that were to unfold throughout Southeast Asia that year.

Another sign of serious trouble was debt. Throughout the 1990s investment exceeded domestic savings by 3 to 4 percent each year. This gap had to be filled by borrowing from foreign financial institutions, especially in the short-term, which now reached $90 billion out of a total of $160 billion in foreign debt. Creditors demanded their money, and pressure rose to devalue the won. World financial leaders tried to protect the won/dollar exchange rate by pouring over $20 billion into the foreign-exchange market. However, when financial crises also emerged in Thailand, Indonesia, and the Hong Kong stock market, foreign creditors began to pull their money out of the country and refused to refinance existing loans. Conditions went from bad to worse when Japanese bankers, suffering from their own recession, withdrew loans. The government denied the existence of a crisis.

Nonetheless, the economic crisis became official on November 21, 1997, when the available foreign-exchange reserves dried up and desperate attempts to support the won failed. The deputy prime minister asked for a bailout package from the International Monetary Fund (IMF). The press immediately reported "a day of national humiliation." In December, the government accepted an IMF program of structural adjustments in exchange for some $55 billion in loans.

Economic Restructuring

What were the basic problems with the Korean economy? First, there was corporate leadership. One person or family dominated the chaebol, and the decision-making process was not transparent. Corporations pursued projects in highly competitive, capital-intensive industries, such as the semiconductor, automobile, chemical, and steel industries, without stockholder oversight. Second, the financial sector supported these speculative projects by providing loans on attractive terms. For example, the Hanbo Group poured almost 6 trillion won—most of which was borrowed from banks—into an unprofitable steel business before it collapsed. Third, the strong ties between conglomerates and politicians facilitated funding for risky projects. What had worked originally to create an economic miracle contributed to a catastrophe.

The principal objectives of restructuring were stabilizing the finances of the conglomerates and lowering the debt-to-equity ratio of the financial institutions. The essential guidelines set by the government and the IMF to achieve these objectives were to improve the transparency and accountability of corporate management, abolish mutual debt guarantees between affiliated companies of a conglomerate, lower the debt-to-equity ratio to less than 200 percent, and increase the responsibility of major shareholders.

Chaebol indebtedness was well out of line with corporate borrowing in other countries. In 1997, the average debt-to-equity ratio of Korean-listed companies was roughly 400 percent. The same figures for U.S. and Japanese firms in 1996 were only about 150 percent and 100 percent, respectively. Large chaebol now had to submit combined financial statements to reveal insider trading among affiliates. Every listed company needed at least one director from outside the company on its board. Also, minority shareholders were to have greater rights to sue the CEO of a company.

In the process of implementing these guidelines, many small and medium-sized companies declared bankruptcies throughout 1998. Large conglomerates, not including the big five, had to prove their fiscal standing in order to get loans from creditor banks. This painful process was called a workout. When a conglomerate was judged unsound, it was forced to downsize: laying off labor and management, selling assets, and replacing top managers, before getting any continued support from creditor banks.

The largest conglomerates, Hyundai, Samsung, Daewoo, LG, and Sunkyung, presented the greatest challenge. More heavily in debt and carrying failed investments on their books, their average debt-to-equity ratio was 477 percent. The government tried to force these chaebol to exchange subsidiaries with one other and focus on their core business. For example, the Samsung Group was to take over an electronics firm of the Daewoo Group and the latter an automobile business of Samsung. This transaction was to be undertaken by the end of 1998; however, because of normal resistance and the intricacy of negotiations, it did not happen.

The workout process turned out to be slower than expected. Of the 65 companies that agreed to improve their financial status, only 9 percent actually implemented their original plans. In order to avoid the traditional use of creative accounting techniques to minimize their debt, both Daewoo and Hyundai announced dramatic restructuring plans, which included huge asset sales in May of 1999.

When the government asked the IMF for a bailout package, the exchange rate soared as everyone tried to get as much hard currency as they could for fear of a moratorium. Within two months the value of the won in relation to the dollar was halved. Financial institutions made no new loans to businesses because they had to meet the Bank of International Settlements (BIS) 8 percent ratio of assets to loans. The stock market collapsed. Even more serious was an increase in the interest rates. The IMF demanded a high-interest-rate policy to stabilize the exchange rate. Rates soared to 30 percent. This resulted in a tremendous number of bankruptcies. Over 20,000 companies became insolvent in 1998, creating even more unemployment.

By the second half of 1998, the exchange rate stabilized and the stock market index and interest rates returned to their precrisis levels. Massive restructuring in the corporate sector was in motion and the number of bankruptcies was in decline. Initially, planners relied on rescheduling foreign debt and on receiving huge loans from the IMF and other international lending institutions, such as the International Bank for Reconstruction and the Asian Development Bank. This approach was very successful; however, the structural problems remained.

When the crisis hit, the financial sector held excessive numbers of bad loans. These were the result of a deficient management system, the lack of accountability to stockholders, and insufficient government supervision. The absence of a responsible management system led to a situation whereby senior bank managers made easy loans to the conglomerates without careful analysis. Because of the regulation that no one could own more than 4 percent of a commercial bank's shares, there were no major shareholders in the banking sector. This allowed bank managers to make decisions without having to be responsible to any stockholders for their mistakes. Another factor that contributed to the crisis was the lack of government supervision of the financial institutions. When commercial banks made loans to troubled countries such as Thailand and Indonesia, the government did not have adequate qualified personnel to stop these hazardous investments.

Upon the recommendation of the IMF, the government established the Financial Supervisory Commission (FSC) to oversee banking, securities, and insurance practices and to pursue reform in two areas: restructuring and liberalization. Its most important assignment was to deal with the huge number of nonperforming loans (NPLs) held by financial institutions. It purchased them, injected new capital, and protected depositors whose financial institutions had merged or closed. Efforts were also made to make the financial sector more competitive with substantial supervision and risk management.

By mid-1998 the NPLs in all financial institutions totaled some 136 trillion won, roughly 22 percent of the total loans. To deal with this problem, the government created the Korean Asset Management Corporation (KAMCO) giving it substantial funding to begin to sell collateral and call in loans. It purchased NPLs at estimated market value, which was to be roughly 50 percent of book value. These actions were similar to those undertaken by the Resolution Trust Corporation in 1989 in the United States during the U.S. savings and loan crisis.

The commercial banks caused the biggest concern because they held the majority of the NPLs. The Bank of International Settlements set a ratio of 8 percent reserves to loans. Of the twenty-four commercial banks, twelve were below this level. They were identified as being unsound and were ordered to resubmit rehabilitation plans. Two of them, Korea First Bank and Seoul Bank, were taken over by the government, injected with 1.5 trillion won, and sold to the Hong Kong and Shanghai Bank of China in early 1999. Five commercial banks were suspended from operating, and 32 percent of the employees (17,000 workers) from nine major commercial banks were terminated.

In addition to these actions, merchant banks, leasing companies, and insurance companies were also forced to restructure. Of the 30 merchant banks that existed before the financial crisis, 11 survived. Only 15 leasing companies initially withstood the process. By August 1998, 4 life insurance companies had closed, and the overhaul of the insurance industry continued. By May 1999, 160 financial institutions disappeared in the financial-sector reform. In order to attract capital, most of the restrictions on foreign investors were removed. Foreign-exchange controls eased.

As financial and corporate sector reforms continued, there were numerous public enterprises that underwent reform. Public sector reform, guided by the Planning and Budget Commission (PBC), was established in February 1998 by the newly elected President Kim Dae-jung to establish guidelines for budgeting and reforming the public sector. As a result of the guidance of the PBC, related organizations were combined and more than 50,000 employees were terminated by the end of 1999. Privatization of major public enterprises, such as Korea Telecommunication, was to take place for greater efficiency and to raise revenue. Since the country had run a budget deficit since 1998, privatization was crucial in financing the deficit. However, this solution was problematic because privatization led to increased unemployment. And since buying out these enterprises required substantial capital, only the large conglomerates could do so. The bane of market concentration persisted.

More Problems in the Restructuring Process

The most serious and painful effect of restructuring was high unemployment. Prior to the crisis the unemployment rate was between 2 and 3 percent. As a result of increased bankruptcies, unemployment reached 8.7 percent, with 1.78 million unemployed by February 1999. To reduce this number the government worked to provide jobs and to establish a social safety-net system at a cost of 9.6 trillion won. Expensive as they were, these endeavors only temporarily relieved the problem. The experts began to focus on job creation in the private sector that in the long run of economic recovery would be a more creditable solution.

Another difficult part of the restructuring process involved the inevitable growth of the government debt as it cleared out bad loans from the financial sector and established a social safety net. It is estimated that budget deficits will continue for years to come. In recent years the budget deficit has been approximately 5 percent of Korea's GDP. The government planned to spend a total of 64 trillion won to restructure the financial sector. It was estimated that 5.8 trillion won would be needed in 1999 and 2000 to pay the interest alone. This money would be raised by privatizing state-owned enterprises (SOEs), reducing government expenditures, and increasing government tax revenues. Because of the increased budget deficits, the public-sector debt was anticipated to peak at 25.1 percent by the end of 2002 and to decrease thereafter.

The Impact of the Crisis on Foreign Policy

Economic cooperation between the Koreas developed before 1997 and continued in spite of the economic crisis. In the late 1980s trade increased, and by the 1990s, some South Korean firms had begun to make investments in North Korea. The volume of trade grew from $18.7 million in 1989 to $308 million by 1997. By the mid-1990s the ROK had become the third largest trading partner of the DPRK. The major initiative of Kim Dae-jung was his Sunshine Policy. Its purpose was to open a dialogue with the North in order to promote economic cooperation. These overtures also had the purpose of lessening military tension with the ultimate goal of reconciliation and cooperation, perhaps even leading to reunification of the peninsula.

Hyundai, the largest of the chaebol, agreed to develop the Mount Kumgang region, an area in North Korea renowned for its scenic beauty, as an international resort. For this opportunity, it promised $150 million annually for a period of 6 years. At the June 2000 summit Kim Dae-jung and Kim Il Sung paved the way for rebuilding a railway line across the heavily armed border to connect Seoul and P'yongyang for the first time in 50 years. Since then, the South Korean government has earmarked $49 million to restore the railway, which ultimately will link with railroads in northern China, Mongolia, and Europe.

When the people of North Korea experienced their sixth consecutive year of bad harvests, the South made plans to furnish imported grain. The ROK provided domestic rice, but it was more expensive than grains grown in other regions of Southeast Asia. The North needed 4.7 million tons of grain to feed its 22 million people annually, but it usually produced less than 3.5 million tons. P'yongyang's repeated requests for fertilizer, food, and electric power led to growing uncertainty about the South's capacity to meet the needs of the North.

Since the economic crisis had begun, the role of the three major powers (United States, Japan, and China) had changed. The importance of the United States increased. Both the United States and the IMF played key parts in providing assistance during the crisis. Koreans acknowledged that their recovery was tied to continued U.S. imports and expressed an increased interest in the continued health of the U.S. economy. Also, in the process of restructuring, they saw elements of the U.S. economy that seemed worth modeling, such as the efficient corporate sector and the sound financial institutions. The importance of the U.S. economy was also seen in terms of the foreign direct investment (FDI) flow into Korea. At the same time, the importance of FDI from Asian firms, mostly Japanese, decreased. Meanwhile, the standing of China improved with its commitment to maintaining the value of the yuan, its accumulation of foreign-exchange reserves, and its ability to control the domestic currency market.

The Korean Economy: Current Conditions and Prospects for the Future

The crisis again provided an opportunity for resolving basic economic problems. Together with the other Asian nations that were suffering from the economic crisis, Korea emerged from the financial crisis in 1998 largely by feeding the insatiable U.S. appetite for imports. By 1999, the economy showed clear signs of recovery: the GDP growth was 10.7 percent, the highest since a rate of 11 percent in 1987. National income also climbed 8.9 percent. The trade surplus was 25 billion won, inflation was in check, and the won was stable. Gross exports of goods and services jumped 16.3 percent in the year, compared with the previous year's 13.2 percent increase. The industrial output rose 24.2 percent, a reversal from the previous year's 6.5 percent decline. The labor market was more flexible. Liberalization allowed significant foreign investment in domestic enterprises. The upward movement of the economy and the government's positive employment policy improved the employment picture.

Conglomerates sped up efforts to improve efficiency and to lower debt-equity ratios below 200 percent, but some of their affiliates had to close. President Kim Dae-jung insisted that the chaebol continue strong restructuring. Four of them (Hyundai, Samsung, LG, and SK) succeeded by attracting foreign investment and offering rights to new stock issues. However, over one third of the thirty top groups (including Daewoo) confronted serious management crises, and many were put under legal management or workout programs. In spite of the need for additional reforms of the corporate structure and financial institutions, a breakdown of the system was prevented. International confidence was restored, and Korea was praised around the world for bouncing back so quickly.

Economic expansion continued through 2000, though at a more moderate pace, in the face of continued restructuring and concerns about failures among the large chaebol, such as Daewoo Motors, which was declared bankrupt. Unemployment was reduced to under

4 percent, while inflation appeared to have been limited to around 2.5 percent for the year. Reforms had indeed brought a quick turn-around of the economy, yet a convincing sustainable recovery did not emerge. Opponents of reform stalled and subsequently impeded the momentum for change. Despite all the pledges of reform, the nation still balked at closing assembly lines and factories in the face of rampant overcapacity, no matter how unprofitable or debt laden they were. The IMF warned in November 2000 that unsound companies endangered a financial system already weighted down with $100 billion in nonperforming loans. Approximately 25 percent of the nation's companies were technically insolvent but continued to muddle along with government aid.

That aid in itself was part of the problem. The government owned many of the insolvent banks, yet no significant management changes occurred to force banks to take full responsibility for loans they authorized. Banks still manipulated interest rates and made loans to favored sectors. The government maintained what is referred to as a positive list of eligible participants. Three years after the onset of the crisis, restructuring was still incomplete, much new capital was needed, and, for the majority of institutions, new private owners were required. The increased government ownership of banks and other financial institutions remained an obstacle to future reform.

In spite of the fact that the stock market was the sixth largest in the world, access to the securities remained difficult. Foreign investors were required to obtain a special identification card before they could purchase equity. Finally, lack of transparency continued to create obstacles for foreign firms trying to enter the domestic market. English translations of laws and regulations had to be provided by local lawyers, and foreign firms had limited access to the authorities.

Of the various components of Kim Dae-jung's first round of reforms, the least successful was that of the large chaebol. Size had traditionally been the most important measure of status; and the chaebol's reckless pursuit of that prize over profitability was the main cause of the economic crisis. Clearly, the chaebol needed to be restructured for sustained economic growth, but they remained resistant. Samuel E. Kim, Associate Director of the Center for Korean Research at Columbia University, has speculated that the chaebol's size-driven and aggressive behavior might have compensated for Korea's national small size. With Kim Dae-jung's reforms, companies were forced to improve their immediate financial prospects; however, the reforms did not extend to significant restructuring of their operations. Labor and wage reductions were often the driving force behind improvement in cash flows.

Meanwhile, the largest corporations dismissed more than one-quarter of their workforce. Payrolls dropped 34 percent. Because Korea had no national unemployment insurance system, labor opposed unrestricted layoffs. It appeared unwilling to make any significant concessions because it had shouldered the burdens of the economic crisis. When in December 2000 two of the largest banks announced their plans to merge, 13,000 workers went on strike in the belief that there would be massive layoffs. With the growth of animosity and mistrust between labor and management, economists were concerned that labor discontent could further hurt production in an economy that was expected to slow in 2001.

Kim Dae-jung implemented a second round of restructuring and committed to complete the process by March 2001. The immediate tasks of the second round were to continue financial and corporate sector reforms, increase flexibility in the labor market, extend the social safety net, enforce labor laws, improve relations between labor and management, and continue deregulation and privatization. In spite of initial optimism, the economy steadily weakened. Oil prices soared, inflation was on the rise, the stock market lost half its value, and consumer confidence fell. Semiconductor prices softened and the export market declined.

The fact that Japan's national debt had swollen to 114 percent of economic output also had implications for Korea's exports. By January 2001 a sharp slowdown in U.S. economic growth indicated that it too might be headed for a recession. The possibility of a downturn in overseas markets heightened fears of falling exports. In October, Kim's Millennium Democratic Party experienced a major defeat in the parliamentary elections. Amid fierce internal bickering, the president stepped down as head of the ruling party. This decision left the country's economic reform and several foreign investment programs in limbo.

For comprehensive reform, strong leadership is paramount. Kim Dae-jung did not have initial support to implement his comprehensive reform program; however, his overtures to North Korea led to the Nobel Peace Prize and increased national and international political support. Although his term runs until February 2003, it will be difficult for him to get crucial legislation passed by the National Assembly. During this time Kim must continue to receive public support in order to force the assembly to continue reforms to create sustainable growth, a higher standard of living for the hardworking Korean people, and the full integration of the nation into the global economy.

NORTH KOREA

North Korea was established as the Democratic People's Republic of Korea (DPRK) on September 9, 1948, amid the uncertainty following World War II. It was created by the dedication of Korean communists with the support of the Soviet Union, whose troops occupied the North at the end of the war. The communists rejected the UN recommendations for the establishment of a unified Korea, adopted their own constitution, and elected Kim Il Sung premier. Since then a communist regime has extended totalitarian control over the state and established a socialist economy, creating a vastly different society than the one in the Republic of Korea.

In a shrinking world the DPRK remains a hermit kingdom, withdrawn from the capitalist world system. In the past fifty years communist leadership has constructed an independent, self-contained economy that continues to be the most independent industrial

P'yongyang, the capital of North Korea. The high-rise structures are condominiums. The city is the North Korean government's idea of a modern, progressive city and a model communist capital. (Photographed by Cheong Wa Dae, Presidential Residence of the Republic of Korea, Photographer's Press Pool)

economy in the most closed society in the world. In the 1990s with the collapse of the Soviet Union, the death of Kim Il Sung, a faltering economy, floods, and famine, observers predicted that the communist regime could not possibly survive; however, Kim Jong Il, the son of Kim Il Sung, remains at the helm. The attention of the world was focused on the Koreas in June 2000 when the leaders met for the first time in fifty years. In spite of this meeting North Korea remains the most mysterious nation in the world. Many basic facts remain unknown. The government operates in secrecy and controls virtually all information and is particularly reluctant to publicize data on economic and social conditions.

Economic Development: 1948–1965

From the beginning Kim Il Sung stressed self-reliance, but his country received substantial economic aid and technical help from the USSR and China, though nothing as extensive as the South's aid from the United States and Japan. Still, unlike nearly every other communist state in the world, North Korea never joined COMECON, the socialist equivalent of the common market. The state took from Marxist-Leninism what it wanted and rejected the rest. It was high on motivation and results. Laborers were to be paid according to the quality and quantity of work.

In 1948 the key policy objectives expressed in the Workers' Party Charter were "to ensure the complete victory of socialism and the accomplishment of the revolutionary goals of national liberation and people's democracy in the entire area of the country" (apparently meaning the entire peninsula). The ultimate goal of the nation was to indoctrinate all the people with the idea of juche (self-reliance) while establishing a socialist system on a Stalinist model that included an emphasis on heavy industry. There was to be a very limited role for market allocation, mainly in rural areas where peasants would sell produce from private plots. Small business was essentially not part of the plan.

Before 1945 most of the industry of Korea was located in the North and almost all the agricultural production was in the South. Since Kim Il Sung inherited half an economy, he embarked on a series of popular reforms to create a more balanced and self-sufficient economy, which included the redistribution of land and nationalization of Japanese property.

Life in rural areas changed significantly. The landlords lost their land, but they could have the same amount of land as the peasants if they tilled the soil. The reform did not compensate them for their land, but it left them with their lives and a means of support. This reform was relatively painless and certainly less violent than the land reform of the Chinese communists.

Under the communist regime dramatic changes occurred in industry. Skilled Korean technicians, who gained experience working in Japanese industry during the war, came to the forefront of the economy. The North was pragmatic in its use of their expertise and received little criticism, whereas the South tended to employ technicians with no experience in industry and received endless criticism. Under the strong direction of Kim Il Sung, the state transformed the economy within a relatively short period of time. While the South struggled with recession and high rates of unemployment in the 1950s, the North's economy generated full employment and rapid growth.

The Korean War temporarily interrupted economic progress. It left the country divided and economically and socially devastated. Almost as soon as the armistice was signed, the North began an impressive building program, which was described as the most centralized and planned economic development program in the world. Between 1954 and 1956 a program was implemented that gave priority to the development of heavy industry. It was so successful that it achieved its goals six months ahead of schedule and established the foundation for an independent economy. In agriculture, private ownership of farms ended when collectivization was completed in 1958. This was a process necessitated by the war that pooled the limited resources and labor essential for survival. All of the rural population lived and worked in some 13,309 cooperatives, with an average of seventy-nine households each. These units corresponded to traditional villages and drew upon a long history of cooperative labor and mutual aid. Although the peasants did not own the land they worked, they were compensated according to the labor they contributed. The majority of the peasants approved of these agrarian conditions. In 1961, a seven-year plan was implemented for further modernization, which included more technological industries.

Achievements were notable. Agricultural production grew by an average of 10 percent per year during the 1950s and 6.3 percent in the 1960s. By the end of the 1960s, the government announced that the country had achieved food self-sufficiency. Industrial growth was even more impressive. The emphasis on industrialization, combined with vast amounts of aid from the Soviet bloc, pushed growth to an increase of 25 percent per year in the decade after the Korean War and about 14 percent from 1965 to 1978. These achievements were so extraordinary that economists spoke of a North Korean miracle. Because the DPRK progressed more rapidly than the ROK, 450,000 Koreans left Japan in 1960 to permanently settle in the DPRK. What makes this particularly striking is the fact that most of these people were originally from the South.

Economic Development: 1965–1994

By the second half of the 1960s the North Korean economy began to slow. The seven-year plan of 1961 was extended for three additional years. In spite of the slowdown, it was still out-producing the ROK in per capita terms in almost every sector from agriculture through electric power, steel and cement, to machine tools and trucks, but not in television sets and automobiles. Sometime in the mid-1970s the South caught up with the North in per capita GNP and then pulled ahead.

There were several reasons for North Korea's economic difficulties. Among the most important were the decline in aid from the Soviet Union and the diversion of scarce materials into defense. Although the North prided itself on self-reliance, it did receive considerable aid not only from the Soviet Union but also from Eastern European countries. The Soviet Union gave essentially free scientific and technical aid. Technical support allowed North Korea to produce many industrial products, including trucks, agricultural machinery, electric motors, transformers, and tractors; all of this contributed significantly to the country's rapid economic development.

Because the DPRK supported China during the Sino-Soviet dispute in the early 1960s, the Soviets withdrew aid and technical support and later reduced trade between the two countries. This led to the postponement of the seven-year plan. When Soviet relations later improved, Chinese–North Korean relations deteriorated. Kim concluded that he could not count on the support of either of these allies and subsequently developed ties with Third World nations. Because of the uncertainty between the country's relations with China and the Soviet Union together with Park Chung Hee's anticommunist policies, Kim determined to increase military capabilities. This represented a major drain on resources and prevented the achievement of established goals. From this point on, international developments continued to be unfavorable for the DPRK. In response to Park's plans to produce nuclear weapons, the North Korean military budget rose to $1.4 billion in 1974. The North received $2 billion in economic aid and less than $1 billion in military aid from the Soviet Union, China, and Eastern Europe, while the ROK got approximately $9.1 billion in economic aid and $6.3 billion in military aid from the United States, Japan, and other countries.

Economic prospects declined throughout the 1980s and 1990s. For the most part, leaders refused to change the country's basic economic structure and institutions. They readjusted planning, enlarged the number of trading partners, mobilized workers, and attracted foreign capital. As a result, from 1961 to 1976 most of the country's total industrial investment was directed into heavy industry. Recognizing the need to balance the economy, the leadership attempted to develop light manufacturing in the provinces; however, this strategy failed because of insufficient resources and lack of incentives.

The state tried to boost the economy by opening trade with the capitalist world. It purchased Western technology and capital equipment on credit. By 1974 North Korea purchased perhaps twice as much from capitalist countries as from its communist partners. It planned to pay for these imports with earnings from exports; however, when the international recession hit in 1974, North Korea could not pay its debts. Unlike other countries, the state was unwilling to accept International Monetary Fund structural adjustment policies and stopped making interest payments. Without financial aid, the country's trade fell by a third in the mid-1970s. The DPRK has never paid its debts from this period.

Between the 1970s and 1990s the leadership launched a series of mass campaigns to increase productivity. Whether any of the mobilization campaigns were successful is an open question. The primary efforts of the 1990s were to attract export-oriented foreign investment, but little foreign capital was generated. With the collapse of the Soviet Union in 1989 and the liberation of Eastern European nations, the overall trade between North Korea and the former Soviet bloc fell by approximately 67 percent in 1991. Left with limited foreign exchange, the state could afford few imports. Nevertheless, it has insisted on maintaining a high level of military outlays from shrinking economic resources. Manufacturing has continued to center on heavy industry, including military industry, with light industry lagging far behind. Despite the use of improved seed varieties, expansion of irrigation, and the heavy use of fertilizers, North Korea has not succeeded in self-sufficient food production. Since the 1990s its GNP has been in decline.

Recent Economic Development and Prospects

During the early 1990s many experts predicted that the North Korean regime, already struggling with economic decline, would not survive Kim Il Sung's death. When Kim died in 1994, it became apparent that his son, Kim Jong Il, had been running much of the government since the 1980s. In 1995 devastating rains and floods ruined nearly half the country's farmland, and 500,000 people were homeless. Despite these disasters, Kim Jong Il solidified his control over the country. He appealed for international support to help the North recover from the flooding. The so-called Agreement of 1994 obliged the DPRK to freeze the nuclear program in exchange for billions of dollars' worth of aid from the United States, Japan, and South Korea, including help in building two nuclear power plants.

North Korea essentially rejected Western advice to follow the example of the Soviet bloc and embrace market forces, pointing out that in spite of substantial Western financial aid, the former Soviet Union had suffered a worse economic collapse than it had. In 1996, the state television station began airing programs on the situation in Russia, programs that highlighted the economic difficulties and social decay that resulted from market forces. Throughout the 1990s the North Koreans blamed their problems on outside forces, such as droughts, floods, and hostile capitalist countries.

As fragile as everything seems, somehow the nation continues to defy expectations that it will simply disintegrate under continued hardships. One reason is the resiliency of the people. In spite of the stress of food shortages, starvation, and poverty, they survive. By 1999 it was estimated that the GDP per capita was $900. (The GDP per capita in Cuba at that time was $1,700, and in the Russian Federation, it was $4,200.) Nevertheless, with estimates of some 2 million deaths by starvation by the year 2000, it appeared that the nation was beginning to change its policies toward the noncommunist world. Yet, policy makers still refused to acknowledge that overly centralized planning and management practices contributed to economic difficulties.

As a sign that North Korea might be ending its international isolation, the reclusive Kim Jong Il visited China in late May 2000 on his

Rice fields outside P'yongyang. (Photographed by Cheong Wa Dae, Presidential Residence of the Republic of Korea, Photographer's Press Pool)

first foreign trip in seventeen years. In his brief Beijing visit, Kim was shown some of the impressive economic gains made by China since its shift toward a market economy. In June, he agreed to meet with the leader of South Korea, Kim Dae-jung, the first meeting between leaders of the Koreas in fifty years. They spoke of promoting a balanced national economy and the reconnection of a cross-border railroad, which was destroyed during the Korean War. In October Madeleine Albright, the U.S. secretary of state, traveled to North Korea to meet with its leader to discuss a number of issues, some of which could lead to closer economic cooperation.

It may be that the DPRK was not moving in a new direction, but only attempting to get more outside help to alleviate famine and poverty. There may be other motives. China has been pressuring Kim Jong Il to open up—mostly to avert greater U.S. presence in Asia. Some observers believe that North Korea has refrained from major policy changes because it believes that economic recovery will occur even without improved relations with South Korea. It may entertain the hope that normalization of relations will work to its advantage without opening up to the global capitalist system.

North Korea needs money, food, and technology. Kim wants to stay in power and is bright, shrewd, farsighted, and pragmatic enough to know that his nation must to some extent engage the outside world. Whether or not fundamental national objectives are changing, there are signs that the leadership is reaching out. Kim's tactical skills are evident as he continues to extract huge amounts of aid from the United States and other donor nations while giving little in return. It remains to be seen whether he will agree to curb ballistic-missile development and export or reduce the military presence near the border with South Korea, the most heavily fortified region of the world.

Table 2. A Comparison of North and South Korea

	Democratic People's Republic of Korea	Republic of South Korea
Population	21,687,550 (July 2000 est.)	47,500,000 (2000)
Size	46,500 sq. miles	38,000 sq. miles
Government	Authoritarian socialist; one-man dictatorship	Republic with powers shared between the president and the legislature
Capital	P'yongyang	Seoul
GDP	$22.6 billion (1999 est.)	$406.7 billion
GDP per capita	$1,000 (1999 est.)	$8,581 (1999 est.)
Literacy	99%	98%
Exports (1998)	$559 million	$132,313 billion
Arable Land	14%	22%
Agriculture	Rice, corn, potatoes, soybeans, cattle, pigs, pork, eggs	Rice, vegetables, fruit, barley
Labor Force	36% agriculture	11% agriculture
Natural Resources	Coal, lead, tungsten, zinc, magnesite, iron ore, copper, gold pyrites, salt, flourspar, hydropower	Limited coal and tungsten, iron ore, limestone, kaolinite, and graphite
Industries	Textiles, chemicals, machinery, food processing	Electronics, autos, chemicals, ships, textiles, clothing, footwear
Electricity Production (1997)	33,705 billion kWh	212,015 billion kWh
Defense	27% of GDP	3.3% of GDP
Active Troops	1.2 million	700,000

Note: North Koreans believe that their current economic difficulties are the result of U.S. economic sanctions, poor harvests, and the collapse of the Soviet bloc.

Sources: Information was obtained from The World Factbook (www.odci.gov/cia/), the U.S. Department of State (www.state.gov/), *New York Times World Almanac* (2000), and the Korean National Statistical Office.

References

A Handbook of Korea. 1993. Seoul: Korean Overseas Information Service.

About Geography, "Geography of North Korea," http://geography.about.com/ . . ./geography/library/cia/blcnorthkorea.htm (cited August 13, 2000).

Amsden, Alice H. 1989. *Asia's Next Giant: South Korea and Late Industrialization.* New York: Oxford University Press.

AsiaNow, "South Korea Begins Work on Cross-Border Link," http://www.cnn.com/2000/ASIANOW (cited September 19, 2000).

AsiaNow, "South Korea Plans to Loan Imported Grain to North Korea," http://www.cnn.com/2000/ASIANOW (cited September 10, 2000).

Breen, Michael. 1998. *The Koreans: Who They Are, What They Want, Where Their Future Lies.* New York: St. Martin's Press.

Cumings, Bruce. 1997. *Korea's Place in the Sun: A Modern History.* New York: W.W. Norton and Company.

Eckert, Carter et al. 1990. *Korea Old and New: A History.* Seoul: Ilchokak Publishers.

Financial Services Liberalization in the WTO, "South Korea Case Study," http://www.C/dobkorea.htm (cited May 4, 2000).

Hart-Landsberg, Martin. 1998. *Korea: Division, Reunification, and U.S. Foreign Policy.* New York: Monthly Review Press.

Kim, Byoung-Lo Philo. 1992. *Two Koreas in Development: A Comparative Study of Principles and Strategies of Capitalist and Communist Third World Development.* New Brunswick, NJ: Transaction Publishers.

Kim, Dae Jung. 1985. *Mass-Participatory Economy: A Democratic Alternative for Korea.* Lanham, MD: University Press of America.

Kim, Samuel S. 2000. "Korea's Segyehawa Drive: Promise versus Performance," in *Korea's Globalization.* Kim, Samuel S., ed., New York: Cambridge University Press.

Korea Herald, "Kim Calls for Government-Business Cooperation to Cope with Looming Crisis," http://www.koreaherald.com (cited September 19, 2001).

Korea's Economic Trends (weekly), "Privatizing State Owned Companies: Foreign Cases of Privatization and Their Implications for Korea," http://www.koreaeconomy.org (cited December 28, 2000).

Korea's Economy Seminar: Transformation of Korea's Economy: Reform and Future Prospects. Korean Consulate General, Los Angeles, CA. 29 November 2000.

Lee, Doowon. 2000. "South Korea's Financial Crisis and Economic Restructuring," in *Korea Briefing: 1997–1999, Challenges and Change at the Turn of the Twentieth Century.* Oh, Kongdan, ed. New York: Asia Society.

Magnier, Mark. "A Nation's Moment of Truth," *Los Angeles Times.* 26 November 2000, C1–5.

Oberdorfer, Don. 1997. *The Two Koreas: A Contemporary History.* Reading, MA: Addison-Wesley.

OECD Economic Outlook, "The OECD Economic Outlook Released on November 21," http://www.mofe.go.kr (cited December 28, 2000).

Roh, Jeong Seon, ed. 2000. *Korean Annual.* Seoul: Yonhap News Agency.

Root, Hilton. 2000. *Korea's Recovery: Don't Count on the Government.* Santa Monica, CA: Milken Institute.

Samsung Economic Research Institute, "Urgent Problems Surrounding the Korean

Economy and Related Suggestions for Government Policy Direction,"
http://www.koreaeconomy.org (cited October 30, 2000).

Soh, Changrok. 1997. *From Investment to Innovation? The Korean Political Economy and Changes in Industrial Competitiveness.* Seoul: Global Research Institute, Korea University.

Song, Byung-Nak. 1997. *The Rise of the Korean Economy.* New York: Oxford University Press.

Song, Meeyong. "Indexes Track Web Stocks Off a Cliff," *Wall Street Journal,* 2 January 2001, R22.

Steinberg, David I. 1993. "The Transformation of the South Korean Economy," in *Korea Briefing, 1993: Festival of Korea.* Clark, Donald, ed., New York: Asia Society.

Wright, Robin. "A Quirky Person Lurks behind North Korea's Cult of Personality," *Los Angeles Times.* 27 October 2000.

Wright, Robin. "North Korean Leader Pledges to Scrap Missile Launches," *Los Angeles Times.* 25 October 2000.

CHAPTER THREE

Political Development since 1945

Around midnight on August 10, 1945, the day after the second atomic bomb was dropped on Japan, the United States made a fateful decision about Korea. Fearing that the Soviet Union was about to swoop down the peninsula and establish a communist regime, the United States hurriedly urged its recent ally to accept a division of the country at the thirty-eighth parallel. The agreement shattered 1300 years of unity. And since that day virtually every political consideration on both sides of that bisection has been chilled by the Cold War.

For forty years Korea had heroically resisted Japanese oppression by clutching the dream of an eventual national government with social and economic justice for all. After liberation the Democratic People's Republic of Korea and the Republic of Korea promised, each in its own way, to give the Korean people what they wanted: stability on the peninsula and self-determination in their national destiny. Nonetheless, those people continued to endure hardships under authoritarian regimes in both North and South.

From June 13 to 15, 2000, the leaders of both sides met for the first time since the division. At that summit Presidents Kim Dae-jung and Kim Jong Il pledged to take concrete steps toward reunification. In the process they attempted to redefine relations that have remained suspicious and hostile for more than a decade after the Cold War ceased everywhere else. In spite of the hopes raised, major

Syngman Rhee, Yun Poson, Park Chung Hee, Choi Kyu Hah (Courtesy of the Korean Information Service)

Chun Doo Hwan, Roh Tae Woo, Kim Young Sam, Kim Dae-jung (Courtesy of the Korean Information Service)

obstacles to unification remain. Political experts throughout the world continue to voice concern that problems on the peninsula pose a dangerous military threat to the stability of East Asia and even to the United States.

THE IMPACT OF TRADITION ON POLITICAL DEVELOPMENT

Until the late nineteenth century political and social traditions throughout the peninsula had been stable and unchanging for centuries. Korea was an agrarian society until two generations ago. Until 1910 it had a monarchical system of government. The centralized court and aristocracy monopolized wealth, power, and status, while the majority of people remained poor. During the Choson dynasty eligibility for state examinations was limited to a small portion of society, the yangban, or aristocratic class. Because few other career paths existed, attaining a government post was the ultimate goal of the yangban. This fact tended to sanction any means, often including bribery, of securing positions.

Both the Koryo (936–1392) and the Choson (1392–1910) dynasties adopted Confucian principles of government. That system incorporated concepts of loyalty, filial duty, respect for age and status, and veneration for learning. Loyalty governed the relationship between ruler and subjects. The bonds were hierarchical, strict, and unequal. Kings sometimes exercised power compassionately, but more often cruelly.

This tradition also incorporated the notion that the ruler and his officials must be virtuous to retain their mandate to rule. If they are no longer virtuous, people have the right to revolt. However, when a king was overthrown, reforms did not necessarily improve lives or change class structure. Periodic revolutions by the common people and slaves, usually triggered by their desperate economic circumstances, were brutally crushed. In the nineteenth century, followers of the Tonghak movement instigated the first nationwide peasant uprising in the country's history. Based on the Confucian notion of a justifiable revolution and beliefs borrowed from Catholicism, Buddhism, Daoism, and Shamanism, the Tonghaks directed themselves to improving the conditions of the people. They held the revolutionary notion that all humans embody the divine, thus rejecting class distinctions that had for centuries condemned the majority of people to lives of poverty. They also believed that the righteous may overthrow the government to correct political wrongs. Their call for equality between men and women and social and economic justice for all continues to have an enormous impact on the yearnings of the Korean people.

The Confucian legacy is still operable today. Most Koreans look to their leaders for major decisions. Family ties constitute the central element in people's lives and organizations. In the South family-owned and family-operated conglomerates predominate. In the North Kim Jong Il was carefully groomed to carry on the ideological work of his father, Kim Il Sung. Tradition dictates that each family member must be diligent in fulfilling his or her role. What is done in the interest of the family, even misconduct, may be overlooked.

THE IMPACT OF THE JAPANESE COLONIAL PERIOD ON CONTEMPORARY LIFE

Colonial policies destroyed the foundations of a remarkably stable nineteenth century hierarchical agrarian society. After overthrowing the Choson dynasty, the Japanese replaced it with a strongly authoritarian regime headed by a governor-general who was inevitably a military man. What came about was a highly centralized colonial government that resembled that of Japan: state intervention in the economy to create new markets and industries and the vigorous suppression of dissent. The authoritarian model, which played an integral role in shaping economic development, was to manifest itself again in both Koreas during the post-1945 period.

The one thing the Japanese did not destroy from the Choson dynasty was the position of the aristocracy. The Japanese did remove most yangban from positions of authority in the colonial government, but landlords were allowed to maintain their estates, dominate the

The Government-General Building, the symbol of Japanese colonialism, was located in Seoul. It was torn down in 1996. Photograph was taken by Steve Smith, U.S. specialist fourth class, during his tour of duty. (Courtesy of Steve Smith)

peasants, and export rice to Japan. The colonial period created a whole new set of future political leaders, molded either by their resistance to or collaboration with the colonizers. Those on the right were the majority of propertied and educated citizens, many of whom cooperated with the regime. Those on the left came from varying backgrounds, including students, intellectuals, peasants, and workers who became politicized by their negative experiences of occupation. They were attracted to communism because it opposed foreign rule and advocated justice for the poor. When the colonial system suddenly ended with liberation on August 15, 1945, they were committed to a complete purge of the collaborators from all positions of power and influence.

THE IMPACT OF U.S. AND SOVIET OCCUPATION AND THE KOREAN WAR ON POLITICAL DEVELOPMENT

After 1945 and the division of Korea at the thirty-eighth parallel, U.S. military authorities backed Syngman Rhee and other conservative

politicians with ties to the yangban and former Japanese collaborators. Because of the paranoia of the early Cold War years, the Americans, ignorant of local history, language and culture, had difficulty
distinguishing communists from persons with understandable
demands for self-government and land reform. Although U.S. officials
came to dislike Rhee's authoritarianism and the corruption of his
government, he appeared to be their best hope of avoiding a communist government in Seoul. Frustrated and prodded by communist
agents, many turned to guerrilla warfare in the South prior to and
during the civil war.

In the North, Soviet occupation forces supported Kim Il Sung as
interim ruler. Highly admired as a former anti-Japanese guerrilla
leader, Kim redistributed land and raised the social status of the
peasants, but his policies made life difficult for Christians, professionals, and landowners. He moved in ways that would eventually
establish him as the autocratic ruler of North Korea.

The most profound effect of the U.S.–USSR occupation of Korea
was institutionalization of the sociopolitical divisions created after
World War II. The DPRK's programs emphasized socialism, land
reform, and independence from outside powers. The regime in South
Korea was capitalist, pro-yangban, largely Japanese-trained, and
dependent on American aid, advice, and approval.

Each of the Koreas has continually blamed the other as the sole
aggressor in the Korean War. Kim Il Sung survived politically despite
the fact that the Chinese had to rescue him and that he failed to
reunify the nation as promised. He purged his critics, eliminated enemies and rivals, blamed others for the unsuccessful conclusion of the
war, and quite miraculously escaped blame. A master of turning
disaster into victory, he actually strengthened his position and generated a formidable cult of personality. He presented himself as a
hero, and his revolutionary deeds were glorified. In South Korea the
1948 constitution made democracy the foundation of the government, but within a short time, the democratic principles were sabo-
taged. The war provided Rhee with opportunities to demand absolute
loyalty, remove potential rivals, and eliminate suspected leftists and
their supporters on a massive scale.

The war, which ended in stalemate, resolved nothing and left a
legacy of heightened bitterness, tension, and mutual paranoia. What
had begun as hostility between two governments and conflicting
ideas about the economic and political direction of Korea now
affected everyone throughout the peninsula. Most Koreans suffered

greatly at the hands of those on the other side. The results contributed significantly to the growth of authoritarian rule and the suppression of civil and political rights both north and south of the thirty-eighth parallel.

A DIVIDED PEOPLE: THE SOUTH KOREAN EXPERIENCE (1948–2001)

The First Republic, 1948–1961

During U.S. occupation, General John R. Hodge established an interim government under the direction of U.S. authorities to draft a constitution. Subsequently, a committee of prominent Koreans consulted widely among emerging leaders, such as Syngman Rhee, who favored a presidential system of government. For a variety of reasons a democratic constitution seemed to be the most viable solution. On July 12, 1948, the National Assembly adopted the first formal constitution, which was definitely shaped by U.S. influence. The constitution declared that the Republic of Korea "shall be a democratic republic" and that its "sovereignty shall reside in the people from whom all state authority shall emanate."

Certain provisions of the constitution shed light on the course of political development. Chapter I renounced all aggressive wars and placed the military with "the sacred duty of protecting the country." It stipulated that no military officer should be appointed prime minister unless he resigned from active service. Chapter II enumerated basic rights that included equality before the law; freedom from unlawful search; freedom of private correspondence; freedoms of speech, press, and assembly; equal opportunity of education; and the equality of men and women. It is interesting to note that the constitutional guarantees of public education, most likely the result of Confucianism, would have in due time a far-reaching impact on economic growth and political development. These rights held great promise; however, some provisions would pave the way for the violation of civil rights, authoritarian rule, and the prominent role of government in the management of the economy.

Chapter II, Article 28 stated that restrictions upon the rights of citizens could be enacted only when necessary for the maintenance of public order and the welfare of the community. Therefore, when the ruling authorities deemed it necessary for public order, all the above liberties could legally be restricted. Chapter II, Article 57 included an emergency clause that gave the president exclusive powers—if time was lacking—for convening the National Assembly to issue orders during civil war, dangerous situations arising with foreign powers, and natural calamities or financial crises. Chapter V stated that judges were to be free from executive and legislative interference. However, the president, with the approval of the National Assembly, appointed the chief justice, and judges of other courts were appointed for the relatively short term of five years. Procedures within this chapter made it difficult to declare any executive actions unconstitutional. Chapter VI provided for state or public management of important enterprises, such as transportation, communications, banking, and insurance. The economic freedom of individuals was guaranteed, but within the limits of public good.

Notwithstanding the ideals of the constitution, the growth of presidential power was understandable given political tensions on the peninsula. Provisions for immediate and decisive action were essential. Since the majority of people lived at a subsistence level, it also seemed natural that the constitution include provisions for an active governmental role in economic development.

Many people assumed that Syngman Rhee, who spent many years in the United States where he was educated at George Washington, Harvard, and Princeton Universities, had learned about politics in the United States and would model his own presidency on the U.S. style. The early hopes for democratization now seem naïve given the authoritarian traditions of Korea's past, Rhee's own background and personality, and the international political and economic tensions of the time.

Rhee, who was born in 1875, had an impressive beginning. At age nineteen, he attended a school run by American Methodist missionaries. As a young man he became active in the Independence Club and took part in a failed attempt to overthrow the pro-Japanese government. He persisted as an advocate for nationalism and reform but was arrested and imprisoned for seven years. After months of terrible beatings and torture, he was released, went to the United States to study, and ultimately spent forty-one years in exile. Although he spent most of his life in the United States, and even though he had a future president, Woodrow Wilson, as a professor at Princeton, his conduct as president grew to resemble that of a Choson monarch. In the beginning of his presidency he impressed Americans because he was well educated, aristocratic, handsome, charismatic, and anticommunist; however, he established a police state. Throughout his administration he reiterated his hatred of the Japanese, perhaps to deflect attention from the many collaborators serving in his government.

When Rhee was inaugurated, he was seventy-three years old. He assumed the presidency when Korea was weak, desperately poor, and politically unstable. Within his first three years, he was faced with insurmountable problems: severe economic hardship, civil unrest, and war. Even though he espoused concern about the plight of the people, he basically was indifferent to their needs and never proposed an official plan of economic development. Rhee was certainly a patriot, but he had been gone far too long from his country to identify with popular aspirations. When he took over in 1948, per capita income was only $86; the year he was overthrown, per capita income was $80. His fiscal concerns primarily related to obtaining as much foreign aid and military assistance as possible.

In October 1948, a large-scale mutiny of two regiments of the Republic's army broke out at the port city of Yosu. This was the second major rebellion to occur that year. The cause of the uprising was the refusal of the army to follow orders to go on a mission against Cheju Island guerrillas. The rebels attacked poorly armed police stations and defenseless local government offices, won over large segments of the population by urging revenge against the oppressive local police, and declared Yosu a liberated area. Large numbers of people paraded through the streets, waving red flags and calling for the restoration of the people's committees. Some of the demonstrators showed the DPRK flag and pledged support for Kim Il Sung.

The rebellion was suppressed under the direction of Americans and carried out by young Korean officers, even though military occupation had ended and the United States supposedly had no authority to be involved in internal matters. Rhee and his American supporters charged that North Korea had instigated the rebellion, but in effect, it was caused by the frustration of local leftists and resentment toward the United States, especially during occupation. A rebel newspaper called for land redistribution without any compensation, a unified Korea, and a purge of all police who had served the Japanese.

It was under these circumstances that the assembly adopted the National Security Law, which is still in force today, over half a century later. Article 1 states that the law's purpose is to ensure "the national security and interests" by protecting the state from its enemies, defined as "any association, groups, or organizations" that conspire against the state. Harsh punishments were promised. The law restricted press freedom, criticism of the United States, and political activities of religious organizations and labor unions.

During the Korean War the government became a military autocracy. Orders were given to execute leftists, and probably more than 100,000 people were killed without a trial. A U.S. State Department official described a POW camp for North Koreans and Chinese as "a reign of terror," but horrible atrocities were committed on both sides. Rhee's indifference to his own people manifested itself as wartime inflation ballooned increasingly out of control. His solution to the problem was to make a unilateral decision to stop printing money. During one of the most precarious times of the war, Rhee, who was obsessed with being reelected, rammed a constitutional amendment through the assembly; this established a precedent for manipulating the constitution for political expediency. In 1953, when the armistice was to be signed, Rhee refused. He was opposed to any agreements with the North because he believed the war should not end until UN forces achieved total victory. He never did sign the armistice.

A year after the war, he acted again to amend the constitution. By this time he had developed his own political party, the Liberal Party. The party consisted of enterprising men who had served in the colonial bureaucracy but were now intensely loyal to Rhee. With their support he was able to get another constitutional amendment adopted by the legislature. This amendment repealed the prohibition against a third four-year presidential term. Rhee was now seventy-nine years old and his plan was to be president for life. By the late 1950s he made the political system his own. His inner circle became increasingly corrupt and indifferent to the will of the people.

Public opposition grew. Although land reforms were carried out after the war, the farm population remained poor and relatively inactive politically; however, criticism of the administration was growing in the cities. At the center of the urban discontent was a growing population of college and university students. They were Korea's first postcolonial generation to come of age. They had been educated about constitutional democracy and hated the fraud and coercion that they associated with the administration. By 1960 student protest had a long and venerable tradition that reached back to the colonial era.

That year, at the advanced age of eighty-five, Rhee ran for another four-year term. The main opposition was the Democratic Party, which had emerged in 1955. The major objective of this party was to adopt a constitutional amendment to change the government to a parliamentary system in order to gain some leverage over the chief executive. Rhee's supporters were determined that he win a direct popular election according to the "democratic constitution." His party was able to stymie the formal opposition within the assembly. But instead of ensuring a democratic mandate, the president's principal supporters rigged the election. Instructions were sent out to police chiefs ordaining the exact plurality that the Rhee team was to receive. When the results were counted, the public was informed of a landslide victory.

On election day a riot broke out in Masan. Even though voters were convinced that the election was stolen, they felt helpless against the police force. When a fisherman found the body of a nineteen-year-old high school student with a teargas shell imbedded in one eye, the people lost all control. The resulting riot triggered massive student demonstrations in Seoul and other major cities.

On April 19 more than 3,000 students marched to the presidential mansion. The police initially fired teargas shells, but when the students surmounted the barricades, the police began firing into the crowds. Within a few hours over 100,000 people were battling the police. Approximately 125 died, and more than 1,000 were wounded. This event came to be known as the Righteous Uprising of April 19.

President Rhee declared martial law, sent heavily armed soldiers into Seoul, and blamed the communists for the disturbances. The U.S. secretary of state informed the Korean ambassador that the public unrest resulted from conduct in the recent elections that was unsuited to a free democracy . Street demonstrations in Seoul spread to all major cities. Although the president commanded the fourth largest army in the world, he agreed to resign when informed that he would save lives if he did so. The "righteous uprising" was a success. The students protested the political wrongs of the government as the Tonghak peasants had done in the late nineteenth century. Rhee sought exile in the United States and spent the remainder of his life in Hawaii.

The Second Republic (1960–1961) and the Military Revolution

In the early months after Rhee's resignation, restrictions on the press and political activity were lifted. An interim government headed by Chang Myon moved quickly to draft a new constitution. In reaction to the abuses of power during Rhee's presidency, lawmakers made major revisions to the 1948 constitution in order to eliminate the problems in the presidential system of government.

The amended constitution created a bicameral parliamentary government centered on a prime minister and a cabinet that were responsible to the National Assembly. The presidency was maintained; however, powers would essentially be ceremonial except for the right to nominate the prime minister, who would be the chief executive and head the cabinet. The impact of the Righteous Uprising of April 19 was seen in certain provisions intended to guarantee the democratic rights of the people, such as the freedom of the press and of assembly.

On July 29, 1960, a new National Assembly was elected. The Democratic Party gained control over both houses. The assembly elected Yun Poson president and approved his nomination of Chang Myon as the first prime minister. When the Democratic Party split into two factions, the opposition party gained control of the National Assembly. Unfortunately, this led to absolute gridlock in the assembly at a time when the government needed to urgently address innumerable problems left over from the previous regime.

Chang, a devout Catholic, came from one of the most distinguished families in Korea. Although Rhee had been decisive and domineering, Chang was cautious and gentle.

From the beginning Chang found himself in a very precarious situation. The economy was in decline. Partisan politics made long-range plans difficult. Widespread government corruption was exposed. One of the groups that Chang did attempt strong action against was the police. However, his administration dismissed so many police that morale sunk to the point that those remaining were unwilling or unable to preserve public order. When the hwan was devalued, prices soared, and public demonstrations occurred. Within a year there were approximately 2,000 street demonstrations involving nearly 1 million people. Unfortunately, the Chang administration began to practice tactics similar to those of Rhee. The Democratic Party called its opponents in the National Assembly communists and restricted groups considered too radical.

On May 16, 1961, Major General Park Chung Hee ordered tanks into Seoul and seized control of the government in the first successful military coup d'état since the late fourteenth century, and for the next thirty-two years, South Korea would be ruled by military governments. A sixteen-man junta declared martial law, dissolved the

National Assembly and all political parties, outlawed demonstrations, and exercised strict censorship over the press. It moved swiftly to get U.S. support by claiming that the first purpose of the government was anticommunism. Although the United States initially resisted support of the coup, its opposition did not last for long.

Military Rule and the Third and Fourth Republics, 1961–1979

Park was similar to Rhee in his desire for personal power and the continuation of American military and economic support, as well as his hostility towards North Korea, and his desire to eliminate opposition. A point of real departure between Park and Rhee was their origins. Both Rhee and Chang were well born and educated as opposed to Park, the eighth child of an impoverished father who had fought with Tonghak peasant rebels. He grew up in desperate circumstances, struggling just to survive. He joined the Japanese military, a route to gain upward mobility outside Korea's rigid class structure, and trained at an officer's school in Japan. During the time of U.S. occupation he graduated from the Korean Military Academy.

Because of his impoverished origins, Park demonstrated much greater sensitivity than his predecessors to the desperate economic conditions of the common people. He was also keenly aware of the deeply rooted Confucian belief that establishing legitimacy was critical for the success of his government. His coup did not automatically achieve that goal. So he stressed the dangers of the communist threat, made pledges to restore civilian government within two years, and implemented plans to bring about rapid economic development.

The Park era divides essentially into three periods. During the first two years (1961–1963) he ruled through a military junta called the Supreme Council for National Reconstruction (SCNR). He moved decisively to control this group and the whole nation to an extent not seen since the colonial period. A special tribunal was created to purge the military, government, and society of people whom the junta felt to be corrupt or undesirable. After thousands of arrests, trials, and forced resignations in the military, a new generation of officers was in Park's debt. The SCNR created the Korean Central Intelligence Agency (KCIA) with Kim Jong Pil as its head. The organization, established to include domestic and international surveillance, ultimately became one of the main symbols of the repression of the Park era.

In the second period (1963–1972) the Park regime responded to domestic and international pressure to restore civilian rule. It was particularly concerned about pressures from the United States, whose aid programs counted for more than 50 percent of the national and over 70 percent of the defense budgets. In December 1962, after martial law was lifted, a constitutional referendum approved a third republic, promising a strong, popularly elected president and a party-centered unicameral legislature. An important feature of the new system was that parties were to be awarded seats in proportion to the popular vote received in the elections. By March 1963 Park made an attempt to abandon his promise to restore civilian rule, but a U.S. threat to withhold $25 million in economic aid forced him to proceed.

Park and his officers were still determined to surrender as little power as possible. To make himself more appealing to the public and to the United States, Park declared that he was retiring from the military and would run for office as a civilian. To strengthen his position and that of his cohorts, he had the junta pass laws to ban serious rivals from any political activity. The efforts of Kim Jong Pil, head of the KCIA, and the utilization of vast funds to create a highly centralized political organization, the Democratic Republican Party (DRP), helped Park maintain power. After the party was fully operable, the ban was lifted on political activity. The date of the presidential election was not announced until a month before; consequently, opposition parties had little time to organize. In subsequent elections, the DRP won and thus controlled the majority of the seats in the assembly. By the end of 1963 Park established what appeared to be a civilian government—one that he might be willing to sustain.

For a number of significant domestic and international reasons, Park would change his mind. Because party politics was becoming too time-consuming, disruptive, and threatening to his agenda, he and the DRP developed new strategies. When he wanted an amendment passed to give him a third term, the DRP called for a secret early morning meeting and adopted one. When the opposition tried delaying tactics to prevent the Normalization Treaty with Japan from being introduced on the floor, the DRP used force to end the debate. The opposition walked out of the assembly in protest. Without its presence, the treaty was then ratified. The treaty included Japan's regret for the "unfortunate period" of occupation from 1910 to 1945 and promised millions of dollars in grants and credits to serve as compensation. Without question, the treaty contributed significantly to South Korea's rapid economic development.

Opposition to Park also helped the two factions of the Democratic Party join forces to form a New Democratic Party (NDP). The party now had new leaders, such as Kim Young Sam and Kim Dae-jung, who were well-known critics of the Park regime. Popular support for the NDP grew, particularly in urban areas.

After successfully ending term limits on the presidency, Park was more determined than ever to win decisively in the election in 1971. To achieve this, the KCIA and additional progovernment organizations were effectively mobilized. Essentially all military commanders and police chiefs throughout the country backed his election. Huge amounts of money flowed into his campaign. Since big business had prospered enormously from Park's economic plans, that community helped in major ways to finance his campaign. It would benefit directly from his reelection through defense and public-works contracts, low-interest loans, and other special favors.

Park's biggest challenger in the election was Kim Dae-jung, who attacked him for his military-dominated authoritarianism. As Kim's support grew, his critics charged him with procommunist leanings. There was cheating on both sides, but with his enormous campaign war chest and all the resources of the government behind him, Park had a huge advantage in spite of mounting domestic problems and international concerns. He was reelected with 53.2 percent of the vote, a much smaller victory than anticipated.

International developments were a cause of growing concern before and after the election. Dramatic changes in U.S. foreign policy had recently shocked Seoul. Nixon announced in his doctrine in 1969 that the United States could no longer afford to sustain its many overseas commitments. This would translate into troop reductions not only in Vietnam, but the withdrawal of 20,000 troops that had been stationed in South Korea since the end of the war. This came at a time when 50,000 Koreans were still fighting in Vietnam. Nixon's visit to China in 1972 ended U.S. support for Taiwan, a close anti-communist ally of South Korea.

These dramatic developments plus increased tensions between North and South led Park to fear for the very survival of the ROK. At about the same time the DPRK was suggesting direct talks with the South. A meeting was arranged between Kim Il Sung and Lee Hu Rak, the director of the ROK intelligence agency. On July 4, 1972, the historic South-North Joint Communiqué was issued; both sides agreed to work for peaceful reunification. Park had no real desire for it, but the world responded with surprise and optimism for rapprochement

Gate of Kyongbok-kung Palace, Seoul. In 1972 President Park Chung Hee announced the Yusin ("revitalizing") policy. This policy included martial law, suspension of the constitution, and dissolution of the National Assembly. Photograph by Steve Smith, U.S. specialist fourth class, during his tour of duty. (Courtesy of Steve Smith)

between the two bitter enemies. Park's fears about North Korea and the rapidly changing international situation led him again to consolidate power.

The period from 1965 to 1971 was one of rapid economic growth, political maneuvering, and relative stability. However, a recession in the early 1970s loomed as an additional threat to the regime. A global economic slowdown triggered a rise in protectionism, especially in the United States. Citing domestic and international insecurity, Park suddenly declared a state of emergency in December 1971. The next year began what was to be the third and final stage of his rule. He imposed martial law, suspended the constitution, and dissolved the National Assembly and all political parties. All colleges and universities were closed. Political activity and civil liberties including free speech were restricted. He claimed that he was eliminating disorder and inefficiency, which were a threat to the developing democracy. The constitution was amended yet again in order to prolong his presidency indefinitely—making Park a legal dictator—and to dissolve the assembly whenever he felt it necessary. The president was also empowered to appoint one-third of the National Assembly, enabling him to control the legislature more directly than ever before. The Yusin ("revitalizing") Constitution was approved by a national referendum when the country was still under martial law. By the end of 1972 Park was the head of the Fourth Republic and appeared to be more firmly in control than ever.

How was Park able to dominate politics for a total of eighteen long years? His rule was solidified by a number of institutional, social, and international forces. He had the support of the national police, the bureaucracy, the KCIA, the military, and the DRP. Economic development also gave him continued support. Businesspeople grew rich, were essentially free from any legal action, and received favors, such as tax and investment credits and low-interest loans. With the rapid expansion of the economy, the middle class grew significantly and thus tolerated Park's tactics. Whatever rural discontent existed essentially disappeared, in part because of anticommunist sentiment, migration to the cities, and the New Village Movement (a program for rural development).

There were also many reasons for the continued international support for Park. Ongoing hostility between the Koreas led many people to accept political conditions that normally would be unacceptable. There were periodic incidents, such as the seizure by North Korea of the *Pueblo,* a U.S. intelligence ship, which heightened security fears. Two assassination attempts generated public sympathy for Park and gave credibility to his authoritarian tactics. In January 1968, a thirty-one man North Korean commando team infiltrated the DMZ and worked its way to Seoul to kill the president. They were 1,000 yards from the Blue House, the presidential mansion, before being stopped. In 1974, a gunman tried to assassinate Park during a speech at the National Theater in Seoul. The gunman missed the president but took the life of his wife. During the early 1970s the United States might have put public pressure on Park to mend his ways, but this was difficult. Because allies for the most part would not support U.S. efforts in its war in Southeast Asia, Park's commitment to send 300,000 Korean troops to Vietnam between 1965 and 1973 made criticism virtually impossible.

The third period of the Park regime (1972–1979) and the Yusin system witnessed growing animosity from the population at large. Kim Dae-jung, Park's popular rival for the presidency in 1971, continued to criticize the government and became a symbol of the growing resistance. However, the most important group in the growing antigovernment movement was the students. The Yusin system stimulated a massive movement that included dissident writers, musicians, and other artists. Protest gradually included new groups of people (intellectuals, the middle class, urban workers, and Christian groups). Regional discontent also developed because of the uneven economic development, which tended to favor the regions of Seoul and Pusan, the home regions of many of the ruling elite, and to neglect two of the Cholla provinces of the southwest. Another reason for dissension was the fact that economic development had been based on low wages and the suppression of organized labor.

In May 1975, Emergency Measure No. 9 made any criticism of the president or of the constitution a crime. Anyone who took a stand against Park or his policies faced arrest, forced confession, imprisonment without trial, and execution. In spite of brutal measures to stop all opposition, the truth about the government spread throughout the nation and overseas. Victims became an inspiration to others to continue the fight. One of the most famous symbols was Kim Dae-jung, whom Park detested. KCIA agents kidnapped him in 1973 from a Tokyo hotel in a murder plot designed to look as if North Koreans committed it. The plan was to dispose of the corpse somewhere between Tokyo and Seoul. Fortunately, a former KCIA director, Kim Hyong-wook, intervened to save him. The U.S. ambassador in Seoul rushed to the Blue House and demanded that Kim Dae-jung be returned alive. Five days later, a bruised and shaken Kim was dumped outside his home and barred from political activity for the rest of Park's term. The former KCIA director who saved him later disappeared in Paris.

It should have been no surprise when the Park Chung Hee regime came to a sudden and violent end, but it was a shock. In spite of Park's effort to maintain control, political and economic problems continued to spin out of his control. They turned worse when OPEC nearly doubled the price of crude oil. Low-paid workers, the main victims of the downturn, expressed their frustrations in increasingly militant labor disputes and strikes. The public became even more aroused when female textile workers were brutally beaten by the police during a hunger strike. A short time later, Kim Young Sam, a vocal opponent of Park from a faction of the NDP, gained control of the opposition. Park's DRP party promptly moved to punish Kim by expelling him from the National Assembly. A week later the opposition walked out of the National Assembly in protest, and in Park's hometown of Pusan, students, workers, and urban residents demanded his resignation and an end to the Yusin system. Within a short time massive demonstrations broke out throughout the country.

On the evening of October 26 Park had a dinner meeting at the KCIA annex near the Blue House. At this meeting an argument broke out about the demonstrations. Park's bodyguard lambasted Kim Jae Kyu, the head of the KCIA, for not controlling the demonstrations. Kim argued that this would mean killing thousands of people. Park then argued that he would be willing to kill 30,000 people. Kim had been frustrated for some time over the politics of his job as KCIA director and Park's criticism of his performance. He left the room and returned with a pistol, shot the bodyguard, and then Park. It was not the demonstrators that brought to an end the life-term of the president, but his trusted security chief.

Political Turmoil, 1979–1981

Park's assassination shocked the nation. More than any other political figure, he had brought economic development to Korea; however, his contributions were both admirable and detestable. Public surveys indicated that the vast majority of the people wanted extensive political reforms and democratization. They also wanted the direct election of the president, limited powers for the chief executive, increased powers for the legislative and judicial branches to check the president, and a system by which there could be more local government control.

After Park was killed, Choi Kyu Hah, a career diplomat and bureaucrat, became acting president of the interim government. Choi pledged that the constitution would be amended "to promote democracy" and announced that elections would be held. He removed emergency decrees of the former regime and restored the civil rights of Park's rivals, such as Kim Dae-jung, religious leaders, journalists, and student activists. These events helped create a sense of national well-being that was known as the Seoul Spring. Kim Young Sam, the head of the National Democratic Party, called for the elimination of the Yusin system, and Kim Dae-jung, who formed the National Coalition for Democracy and Unification, demanded rapid democratization.

The public did not get what it wanted. South Koreans were to experience the greatest violence since the Korean War and control by a military junta. The "12.12" coup occurred on December 12, 1979.

Major General Chun Doo Hwan, a close friend of the murdered Park, led the coup with two key assistants, Major General Roh Tae Woo and Major General Chong Ho-yong. They were all graduates of the Korean Military Academy in 1955 and members of a secret military organization, the Hanahwoe, that included bright and ambitious army officers. Chun was the head of the Defense Security Command, one of the intelligence structures that Park created. This agency was charged with the investigation into Park's assassination. It was decided that General Roh Tae Woo, commander of the Ninth Army Division, would arrest his superior, General Chong Sunghwa, and falsely charge him of being an accomplice with Kim Jae Kyu. Several thousand troops from a secret network within the army overpowered Chong's guards, arrested him, and took over the Defense Ministry and army headquarters. Chun was now in control of the military, and both Chong and Kim Jae Kyu were executed.

In order to pull off the coup, Chun had used the Ninth Army, which was part of the American-Korean Combined Forces Command (CFC). However, Roh had moved the division from the DMZ to Seoul without notifying General John A. Wickham, the commander of the CFC. Wickham was furious and immediately communicated his disapproval to Chun. The U.S. government delivered a strong warning to Chun for violating the CFC's operation control.

Chun's actions resulted in massive student demonstrations calling for his resignation and the immediate end of the Yusin system. Approximately 70,000 to 100,000 students were voicing their opinions in the streets of Seoul. Chun, as new head of the KCIA, extended martial law, dissolved the National Assembly, closed colleges and universities, banned labor strikes, and prohibited all political discussion and activity. His seizure of power essentially complete, he had Kim Dae-jung and Kim Young Sam arrested.

The events of December 1979 brought U.S. officials face-to-face with the limits of their control over South Korea's political situation. When a Korean academic urged William Gleysteen, the U.S. ambassador, to kick Chun out to show that the United States would not support just anyone, Gleysteen, who recognized Chun's intelligence and drive, rejected his idea by saying that he could not act as a colonial governor. Instead, the United States strongly advised Chun to refrain from interfering in the political process or taking political power in his own right, which is exactly what he did.

Some months later, between May 14 and 18, the CFC commander, General Wickham, frustrated by the events, went to Washington,

D.C., to discuss the situation. Meanwhile the Chun forces quietly notified the CFC deputy commander, a Korean general, of their intent to move the Twentieth Division. The deputy commander immediately granted a notification of release.

The tumultuous events moved out of Seoul and into Kwangju, the capital of the province of Kim Dae-jung in South Cholla. This area was historically a center of popular protest against injustice in the tradition of the Tonghak uprising and an area that had been consistently ignored in the economic development plans of Park Chung Hee. On the morning of May 18 about 500 students demanded Kim's release and an end of martial law. They suddenly found themselves up against paratroopers sent into the city by General Chong Ho-yong, commander of the special forces, who had been told that communists were overrunning Kwangju. The paratroopers, who were outside of the U.S. Combined Command, began brutally clubbing protesters with riot gear and rifle butts. Many students were left bleeding or were hauled away in military vehicles. Citizens became outraged and poured into the streets to join the students.

General Chun grew impatient with the events in Kwangju and ordered Chong Ho-yong to take charge of the military operations. Early in the morning of May 27 tanks and armored personnel carriers released their power on the Kwangju citizenry. Loudspeakers from helicopters warned that the ROK Twentieth Division would enter the city and that people should disarm and return to their homes. However, when it was all over, hundreds and maybe thousands were dead. The government announced that the death toll was roughly 240. Witnesses estimated that at least 2,000 must have been killed. The fallout from the events haunted Chun throughout his rule. The Kwangju Massacre became a pivotal event in the country's journey from dictatorship to democracy. Ultimately both Chun Doo Hwan and Roh Tae Woo were arrested and prosecuted as leaders of the massacre.

During the Kwangju demonstrations, residents of the city had appealed in vain to the U.S. embassy to intervene. Since nothing happened, students concluded that the United States supported Chun and had approved his dispatch of forces to the city, especially because the government-controlled media confirmed this fact. There were also accusations that North Korean agents had directed the rebellion.

President Carter based his administration on a commitment to global human rights. Despite discomfort with Chun's takeover and the subsequent massacre, U.S. authorities in Korea and the Carter administration could have used armed forces to intervene, but it would have been unprecedented since the 1940s. Distraught by the simultaneous Iranian crisis and concerned about fictitious KCIA reports of North Korean troop movements, the United States feared taking any step that could weaken the stability of the existing ROK regime and security on the peninsula.

In his last months in office Carter took steps to save Kim Dae-jung's life. After the Kwangju incident, Chun immediately arrested Kim and blamed him for planning the rebellion despite the fact that Kim was in prison at the time. After a show trial, Kim was sentenced to death for sedition. Since Chun wanted to obtain legitimacy for his regime, he was eager to be invited to Washington, D.C. As a quid pro quo for an invitation to the White House to meet the newly inaugurated president, Ronald Reagan, Chun commuted Kim's death sentence to life imprisonment.

The final step to Chun's ascendancy to power was to have the civilian government accede to what was already a reality. On May 31, Chun established a special military-civilian committee that was chaired by Choi, but in effect was a front for Chun and his supporters. When Choi resigned from the presidency, Chun promoted himself to four-star general and discharged himself from the army. Operating under the procedures of a rubber-stamped electoral college established under Park's Yusin Constitution, Chun had himself inaugurated president in February 1981.

The Fifth Republic, 1981–1988

The seven-year rule by Chun Doo Hwan's military regime was the most tyrannical period in the modern history of South Korea. Even though he denounced past corruption and promised a new age of growth, honesty in government, and justice, Chun was consistently more heavy-handed than Park, who could at least justifiably claim credit for rapid economic growth. Before he declared himself president, actions were taken to weaken the press even further. Laws were adopted to curtail workers' rights to strike. The government regularly sided with business, especially those businesses in which foreign investment was high.

Chun's coup and transition to civilian rule were similar to Park's. Chun kept the loyalty of his classmates from the Korean Military Academy. One was Roh Tae Woo, who was given the high-profile task of obtaining authorization from the Olympic Committee to host the

1988 Summer Olympics in Seoul. When Roh got approval in 1981, Chun started a major construction effort to rebuild the nation. He emphasized economic growth over any serious efforts toward democratization; however, he did allow political parties to become more important, and the ban on political activities by former politicians (except Kim Dae-jung) was gradually lifted. Both Park and Chun cultivated building a strong political party in the National Assembly as a means of controlling the legislative process and allowing military personnel to serve as civilian politicians. To stop criticism Chun included a provision in the new constitution that a president could only serve a single seven-year term. He commented frequently that he would turn over his position to an elected successor in February 1988. He hoped that time would allow him to gain public acceptance.

His strategies did not work. Although Park came into power with relatively little bloodshed, Chun's coup involved the death of soldiers and a savage attack on civilians. The fact that he refused to accept any responsibility for the tragedy in Kwangju created even greater public hostility. Students became increasingly hostile to Chun and anti-American because it appeared to them that the United States had backed him during the events in Kwangju. Another reason that Chun had difficulty gaining support was the fact that people basically did not like or respect him. Family members damaged his reputation further—his wife and brother were continually implicated in financial scandals. The new U.S. ambassador, Richard L. Walker, considered Chun one of the most calculating, politically smart people that he had ever known.

As Chun continued to restrain civil unrest and antigovernment activities, students and workers became more militant. This was demonstrated in the early and mid-1980s by seventy incidents of self-immolation. Radical students insisted that Korea's problems stemmed from the country's division by the United States. Many of these students went on to underreport their educational backgrounds and became factory workers in order to organize other workers.

In addition to student and worker activists, the middle class became a force that demanded change. It had grown to expect that economic development would be continuous. The Yusin system gave impetus for democratization from political organizations, religious groups, intellectuals, and human rights groups. By 1974 the number of Christians in South Korea numbered 4.3 million, approximately 13 percent of the population. Many Christians were better educated and belonged to an increasingly political middle class that believed in

democracy. Groups that had been apathetic to political developments, such as professionals, white-collar workers, technicians, factory managers, small-business owners, and lower level bureaucrats
increasingly supported real democracy. A new political party, the
New Korean Democratic Party (NKDP) became the largest opposition
bloc in the National Assembly after the 1985 elections. The two leading members of the NKDP were Kim Dae-jung and Kim Young Sam,
both Christians who championed democratic reforms. There was
now a broad base for challenging the authoritarian regime of Chun.
All that was needed was another explosive incident. No one had to
wait very long.

Early in 1987, a twenty-one-year-old student from Seoul National
University died in police custody. The police had continually dunked
his head in a bathtub and smashed his windpipe in the process. They
tried to cover it up, but details leaked and inflamed the populace
against the regime. Memorial services and protests were held throughout the country. After years of indifference to youthful demonstrations, citizens rose up and demanded democratization and reform.

Although riot police and teargas assaulted street demonstrators,
Chun appeared agreeable to a constitutional amendment to allow a
direct, popular election to choose his successor. However, on April
13, 1987, Chun announced that he had changed his mind. Two
months later he met with his key supporters from the ruling Democratic Justice Party and announced his decision to appoint Roh Tae
Woo as his successor. His audience applauded his decision and a
moist-eyed Roh thanked his chief. On June 10 the ruling party held
its convention, and 99 percent of the delegates rubber-stamped the
Roh candidacy in an indirect election to the presidency.

Chun had a sense of urgency that Roh succeed him as president.
He needed a loyal friend to succeed him, one who would not prose-
cute him for his illegal seizure of power before and after the Kwangju
Massacre. It was strongly suspected and later confirmed that Chun
and Park had received huge political donations from the chaebol as
kickbacks for profitable contracts. Chun could pledge Roh all the
money he needed to win the election.

In response to the Roh candidacy, on a day now called the "6.10
Struggle," dissenters organized a coalition of opposition called the
People's Movement to Win a Democratic Constitution and demanded
direct presidential election and a series of reforms. Although there
had been many demonstrations since the founding of the ROK in
1948, there had never been anything as large in size or scope as the

ones in the summer of 1987. For the first time significant numbers of older people and the well-dressed middle class joined students and workers on the streets in urban areas throughout the Republic. This massive protest became a watershed moment in the evolution of democracy in South Korea.

Coming on the heels of the Philippine revolution, the political crisis grabbed international attention. The Reagan administration worried that a full-fledged revolution might overthrow the regime. Believing in its crucial role to protect the external security of the ROK, the United States sent a message via Beijing to North Korea that it should not take advantage of the trouble in the South. President Reagan then sent a letter to Chun. It expressed support for Chun's previous commitment to a peaceful transfer of power as a necessary step in strengthening the institution of democratic government. The president also expressed support for the release of political prisoners to send a signal to the world that South Korea was breaking away from what Chun termed the old politics. At the end of the letter, Reagan held out the promise of a state visit to the United States after Chun peacefully left office in 1988.

Prior to receiving this letter Chun had considered using the army to suppress the riots. Even the military expressed alarm about his extensive preparations to use force against civilians. Chun suspended the mobilization order. On June 29, Roh shocked the nation by accepting the demand for a direct presidential election. His announcement included a program of reform that included amnesty for Kim Dae-jung, freedom of the press, and autonomy for the colleges and universities. In response to public antipathy toward rampant corruption and crime, Roh posed as a moral crusader who said he would build "a clean and honest society." He made his declaration to Chun and stated that he would resign from all public duties if Chun refused to accept it. Two days later Chun publicly accepted the proposals. The crisis was over and the country took a step further in the democratization process.

No one knows exactly why Roh opted for reform or why Chun agreed to it, but the 1988 Seoul Olympics had something to do with it. Chun had made the Seoul Olympics the cornerstone of domestic and international policies. This was South Korea's chance to gain international recognition and respect. Continued political instability could bring possible cancellation by the Olympic Committee. The fact that the overwhelming majority of Koreans wanted reform together with tremendous pressure from the United States to abstain from a military solution made reform more tolerable.

During the next six months there was considerable political activity. In October a national referendum approved the new constitution that had been approved by both the opposition and the ruling parties. This was the eighth time since the founding of the ROK in 1948 that the constitution had been amended or rewritten. By 1987 it was clear that a thorough revision was necessary because it had become the tool of military dictators. The revised constitution contained sweeping changes and emerged on October 29, 1987; it remains the fundamental law of South Korea.

One of the most important elements of the 1987 constitution was that the president be elected for a single term of five years by a universal, direct, and secret ballot of the citizens. The powers of the president were restricted in order to provide a greater balance between the executive branch and the National Assembly, consisting of 273 members holding four-year terms. The latter was given impeachment power over the president, the prime minister, judges of the court, and numerous other positions. The armed forces were charged solely with national defense and were forbidden to be politically active. Gone were the provisions from the 1948 constitution that said that rights and freedoms could be taken away in order to maintain public order. Consequently, restrictions on free speech and the press were disallowed. Workers were given the right to form unions, bargain collectively, and strike. A provision of the former constitution that was retained held that the state had the right to regulate economic affairs in order to maintain balanced growth and stability, to ensure proper distribution of income, and to prevent abuse of economic power. To correct the regional favoritism, an article made a commitment to ensure the balanced development of all regions.

Given the long history of authoritarian rule, the course of democratization in Korea would depend heavily on the character of future presidents, the composition of the National Assembly, sustained economic development, and stability on the peninsula. The December 1987 election, the first by direct popular vote in sixteen years, was a particularly significant test of whether the country would have a civilian president or another retired general loyal to Chun. During his campaign Roh portrayed himself as someone who would finally end military-backed rule. However, there were numerous reasons why change did not occur. He had the advantage of leading the incumbent party, massive funding, and extensive exposure in the media, which was still controlled by the government. The fact that Reagan hosted Roh in the White House a few months before the election must have had some influence on the outcome. But the major factor in the election results was the political rivalry between the two main opposition leaders: Kim Young Sam and Kim Dae-jung. Roh knew that if he granted the latter Kim amnesty, he would run for the presidency, split the Democratic Party, and allow Roh to win. The election results confirmed his calculations; he won with 37 percent of the vote, and the opposition vote was divided 28 percent and 27 percent, respectively, between Kim Young Sam and Kim Dae-jung. If either one of the opposition candidates had bowed out and supported the other, Roh would have lost. There were numerous accusations of vote buying, intimidation, and fraud; however, the election results were generally accepted by a public grown weary from tumultuous politics. The results also revealed that each candidate obtained strong support from his own region. Roh Tae Woo, whose nomination had created civil disturbance and media attention throughout the world, was peacefully inaugurated as president in Seoul on February 25, 1988.

The Sixth Republic, 1988–1993

Roh Tae Woo's inauguration in February 1988 was the first normal constitutional transfer of presidential power in Korea since 1948. In his inaugural address he declared that "with the launching of the new Republic, we will sail steadfastly toward democracy." Although he expressed eagerness to implement the new constitution, it would be a challenge for the new president, a man accustomed to giving orders and being obeyed, to actually implement it. This challenge would become even more daunting because the Democratic Justice Party (DJP) did not get the majority of the votes in the National Assembly elections for the first time in forty years.

To convey to the public that a new era had dawned, Roh blamed Chun Doo Hwan for the coup of December 12, 1979, and for the Kwangju Uprising. However, Roh protected his longtime friend from punishment and jail by allowing Chun the opportunity to check into a remote Buddhist temple for meditation. Although Roh seemed to be more popular than Chun, his selection of cabinet members indicated that a true break with the past had not occurred. The political system under Roh was in no way a true civilian regime. But with the new checks-and-balances system, he lacked the power of previous presidents. His party did not control the National Assembly, which asserted itself with a vengeance.

For most people there did appear important signs of change. In the

National Assembly the opposition used its power to probe the financial scandals of the Chun administration and to reject Roh's nominee for chief justice, the first time the assembly had rejected a Supreme Court nomination. The administration initially indicated a more laissez-faire approach to labor disputes. Many political prisoners were freed. The press was also freer from government interference.

Another sign of change appeared in June 1988 when Roh announced efforts to improve relations with P'yongyang. His Northern Diplomacy efforts were geared to improving communication and ending isolation from the international community of capitalist nations. Although his policies reflected the immediate goal of creating an atmosphere conducive to a successful Summer Olympics, they marked a significant departure from adversarial confrontation with the North, China, the Soviet Union, and other socialist nations. For the past year there had been considerable tension between the Koreas relating to the Olympics. North Korea had attempted to pressure its communist allies to boycott the games. Two months after the North had rejected the final International Olympic Proposal and refused participation in the games, two highly trained DPRK espionage agents blew up a South Korean airliner. One of the agents, Kim Hyon Hui, later confessed that she had been brainwashed to believe that by destroying the airliner she would help to bring about reunification of the Koreas.

An unprecedented political development occurred two years later, in January 1990, when three political parties merged. Kim Young Sam's Reunification Democratic Party and Kim Jong Pil's New Democratic Republican Party joined Roh's ruling Democratic Justice Party to form the Democratic Liberal Party. Three pragmatic politicians had secretly agreed to this merger to establish control over the National Assembly. This was good news for Roh because it would end the gridlock in the assembly. Kim Young Sam defended his alliance with Roh, a man he had previously castigated for being a military dictator and an enemy of democracy. Kim said the merger would save the country by ending the political stalemate, but his political maneuvering was directed toward obtaining the presidency.

Roh had promised greater equity for workers, and labor's hopes were raised. But when the economy slowed down for a variety of reasons, Roh reneged on his promises to support wage increases in the belief that they would threaten economic growth. After the three parties merged, Roh Tae Woo had greater freedom to arrest dissidents under the National Security Law and to crush various labor strikes.

Over 1,000 dissidents were arrested in one year alone. Business was also threatened by Roh's get-tough policies. If businesses granted wage increases, they would be denied loans.

With the end of the Cold War in 1989, Roh continued to make overtures to improve relations with North Korea and former socialist countries. Relations with most of them, including the former Soviet Union and China, were normalized, and thus the Republic's relations became truly global. In September 1991, South and North Korea joined the United Nations simultaneously, a sign of the success of the Northern Diplomacy. On December 13, 1991, the two Koreas came closer than ever before to accepting each other's regime as a legitimate government with a right to exist. They pledged to transform the armistice into a solid state of peace, avoid force against each other, and reduce arms. They also pledged to develop economic, cultural, and scientific exchanges, to allow correspondence between divided families, and to reopen roads and railroads between the Koreas. In a final agreement on December 31, both North and South agreed not to "test, manufacture, produce, receive, possess, store, deploy or use nuclear weapons" and not to "possess nuclear reprocessing and uranium enrichment facilities." They also agreed to reciprocal inspections of facilities to be carried out by a Joint Nuclear Control Commission. Suddenly life on the Korean peninsula seemed safer.

Despite Roh's achievements in diplomacy, the rate of economic growth slowed to the lowest point in decades. Anxiety about the economy clearly showed in the results of the March 1992 elections for the National Assembly. The Democratic Liberal Party created by the merger lost control over the Assembly by one vote. The opposition party, the Democratic Party led by Kim Dae-jung, made a strong showing. The honorary chairman of the Hyundai Group, Chung Chu-Yong, won thirty-one seats. The public, in effect, repudiated the three-party merger and helped to reconfigure the political makeup of the National Assembly.

As Roh's single-term presidency was ending in 1992, there was no question about duly electing the next president through a direct popular vote. It was certain that Kim Dae-jung, who had aspired to the presidency since 1971, would run again. In May, the ruling Democratic Liberal Party had its convention and nominated Kim Young Sam the government party candidate. As Kim celebrated his nomination, students led anti-Kim and anti-ruling-party demonstrations in twenty-two urban centers, including Seoul, Pusan, and Kwangju. Students denounced the ruling party as being an illicit union of three parties and that it had betrayed the wishes of the people in the 1987 and 1992 National Assembly elections. The government immediately called out the riot police and quickly ended the demonstrations. As expected, Kim Dae-jung received the nomination from the opposition party. Chung Chu-Yong organized his own political party, the United People's Party, and announced his candidacy. His entrance in the race indicated a growing disillusionment among business conglomerates with the government and the candidates in the presidential race.

The election was to be one of many firsts. For the first time citizen groups organized on a massive scale to ensure a truly democratic election. Grassroots movements arose to oversee a fair election. They promised to expose any corrupt or coercive practices in electioneering, such as the distribution of gifts or pressure by local officials, including the police. Another first was the fact that all three candidates were civilians with no military background or backing by the military.

Throughout the campaign Kim Dae-jung proved to be an articulate and charismatic campaigner who stressed democratization and reunification. However, he did not have the financial resources of his rivals. He was limited to taking commercial flights, which allowed him to make contact with only urban dwellers. Kim Young Sam, a hiking enthusiast and daily jogger, had unlimited energy and abundant funds from the ruling party and could travel by helicopter essentially everywhere. He took a more moderate position, emphasizing "reform amidst stability."

When the ballots were counted, Kim Young Sam emerged with 41.4 percent to Kim Dae-jung's 33.4 percent. Chung Chu-Yong received only 16.1 percent of the vote. As in previous elections since 1971 the results were clearly regional. Aside from the deep-seated regionalism, it was also clear from the results that Kim Young Sam obtained more widespread support from different social classes, educational backgrounds, age groups, and occupations than the other two candidates. Kim Dae-jung gave a prompt and gracious concession speech, which was also unprecedented in Korean politics; this conciliatory gesture was believed to have earned him considerable respect. The inauguration took place on February 25, 1993; it was the first peaceful transfer of power to a duly elected civilian president in thirty-two years.

The Seventh Republic, 1993–1998

At the time of Kim Young Sam's inauguration his political career had already spanned four decades. His election to the National Assembly on a government ticket at age twenty-five made him the youngest national legislator on record. His youth was shaped by the last years of the colonial period, the financial success of his father, and education at an elite high school in Pusan and Seoul National University, the nation's most prestigious university. During his many years as an opposition politician he held the dream of becoming the president of South Korea.

As he launched his regime as the legitimate leader of his nation, Kim announced that the Seventh Republic was "the Second Founding of the Korean Republic." He set high standards for his administration and ones by which he too was eventually judged. In his inaugural address he declared that the Seventh Republic would open a civilian and democratic era for a new Korea by rooting out the disease of corruption and misconduct. Kim, who had organized and led the June 10, 1987, march that demanded political democratization through direct presidential election, ultimately freed over 5,500 political prisoners and erased the conviction records of more than 500,000 political prisoners from former military regimes. Within a month he announced a new plan to revitalize the economy.

Regardless of the fact that Kim was a skilled politician, he had limited administrative experience. He came into office with little knowledge of or conviction in economic policy matters at a time when the chaebol dominated the financial sector. What was not apparent at the time of his inauguration was that he owed considerable political debts to business for its part in the unscrupulous merger in 1990 of the three parties. He joined Roh Tae Woo's ruling group as a means of obtaining the presidency.

His cabinet appointments were a hopeful sign of change; nearly all the members were reform-minded and outsiders, unlike those of his predecessor. For the first time several women received cabinet posts. The next step in reform was the realignment of the military, the principal force threatening the government. Within two weeks of his inauguration, Kim began dismissals, early retirements, and demotions of powerful military figures. These moves were referred to as a revolutionary cleansing and brought the military under the control of a civilian government. In the past military service had been a means of attaining power and status for those with humble backgrounds; this was no longer the case.

From his involvement in politics for many years, Kim was well acquainted with the powerful ties between business and government.

Politicians were known to accept huge donations from heads of the largest conglomerates. It was commonly known that when Chun Doo Hwan was in power, he accumulated a giant slush fund to help his friends and silence his opponents. After Roh was nominated for the presidency, Chun provided enormous amounts of money for the party and, specifically, for Roh's campaign.

Only two days after his inauguration, Kim Young Sam surprised everyone by taking the unparalleled step of making public his financial assets and those of his extended family. He also promised that during his presidency he would accept no political contributions. Although the public was delighted by the news, the publicity was such that pressures mounted for other officials to follow suit. Over 1,500 were either dismissed or resigned voluntarily. Legislation was also adopted to ensure fair elections, limit campaign expenses, and prevent the recurrence of corrupt and violent elections.

In 1994 President Kim declared his vision of *segyehwa* (globalization) to prepare for the monumental changes taking place throughout the world and to build the Republic into a first-rate nation in the twenty-first century. His plan was to open Korea to the world in all fields (political, economic, and social) and to meet global standards of excellence in all areas. At a time when the economy was eleventh highest in the world, he was very confident that his country could compete economically with any trading partners and could establish standards of excellence in all areas, such as the protection of human rights and workers' rights.

At the same time that Kim was promoting his vision of globalization, a major crisis was building up on the peninsula. When the International Atomic Energy Agency was denied access to inspect North Korea's nuclear sites, it turned the matter over to the United Nations Security Council, where the United States hoped to get enough votes to impose sanctions on P'yongyang. North Korea denounced sanctions as a declaration of war and threatened to turn Seoul into "a sea of fire." In response, President Bill Clinton sent substantial reinforcements to South Korea. As developments seemed to be spinning out of control, former president Jimmy Carter, alarmed by the depth of the crisis, offered to go to North Korea as a private citizen. In spite of Kim Young Sam's belief that the visit was "ill-timed," Carter met with an ailing Kim Il Sung and defused the crisis. His meeting paved the way for an agreement that became the October Framework; P'yongyang would freeze its graphite reactors and accept full inspections under the Nuclear Non-Proliferation Treaty (NPT), and in return, a consortium of nations would supply light-water reactors to help solve the North's energy problems.

In 1995 Korea took a significant step in the democratization process. For the first time there were full-scale local democratic elections. While the 1948 constitution had mandated local self-rule, Park terminated local autonomy until reunification was accomplished. When Kim Young Sam was inaugurated he expressed that one of his reforms was to establish functioning local governments. In June, direct elections throughout the country chose over 5,500 local officials from over 15,000 candidates. In these elections, voters selected mayors, heads of local units, and councilors for local and wide-area governments. Over 68 percent of the electorate voted in what was determined by observers to be a free and fair election devoid of any violence.

Although the local elections were a significant success for democracy, they were a tremendous setback for President Kim, and the results signified the growth of the opposition. In the first year of his presidency he had an approval rating of 90 percent; however, by 1995 anti-ruling-party hostility grew from those who had been adversely affected by government reforms: the military, businesspeople, and government officials who had served in the Park, Chun, and Roh regimes. In spite of Kim's efforts to improve Korea's standing in the world, he failed to sustain public support. Many could not forgive him for the merger of the three parties, particularly because he had formerly denounced Roh and Kim Jong Pil as enemies of democracy.

The June 1995 local elections also signified the persistence of regionalism. Kim Young Sam's party did well in his native South Kyongsang Province. The opposition Democratic Party, identified with Kim Dae-jung, was victorious in Kim's native South Cholla Province, and Kim Jong Pil's party won substantial support in his native South Ch'ungch'ong Province. The country was clearly divided into three prominent camps, and Seoul emerged in support of the opposition Democratic Party. If Kim Dae-jung declared his candidacy in the next presidential election, it appeared that he could win.

Several developments strongly influenced the remainder of Kim's presidency. His detractors, knowing that he had risen to be the leader of the ruling party during Roh's presidency, suspected that Kim must have been involved in some aspects of its corruption. All the time he continued to convey the impression that he knew nothing or was indifferent about Chun's and Roh's deeds or past activities. Several events in 1995 brought charges of corruption to the forefront. In

October a representative in the National Assembly startled everyone with the announcement that Roh had a secret fund of approximately $500 million that was deposited in commercial banks under forty false-name accounts. He then showed the Assembly copies of Roh's savings accounts. Eight days after this disclosure a tearful Roh apologized to the nation for collecting approximately $650 million in slush funds while in office. At the time of his apology the country's per capita income had only reached $10,000.

A huge rally, organized by Kim Dae-jung, demanded that Kim Young Sam prove that he did not receive money from Roh's slush fund. The president then amazed everyone by announcing that legislation would be adopted to deal with the corruption and military activities of former administrations. The Constitutional Court ruled two days later that those involved in the Kwangju Massacre could be prosecuted. This surprise development paved the way for criminal prosecution of those involved in the coup of December 12, 1979, and the massacre led by Chun and Roh. The president said that he would personally show that justice was alive in Korea. Critics responded by saying that Kim's motivation was to influence the upcoming National Assembly elections and the 1997 presidential election in the ruling party's favor. A special law to deal with political scandal and the massacre was quickly adopted by the National Assembly and paved the way for the indictment of Chun, Roh, and other former army officers on charges of mutiny, treason, and bribery.

Their trial began in December 1995 in a heavily guarded courthouse in Seoul. Chun admitted that he had received donations, but not bribes. He revealed that he had sent some $240 million directly to Roh for his 1987 presidential campaign. Chun reported that he had given $70 million to Roh to celebrate his election and start his presidency. Roh also said he had received only donations and that they amounted to approximately $575 million from 35 of the nation's leading conglomerates. Roh remembered spending $175 million to help ruling-party candidates in the 1988 and 1992 National Assembly elections, but he evaded questions that related to the possible financial support of Kim Young Sam's election. When Chun suggested that he might reveal recipients' names if he were treated harshly, the public trial was conveniently postponed, preventing any revelation embarrassing to President Kim or the ruling party from being made before the Assembly elections. The entire membership of 299 seats in the assembly was at stake, and Kim knew that the election would be a test of his presidency and democratization.

Kim was determined that his ruling party would fair well in the election, especially after the setback in the local elections. He also knew that if the ruling party did not maintain a majority in the assembly, he would be a lame duck for the last two years of his presidency. As part of his drive to show that his party was creating a new Korea, Kim changed its name from the Democratic Liberal Party to the New Korea Party. He warned the public that there would be no further reforms if the opposition got control of the seats in the National Assembly. He said a vote against his party would mean social disorder and paralysis in government.

Encouraged by the results of the local elections, Kim Dae-jung created a new political party, the National Congress for New Politics, and announced that he would run for the presidency for the fourth time. Immediately, nearly 100 members of the Democratic Party joined Kim Dae-jung's new party, which made it the largest opposition party in the assembly. Two other candidates announced their candidacy: Kim Jong Pil of the newly formed United Liberal Democratic Party and Yu Ju-taek, who led what was left of the Democratic Party in the assembly.

Kim Young Sam stressed that stability was the key election issue, and Kim Dae-jung made economic prosperity the focus of his campaign. But in the public's eyes the economy appeared strong despite signs that the country's competitive edge was weakening. In the final days of the sixteen-day campaign period, another scandal erupted. Kim Dae-jung's new opposition party charged that a personal assistant to the president and the first lady had received approximately $1 million in bribes. Kim promptly fired the assistant and went on to spend wildly, thus violating the new reform laws that his own administration had adopted. He won the election.

Another shock occurred six days before the elections. On the night of April 5, hundreds of armed DPRK soldiers entered the northern sector of Panmunjom in violation of the 1953 armistice agreement. The troops came into the area three times, and in one instance staged field maneuvers in the buffer zone, the most heavily fortified region in the world. President Kim placed the military on its highest level of readiness, and the U.S. forces were put on alert. He also capitalized on this crisis by urging the public in the final stages of the campaign to support the ruling party in order to secure peace and stability on the peninsula. The election results clearly reflected the impact of the North's activities along the DMZ.

The ruling party achieved a first in that the New Korea Party won in Seoul, which had previously been a stronghold of the opposition party. Another first was the fact that nearly half of the elected assembly members were well-educated professionals new to politics, certainly a development that reflected voter disillusionment with traditional party politics. Despite these indications of change, the same regionalism surfaced that had occurred in the 1996 elections. Candidates nominated by Kim Dae-jung's National Congress for New Politics were successful in the Cholla Provinces, but failed to win a single seat in the Kyongsang Provinces, Kim Young Sam's stronghold. The only locations where candidates of Kim Young Sam's New Korea Party lost were in the Cholla Provinces, Kim Dae-jung's home base. In spite of the ruling party's strong showing, it was eleven votes short of majority. Nevertheless, this was much better than the clear defeat in local elections the previous year.

Shortly after the elections, prosecutors in Chun's trial revealed that they discovered some $8 million that Chun had not disclosed. This was known before the election, but the fact that it was not made public until afterwards is a sign that the Kim government needed to protect itself. As the trial resumed after the elections, both Chun and Roh defended their actions in the December 1979 coup because of Park's murder and the fear of domestic unrest followed by possible aggression from North Korea. In August 1996 both former presidents were charged with the illegal seizure of power, amassing illegal wealth by abusing their power, and murdering innocent citizens. The prosecutors demanded the death sentence for Chun and a life sentence for Roh for mutiny, treason, and corruption.

Kim Young Sam benefited from the political prize of Chun's and Roh's trial. The trial itself was made possible by his civilian government and stood as a lesson that former presidents could be punished for their actions. Newspapers reported that democracy was now stronger. Nevertheless there was deep suspicion that Kim Young Sam had probably received slush funds from Roh during his 1992 campaign. Another scandal shortly thereafter revealed that one of Kim's sons was involved in bribing high-level officials. Meanwhile Kim was beset with a worsening economic crisis.

As the economy took a sharp downturn in 1996, the mass media, some of which were owned or heavily dominated by the chaebol, appealed to citizens "to tighten the belt" and not to expect wage increases. Korean workers, known internationally for their hard toil and for working the longest workdays in the world, had seen little improvement in their wages over the years and resented the obvious extravagance of high-ranking government officials and the chaebol tycoons. The labor bills that were adopted by the National Assembly made it clear that there were no prolabor voices in the legislature. Predictably nationwide strikes spanned the range from assembly-line workers at Hyundai to subway engineers. Despite the hopes raised at the time of Kim's inauguration and by his bold reforms, government was still corrupt, antilabor, and probusiness.

While the public was preoccupied with the declining economy and worker strikes, the Hanbo Steel Industry, the second largest steel manufacturer, declared bankruptcy in January 1997 with $6 billion of debt, mostly in bank loans. Prosecutors accused Hanbo's president of bribing high government officials to receive preferential bank loans at very favorable rates. It was particularly disturbing to learn that several of President Kim's closest friends were receiving large bribes. Ultimately some thirty high-ranking officials were implicated in the scandal, but the worst part was that Kim's second son was also deeply involved. It was unprecedented that a sitting president's son could be charged by the court system with wrongdoing. This positive step in the evolution of democracy was nonetheless quite disturbing to an increasingly cynical public.

The question of funds in the 1992 presidential campaign again surfaced at this inopportune time. Kim Jong Pil charged that Kim Young Sam received approximately $75 million from the Hanbo group and $375 million from Roh Tae Woo. If accurate, it meant that Kim had received more than ten times the legal limit in a presidential race. The National Assembly initiated televised hearings on the matter, but the results were inconclusive. Most witnesses denied the charges and no one could produce any hard evidence. When the public demanded a thorough investigation by the prosecution, Kim's son was questioned for three days. As a result, he was charged with taking some $3.6 million in bribes from the business community.

With the beginning of his son's trial in July, the popularity of the president hit a low. When Kim took office in 1993, he had promised to clean up the so-called Korean disease of corruption. While his zeal led to the imprisonment of two former presidents, he began to contemplate the bitter ironies of laundering his country's politics. A public opinion poll indicated that he was even less popular than the imprisoned Chun. As the economy continued to decline, it became evident that Kim was absorbed in his son's trial and incapable of dealing with the nation's mounting problems in his final months in office.

Two former presidential aspirants declared themselves candidates. Both Kim Dae-jung (National Congress for New Politics) and Kim

Jong Pil (United Liberal Democratic Party) were in their seventies and thought they would try one last time. The New Korea Party established a historic first by establishing a competitive nomination process. After seven party aspirants registered, there was intense competition to get the nomination. For the first time in the South, the government party held an open and competitive nominating convention. Lee Hoi Chang became the clear winner. Shortly thereafter his popularity plummeted when it was revealed that his two sons had evaded military service on the basis that they were supposedly underweight. In a country that has placed a high value on military service, the avoidance of compulsory service by those who possessed wealth and power was unacceptable.

While the nation was preoccupied with the approaching December 18 presidential election, the public was shocked to learn that the government would apply for a bailout from the IMF to avoid national bankruptcy. Kim Dae-jung, who was leading the polls, charged that the bailout would place the country in an "economic trusteeship." Lee Hoi Chang charged that Kim was seeking the favor of voters who felt humiliated by the IMF.

Prior to the election Kim Dae-jung and Kim Jong Pil agreed to end their thirty-six years of political enmity and forged an alliance. Kim Dae-jung would be the presidential candidate and Kim Jong Pil the prime minister designate. They also agreed that during Kim Dae-jung's presidential term the constitution would again be amended to convert the presidential system into a parliamentary one, a change that Kim Jong Pil had long advocated. This alliance was particularly remarkable because Kim Jong Pil was the nephew of Park Chung Hee and first head of the KCIA, the agency responsible for Kim Dae-jung's kidnapping in Tokyo. To counter this alliance, Lee Hoi Chang, the ruling-party candidate, and Cho Soon, the Democratic Party candidate, whose popularity was lowest among the major candidates, also joined forces. Cho agreed to give up his candidacy and to accept the presidency of the ruling party, which was renamed the Grand National Party. As a result of the these alliances it appeared that the leading candidates were now Kim Dae-jung, Lee Hoi Chang, and Rhee In-je, the candidate for the New Party for the People.

The presidential election of 1997 turned out to be the least violent and most inexpensive campaign ever and was closely monitored by civic groups. A new development was the broadcast of televised debates, which aroused voter interest and eliminated the expensive outdoor rallies of the past. Kim Dae-jung appeared particularly well informed, articulate, and presidential. When he took the lead in public opinion polls, attempts were made to discredit him.

Eighty percent of the qualified voters, more than 26 million people, voted on election day. Kim Dae-jung won by a very slim margin; he received 40.3 percent of the vote compared to Lee Hoi Chang's 38.7 percent and Rhee In-je's 19.2 percent. Four other candidates received a total of 1.8 percent. If Rhee had not split the ruling camp, Lee might have been the winner. Kim's victory was the result of his clever manipulation of regionalism and his alliance with Kim Jong Pil. Public opinion polls prior to the election indicated that the financial crisis also became his ally and frustrated Lee's efforts to engineer an upset victory.

The Eighth Republic, 1998–2003

Kim Dae-jung's outdoor inaugural celebration, attended by more than 40,000 people, took place in Seoul on February 25, 1998. The inauguration of South Korea's eighth president was particularly memorable as it signified another important step in the process of democratization. It was the first peaceful transfer of power from an entrenched ruling party to an opposition leader since the founding of the Republic in 1948. As a man hounded for decades as an enemy of the state, Kim called for reconciliation with the country's authoritarian past and for a strong national effort to overcome the disastrous economic crisis. It was also a very extraordinary event because Chun and Roh, attended the ceremony. As a sign of Kim Dae-jung's message of conciliation and forgiveness, he agreed to pardon the former presidents from their lifetime prison sentences for corruption.

A key factor in Kim's victory was the indomitable man himself. The seventy-three-year-old devout Catholic from a remote island in South Cholla Province had become president, the dream of many Korean fathers of very bright sons. Conscious of the lack of a formal education in a country where it is highly valued, he compensated by voracious reading and occasional attendance at universities when he had the time and money to do so. Prior to his inauguration he faced death five times. One assassination attempt left him with a broken arm and a permanent limp. For six years he was in prison, and for ten years he was in exile or under house arrest. To satisfy his thirst for knowledge, he read constantly whether in prison, under house arrest, or in exile. For twenty years Kim pushed for democratic reform, earning the nickname "Indongch'o," a kind of wild grass that

Kim Jong Il and Kim Dae-jung in P'yongyang, June 2000. The summit between North and South Korea began with a warm handshake, ending 55 years of opposition and separation. (Photographed by Cheong Wa Dae, Presidential Residence of the Republic of Korea, Photographer's Press Pool)

grows even in the winter and is almost impossible to kill. Kim taught himself English with help from occasional tutors, and his command of the language became vastly superior to any of his predecessors. Prior to his inauguration, he said, "I never lost hope that someday there would be something like this."

In his inaugural address Kim said: "Let us open a new age during which we will overcome the national crisis and make a new leap forward." In his famous Sunshine Policy he declared that he intended to bring to a gradual end the shame of a divided Korean peninsula through a cooperative reunification with rival North Korea. He said he would push for immediate improvement in communications with the communist North. He called for the reunion of separated families, the expansion of cultural and academic exchanges, economic cooperation, and the exchange of special envoys. President Kim's goals revealed a more humane Korea that would balance market economics with the kind of democracy for which he had long struggled. He promised the people: "I will consult with you on all issues; you, in return, must help me, if only for one year—this year—when the nation is standing on the brink of disaster."

After his election on December 18, Kim moved quickly as the de facto president to initiate structural reforms in response to the economic crisis. Significant changes took place within a short period of time, a remarkable achievement considering his slim power base. Kim headed a minority political party with only 78 followers in a fractious 299-member National Assembly. Even with support from Kim Jong Pil's United Liberal Democrats, who held 43 seats, Kim Dae-jung remained a minority president facing a resistant Grand National Party with a total of 161 National Assembly members.

Given these political realities and the economic crisis, political instability loomed as a strong possibility. Nevertheless, Kim was able to consolidate his authority as president in part because the public blamed Kim Young Sam and the Grand National Party for its economic woes. Because of solid support from the United States for an IMF bailout, the president was able to look at economic problems in a straightforward manner and to embrace a solution without intolerable political risks. The bailout was seen by most as a means to reform the underregulated and overexpanded economy. Another fortunate factor that garnered support for reform was Kim's reputation as a progressive politician who had always been ahead of his time by supporting economic reform, democratization, and improved communication with North Korea. When he appeared on his first televised talk, "Let's show the world the great potential of Koreans," he seemed to be the right man for the times.

Fortunately, society gave Kim a brief honeymoon period prior to his inauguration to devise a strategy to deal with the economic crisis. Had he not hurriedly assembled his financial, labor, and chaebol reform through a special tripartite committee and legislated key reform bills before his inauguration, Korea's financial situation would have looked very different from what it became in 1999. Immediately after his inauguration, intense partisan politics set in, and the National Assembly became essentially deadlocked in a contest of political wills between Kim and his foes.

Neither Kim's election nor the severity of the financial crisis altered traditional politics. Since 1948 South Korea has upheld representative democracy as its ideal; however, political parties tend to serve the interests and aspirations of those in power and remain the weakest link in the democratization process. They continue to be loose combinations of regional factions that coalesce around individuals rather than policy issues. They are not based on ideology, group affiliation, or class. Party bosses avoid taking positions on issues. The objective is to bring rival regional leaders into winning coalitions and to build electoral machines through the distribution of financial rewards and privileges to those who join together by bloodlines, school networks, or regional ties. Regional prejudices and money politics, not policy, are the primary instruments for achieving mass support in electoral politics.

What Kim Dae-jung inherited is a system that arose from Confucian familism. Korean regionalism is basically emotional and psychological and is based on affection for one's place of birth. In itself this attachment is not enough to secure an election victory. Regional leaders need to create incentives, which tend to be financial. Businesspeople contribute money to the campaigns with an implicit or explicit agreement for political and financial support. Recipients see these funds as a rightful reward for their efforts. Party leaders regard the distribution of funds as a manifestation of Confucianism or paternal affection and benevolence to their loyal followers. As a result corruption permeates the system of politics, contributes to astronomical campaign expenses, curtails reform, and diverts scarce resources from productive economic activity.

After Kim's inauguration bitter partisan rivalry appeared. When the president moved to fulfill his campaign promise to appoint Kim Jong Pil as his prime minister, the Grand National Party attempted to stop him. He successfully maneuvered the appointment and then launched a series of investigations into the illegal activities of his predecessor. The Grand National Party retaliated with a strategy of obstruction and paralyzed the legislative process. Five special sessions failed to produce a single bill. When legislation could no longer be delayed, the National Assembly members rushed into a flurry of activity without carefully reviewing the content of the measures.

The year 1999 saw continued useless political conflict and lost opportunities for significant structural reforms, with the ruling and opposition parties showing no signs of compromise on almost any issues. The political impasse put the breaks on reform in each sector of society and increased public disgust over politics. The National Assembly lost stature and appeared impotent in the face of partisan strife. Individuals responsible for answering to the needs of society appeared to be totally self-absorbed in conflicts that had no bearing on substantial reform of institutions or the economy.

The opportunity lost for Korea was an opportunity gained for Kim Dae-jung. In the process of the investigation of the Grand National Party, individuals were arrested for neglect of duty, violating campaign laws, and political conspiracy to prevent Kim's victory in 1997. Since corruption was so rampant, opposition politicians and independents feared for their careers and flocked to Kim's governing coalition. By September partisan realignments gave him and Kim Jong Pil a parliamentary majority and saved the president from becoming a target of political intimidation by the Grand National Party.

Through this process of political realignment, Kim was able to build a policy network for devising viable reform strategies. He selected distinguished career bureaucrats unaffiliated with political parties for guidance in economic policy. Their appointments yielded visible results: banks were recapitalized and foreign investment increased by 1999. In spite of all the partisan bickering and an all-time high unemployment rate of 8.7 percent in Kim's first year of office, his public approval rate was 80.2 percent in early 1999. By the end of that year the government announced the encouraging news that economic growth had hit 9 percent, compared with the negative 5.8 percent in 1998. By October the unemployment rate was down to 4.6 percent.

Between February 1998 and the spring of 1999 the Kim government effectively dealt with foreign-policy issues. First, it was able to obtain loans from Japan to assist with the devastating economic crisis. It also succeeded in obtaining, for the first time, a written apology from Japan for its harsh colonial rule. Second, the adoption of Kim's Sunshine Policy toward North Korea strengthened relations with the United States. Third, Kim improved relations with China, allowing the country to deal more effectively with the issue of peace and stability on the peninsula. Fourth, he enhanced relations with Russia as a result of his state visit to Moscow in May 1999. Fifth, Kim actively sought multilateral approaches to economic and political issues in East Asia by his active participation in Asia-Pacific Economic Cooperation (APEC) and the Association of Southeast Asian Nations (ASEAN).

In 1999 there were two particular potential sources of trouble for Kim Dae-jung. The deadline set by his 1997 campaign pledge for a constitutional amendment to adopt a parliamentary cabinet system was approaching. While he did not wish to renege on his promise, the adoption of such a system would weaken his hard-won accumulation of power. After triumphing in several disputes with the president,

Kim Jong Pil, who had campaigned for years on behalf of a parliamentary system, backed off on the idea. In May a scandal broke out that involved the wife of a high official of the ruling party who accepted expensive clothing in return for political influence. It dealt a severe blow to the integrity of the government.

By February 2000, Kim had met with foreign officials and businesspeople more than ten times per month, attended domestic events four times a day, and held nine state visits in order to overcome the economic crisis and improve foreign relations. In spite of this schedule, voter apathy and cynicism were pervasive during March and April when the campaign for the National Assembly began. It was clear that the election results would be a test of his achievements. His successes in terms of economic recovery were respected and acknowledged even by the opposition party; however, his record on the Sunshine Policy was in question because P'yongyang had not responded in any significant way to Seoul's overtures. Kim had promised to revamp a number of areas, notably politics, finance, the chaebol, and labor, but his efforts met strong resistance. Many labor leaders saw him as a traitor to their cause. In anticipation of the elections he renamed his National Congress for New Politics the Millennium Democratic Party (MDP) and pledged that its members would reform themselves in an effort to improve the nation. When Seoul and P'yongyang jointly announced a summit to be held in June, the initial reaction was mixed. Many people were skeptical about the timing of the announcement only three days prior to the elections.

As a result of the elections the opposition Grand National Party remained in control of the National Assembly, which guaranteed continual political strife and further deadlock. The outcome also indicated the continuing role of regionalism in national politics. There were, however, some signs of change. Freshman legislators held over 41 percent of the assembly seats. A particularly promising sign of change was the role played by civic organizations during the elections. They worked successfully to defeat candidates seen as unfit because of tax evasion and political corruption.

An even more momentous development occurred in the weeks following the elections. At the June Summit (June 13–15) the leaders of North and South Korea met for the first time since the division. Although relations between them were precarious during the Cold War, the ROK policy was based primarily on deterring P'yongyang's military and ideological threats. With the end of the Cold War it appeared that a more durable peace might in time become a reality. However, in the 1990s with the collapse of the Soviet bloc and deteriorating economic conditions in the North, the situation between the Koreas remained precarious. The Cold War had not ended on the peninsula.

During the 1990s Kim Jong Il assumed power and was determined to preserve a system that had been failing for some time. A major concern was the fact that North Korea began to develop weapons of mass destruction. Since the beginning of Kim Dae-jung's administration, there were several near-crisis situations over the DPRK's weapons program, particularly related to a suspected underground nuclear facility and the test-launch of a long-range ballistic missile over Japan. These incidents triggered loud protests from the United States and Japan and prompted hard-line responses toward the North. Nevertheless, Kim Dae-jung pursued his policies of reconciliation as the principal means for bringing permanent peace and possible reunification.

In June 2000, using protocol and pageantry to signal an end to their historic enmity, the leaders of North and South Korea pledged concrete steps toward reconciliation along the lines of a confederation. The idea of a confederation was not new. Since the 1990s, the North had expressed hopes for the formation of a Korean confederacy consisting of "one nation, one state, two systems, and two governments." At the summit President Kim Dae-jung acknowledged that national unification was the ultimate objective, but recognizing the realities facing the nation at the time, he joined Kim Jong Il in support of the creation of a confederacy. They agreed that they would first lay a foundation for reunification through peaceful coexistence, reconciliation, and cooperation. Kim Dae-jung and Kim Jong Il agreed to allow visits in August of an unspecified number of the estimated 1.2 million family members separated since the war five decades earlier. They also agreed to resolve additional human rights problems, narrow the gap between their two economies, and speed cultural, athletic, medical, and environmental cooperation and exchanges. Also, the North Korean leader accepted an invitation to visit Seoul at an appropriate time. Two months later euphoria swept the South in the aftermath of the dramatic reunions between families from both sides. After half a century 200 Koreans, 100 from each side, experienced tearful if brief reunions with their loved ones.

Although the summit was a positive step, the agreement did not include provisions to reduce tension or deployment of the two countries' armies, which together have more than 1.7 million soldiers facing one another across the demilitarized zone. Nor did it mention North Korea's frozen nuclear weapons program, its development and foreign sales of advanced missiles, or its demand that the United States remove its 37,000 troops from South Korea. The accord, however, far exceeded expectations of what could be accomplished at the first face-to-face meeting since the peninsula was divided in 1945. Through these talks, Koreans finally arrived at a genuine starting point for their march toward national reconciliation and unification.

In September at the Olympics in Sydney, Australia, 180 athletes and sports officials from North and South Korea paraded together hand in hand into the stadium, following a placard that included a blue facsimile of the Korean peninsula with the simple designation of the Korean unification flag. The joint march received thunderous standing ovations from 110,000 spectators. In October the Norwegian Nobel Prize Committee awarded Kim Dae-jung the Peace Prize for his work for democracy and human rights in South Korea and East Asia in general and for reconciliation with North Korea in particular.

While the year 2000 was a year of great promise and the zenith of Kim Dae-jung's political career, he continues to face formidable obstacles in his remaining two years in office. Major tasks include relations with North Korea, the deteriorating economic situation at home, and growing public criticism. When George W. Bush announced early in 2001 that he needed to reexamine U.S. foreign policy with North Korea, an angry Kim Jong Il called off several high-level contacts with the South and criticized the United States, raising fears that a fragile rapprochement between the Koreas could be derailed.

Kim Jong Il said that his next summit with South Korea would only take place after Bush completed his policy review on North Korea. Needless to say, Bush's harder line against the DPRK gave Kim Dae-jung's critics further ammunition. When terrorists attacked the World Trade Center in New York and the U.S. Pentagon on September 11, 2001, both Kim Dae-jung and Kim Jong Il condemned the attack. However, the fact that North Korea was one of the world's leading exporters of ballistic missiles and related technology to the volatile Middle East also worked against support within South Korea for the Sunshine Policy.

While Kim was quite successful in his initial efforts to effectively restructure the economy, it began to slow significantly in the final months of 2001. Unemployment rose and exports dropped dramatically. Politics remained highly confrontational and economic reforms slowed. As a result of the terrorist attack on the United States, South Koreans have begun to fear the implications for stability in the world and their own economy, dependent as it is on exports to the United States.

President Kim Dae-jung continues to be widely respected throughout the world; however, he is the subject of constant controversy and is strongly criticized at home, particularly by intellectuals who consider him to be no different than previous leaders. Some say that he is more dangerous than the military leaders because he believes that he is the symbol of democracy. They ironically note that with his efforts to respond to the economic crisis, the government has actually become more powerful than before, and Kim's supporters use whatever means necessary to undermine the opposition.

Former U.S. Ambassador to South Korea Donald P. Gregg says: "Kim is facing what all modern Korean leaders have faced in the last years in office—the growing cynicism and disillusionment on the part of the people." This may be a lingering echo of traditional Confucianism. Much confidence is placed in the leader; but when events do not turn out well, great disappointment follows, perhaps even resentment. He bemoans the fact that "many Koreans seem utterly indifferent to the international stature of the man who is their president, and I am not sure how much that sad pattern will change in the months remaining in President Kim's term in office."

Since his inauguration, Kim Dae-jung has met the challenge of the economic crisis, the greatest challenge since the Korean War. He paved the way for the summit in June 2000, one of the most inspiring and hopeful events since the liberation from Japan in 1945. The remaining months in office provide the president an opportunity to lead his nation to a more mature democracy and to continue down the path of ultimate reunification. His Nobel Peace Prize provides Koreans with a golden opportunity.

A DIVIDED PEOPLE: THE NORTH KOREAN EXPERIENCE (1945–2001)

No nation in the twentieth century has constructed an identity so associated with its founder and leader as North Korea. As Dae-Sook Suh put it, the study of Kim Il Sung and his rule is the study of North Korea.

Kim Il Sung, former commander of anti-Japanese guerrilla units and senior officer in the Soviet army, was Stalin's hand-picked candidate for head of state. He adopted Marxism-Leninism as its ruling

philosophy when he established the Democratic People's Republic of
Korea in 1948. In the official history that was constructed after 1945,
he became the embodiment of the regime's legitimacy and symbol of
its virtue. His career at the helm of North Korea over the span of
nearly half a century is remarkable for both longevity and consis-
tency of purpose. The political stability has to be viewed in terms of
the means by which it was achieved: sustained ideological propaganda, punishment of dissenters, and periodic purges.

The constitution states: "The DPRK is an independent socialist
state representing the interests of all the Korean people." Unlike
orthodox socialist societies, however, the North's ruling principle is
juche (self-reliance), an ideology created by the national founder and
sustained as a "man-centered" philosophy by his son, Kim Jong Il,
who has ruled the country since his father's death in 1994.

Juche is firmly rooted in the experience of Kim Il Sung and his
people. It is the most important idea of Kim's rule. He believed that
people should adopt the principles of Marxism and Leninism; however, he took what he wanted from these principles and discarded the
rest. His thought system was based on the idea that the master of
revolution is the people; therefore, the people should be armed with
self-reliant thought, problem solving skills, and a determination to
create a national consciousness unique to Korea. He stressed that
self-reliance is essential for political independence, economic self-
sustenance, and military defense. Last, but perhaps most important,
is the role of the Supreme Leader in the idea of juche.

Although the masses are the masters of the revolution, they cannot
play that role individually; someone must lead. Thus the people are to
obey the instructions of the leader unconditionally. These ideas give
insight into the behavior of the North Koreans: their xenophobia, regi-
mentation, militarism, isolation, and fanaticism toward the personality
cults of Kim Il Sung and his son. In every city, town, and village, there
are statues; and images of the Supreme Leader appear on billboards
and subway and apartment walls. All citizens wear Kim buttons on the
left breast. His portrait is hung in every home and workplace.

Kim adopted the values of Marxism-Leninism, which brought radical changes to society. Land reform led to confiscation of estates
and redistributon of farm plots to peasants. Business enterprises
were nationalized. In spite of the complete devastation that
occurred during the Korean War, the nation used its abundant mineral and hydroelectric resources to develop military strength and
heavy industry in the following decades. Despite its stress on self-

reliance, Soviet and Chinese assistance and machinery were crucial to industrial growth. By 1972, eleven years of schooling became free and compulsory. Public health facilities were comprehensive and free, housing was available, and until the late 1980s and early 1990s food supplies were generally adequate. There is no taxation or unemployment, and compared to most Third World nations, the standard of living is high.

Of all the communist nations, North Korea has one of the most traditional, rigid, and tightly controlled totalitarian societies. It has been described as the closest thing to the Orwellian world described in *1984*. The commitment to "democratic centralism," by which all subordinate bodies submit to the decisions formulated by the Central Committee of the Workers' Party (the principal political institution), ensures the unity considered essential to a socialist society. The Central Committee makes all decisions on government policies and appoints government officials, including cabinet members.

The constitution of the DPRK guarantees its citizens the usual political liberties: a free press; freedom of speech, petition, and religion; free elections; and guarantees against arbitrary arrest. Implementing these freedoms is under the auspices of the state authority, the Korean Workers' Party, which is controlled by the Supreme Leader. In reality, there are no civil rights. The press is strictly controlled and the media offers only elaborate praise for the Kim regime and its policies. Any criticism of the leader, the party, or its policies is illegal and rewarded with imprisonment and hard labor.

The harsh reality of a dictatorship is softened by the way it is presented to the people. As in traditional Korean society, Kim Il Sung's authority as ruler stemmed from his virtue and benevolence and was reinforced by the notion that he was not only a just ruler, but a loving father, a wise general, the sun of the world, and the greatest leader in 1,000 years. In spite of the fact that all religion is officially outlawed in North Korea, there are astonishing continuities from the Confucian authoritarianism of the past. That tradition of loyalty to one's family or lineage is extended to the nation as a whole. Virtues, such as loyalty, obedience, industry, respect, reciprocity between the leader and the led, are highly valued in communist North Korea. The language used to describe Kim Il Sung's virtues are all essentially Confucian. According to Confucianism, what makes people human is their acceptance of social roles that integrate them into the collective whole, a notion consistent with the collective spirit of communism. Family-based politics, authoritarian rule, the succession of the leader's son, and the extraordinary veneration of Kim Il Sung are all dimensions of ancient Confucian traditions.

Kim's vision of creating a socialist paradise became a massive failure. Although located in the heart of one of the most economically dynamic regions of the world, North Korea has, for a variety of reasons, recorded negative economic growth for ten consecutive years. The totalitarian nature of the regime obstructs the innovation and creativity needed for sustained development. Because the twenty-seven volumes of Kim Il Sung's teachings form the core curriculum, education typically does not provide advanced technological and communication skills.

Since the division of Korea, the biggest economic problem has been the lack of farmland. The ideal of juche was impossible to achieve; therefore, the DPRK supported itself by bartering raw materials, heavy manufacturing, and military hardware to other countries to pay for food and oil. However, the continuing U.S. trade embargo and the collapse of the socialist bloc deprived P'yongyang of major markets, leading to a steadily declining GNP. The country has also experienced severe energy shortages exacerbated by a series of natural disasters: floods followed by drought. Since 1995 the nation has suffered famine and relies on international charities to feed its 22 million people.

AFTER THE SUMMIT:
CONCERNS AND PROSPECTS

Korea entered a new phase with the signing of the North-South Declaration in P'yongyang on June 15, 2000. It is hoped that this is genuinely the beginning of the end of the Cold War on the peninsula. There are positive signs of rapprochement as illustrated by reunions of long-separated families and by extended economic, social, and cultural exchanges; however, lingering tensions, created by North Korea's nuclear and missile programs and the huge military force deployed along the DMZ, remain. In 2001 an unprecedented drought will inevitably bring more famine.

Since the summit, substantive problems threaten inter-Korean cooperation. DPRK requests for economic assistance have skyrocketed. Under the circumstances, it is not surprising, but P'yongyang's repeated requests for fertilizer, food, and electric power have forced Seoul to be concerned about whether it can meet those needs, especially when its own economy appears to be weakening.

ROK investments in the North will undoubtedly involve financial risks, lack of adequate infrastructure, shortages of capital and raw material, bureaucratic red tape, differences over management practices, and excessive logistical costs. During the euphoria of the summit, the negative perceptions of North Korea were temporarily put on hold. A year later the public became more cautious. For years textbooks, printed material, and the news media on both sides served to fuel bilateral distrust and confrontation by focusing negatively on the other's political system, human rights abuses, economic conditions, and arms buildup. As a result, the vast majority of Koreans have an extremely negative view of the other side. Although the public praised Kim Dae-jung for what was accomplished, a year later South Koreans were increasingly critical. Many of them feared that the South was doing all the giving and the North all the getting.

The challenge of reunification remains daunting. German reunification is instructive. Even though German reunification occurred ten years ago, the two Germanys remain very much apart. It has been said that it will take another generation for the desired harmony to be achieved. If unity is to be achieved on the Korean peninsula, it will take time, patience, financial risk, and extensive advanced planning. Though Koreans have a common heritage, the North and South represent two very different cultures. Concerted efforts must be made to restore the homogeneity of the people.

The economic differences between the North and South must be narrowed. In 1999 the nominal gross national income of North Korea was estimated at $15.8 billion, or just one-twenty-sixth of South Korea's $402.1 billion. Per capita income of the DPRK amounts to $1,000 compared to the ROK's $8,581. As in the case of Germany's unification process in which inter-German contacts and West German economic assistance to East Germany were vital, South Korea will need to apply economic rather than political logic in dealing with the North. Financial assistance—not political rhetoric—will be essential in working with the mind-set of the North Korean ruling elite. Another obstacle for Kim is the staggering potential cost of reunification. Estimates range from $1 billion to $3 trillion—about five to six times South Korea's GNP.

German reunification was the result of the overwhelming support of the people. Since South Korea can not expect the North Korean people to rise up as did their East German counterparts, it seems inevitable that Korean unification may lie in the distant future. Another major consideration relates to basic freedoms. Without improvement in human rights—freedom of movement, freedom of speech and of the press—unification remains elusive if not impossible.

On September 18, 2001, North and South Korea agreed to hold a new round of family reunions in mid-October and to resume ministerial-level meetings. Both sides intimated that they might be receptive to further plans to set up a cross-border rail link and coordinate flood-control projects. Analysts speculated that these sudden developments were the result of the September 11 attack on the World Trade Center and the Pentagon and the determination of the United States to fight global terrorism. Since North Korea is a state long associated with terrorism, P'yongyang was suddenly eager to appear more moderate and reasonable to avoid becoming a target of U.S. retaliatory action. Skeptics of these developments felt that even if Kim Jong Il visited Seoul, it would not mean very much. Another round of family reunions involving 100 or so Koreans after half a century of separation provides little solace for an estimated ten million people who have relatives on both sides of the border. South Koreans want more palpable steps, such as direct mail service between the two countries, more people-to-people contact, and a North Korean agreement to reduce the production and export of missiles.

If the aftereffect of the June Summit is better inter-Korean relations, many on both sides will noticeably benefit. But improvement will also raise serious questions for the United States about its military presence on the peninsula and about its role in Asia. The United States must understand the changing diplomatic situation if it wishes to shape a more stable and secure Northeast Asia.

References
A Handbook of Korea. 1993. Seoul: Korean Overseas Information Service.
AsiaWeek, "Evaluating Kim: South Korea's Upcoming Polls Are a Verdict on the President's Policies," http://www.cgi.cnn.com/AsiaNow (cited July 30, 2000).
Breen, Michael. 1998. *The Koreans: Who They Are, What They Want, Where Their Future Lies.* New York: St. Martin's Press.
Chang, Dal-Joong. 2000. "Summit Talks and Marshall Plan for North Korea," in *Korea Focus* (March/April). Seoul: Korea Foundation.
Chang, Kyung-sup. 2000. "Are There Any Credible Political Parties in Korea," in *Korea Focus* (September/October). Seoul: Korea Foundation.
Christie, Kenneth, and Denny Roy. 2001. *The Politics of Human Rights in East Asia.* Sterling, VA: Pluto Press.
Cumings, Bruce. 1997. *Korea's Place in the Sun: A Modern History.* New York: W. W. Norton and Company.

Editorial, *Chosun Ilbo.* 2000. "Lessons of German Unification after 10 Years," in *Korea Focus* (November/December). Seoul: Korea Foundation.

Eckert, Carter et al. 1990. *Korea Old and New: A History.* Seoul: Ilchokak Publishers.

Gregg, Donald P. 2001. "Korean Cross Currents," in *The Korean Society Quarterly* (Spring). New York: The Korea Society.

Kim, Byoung-Lo Philo. 1992. *Two Koreas in Development: A Comparative Study of Principles and Strategies of Capitalist and Communist Third World Development.* New Brunswick, NJ: Transaction Publishers.

Kim, Byung-Kook. 2000. "The Politics of Crisis and a Crisis of Politics: The Presidency of Kim Dae-jung," in *Korea Briefing 1997–1999: Challenges and Change at the Turn of the Century.* Oh, Kongdan, ed., New York: Asia Society.

Kim, Dong-Sung. 2000. "The Nobel Peace Prize and Domestic Politics," in *Korea Focus* (September/October). Seoul: Korea Foundation.

Kim, Hong Nack. 2000. "Foreign Relations under the Kim Dae-jung Government," in *Korea Briefing 1997–1999: Challenges and Change at the Turn of the Century.* Oh, Kongdan, ed., New York: Asia Society.

Kim, Tack-Whan. 2000. "Image of North Korea after Inter-Korean Summit," in *Korea Focus* (November/December). Seoul: Korea Foundation.

Kim, Young-Yoon. 2001. "Investment for Balanced Growth between North and South Korea," in *Korea Focus* (January/February). Seoul: Korea Foundation.

Korea Times, "Five Upcoming Tests for Kim Dae-jung's Leadership," http://hk.co.kr/kt_nation/2001 (cited May 22, 2001).

Lone, Stewart, and Gavan McCormack. 1993. *Korea Since 1850.* New York: St. Martin's Press.

Magnier, Mark. "Koreas Agree to More Reunions," *Los Angeles Times.* 18 September 2001, A27.

Murphey, Rhoads. 2001. *East Asia: A New History.* New York: Longman Press.

Oberdorfer, Don. 1997. *The Two Koreas: A Contemporary History.* Reading, MA: Addison-Wesley.

———. "Seeking Truth in Action," *The Wilson Quarterly.* http://wwws.elibrary.com (cited September 21, 2001).

Office of the President of the Republic of Korea, "Policy Series," http://www.bluehouse.go.kr/english (cited August 31, 2001).

Oh, John Kie-chian. 1999. *Korean Politics: The Quest for Democratization and Economic Development.* Ithaca, NY: Cornell University Press.

Oh, Kongdan, ed. 2000. *Korea Briefing 1997–1999: Challenges and Change at the Turn of the Century.* New York: M. E. Sharpe, Inc.

Paik, Jin-byun. 2000. "New Concept of Engagement Policy toward North Korea," in *Korea Focus* (March/April). Seoul: Korea Foundation.

Roh, Jeong Seon, ed. 2000. *Korean Annual.* Seoul: Yonhap News Agency.

Ryoo, Kihl-jae. 2000. "An Evaluation of the Inter-Korean Summit," in *Korea Focus* (July/August). Seoul: Korea Foundation.

Saccone, Richard. 1993. *Fifty Famous People Who Helped Shape Korea.* Seoul: Hollym Corporation.

Suh, Dae-Sook. 1988. *Kim Il Sung: The North Korean Leader.* New York: Columbia University Press.

Time International, "Asia: Destiny's Choice Jailed, Beaten, Marked for Death. To Kim Dae-jung, It Was All Preparation for This Moment," Frank Gibney http://wwws.elibrary.com (cited April 23, 2001).

CHAPTER FOUR
Contemporary Culture and Social Problems

RAPID CHANGE AND THE PERSISTENCE OF TRADITION

The dramatic events of the twentieth century brought rapid cultural and societal changes to Korea. There has been so much upheaval that each new generation has faced a completely different world from that of its parents. Colonialism, national division, communism, war, industrialization, and urbanization devastated old structures. In North Korea, land redistribution and industrialization under a socialist system brought revolutionary change to society and its value system. In South Korea, rapid industrialization, urbanization, and Western influence had a great impact on class structure, the family, and daily life.

Although the generations experienced radical dislocation, certain core beliefs remain strong. The common heritage of the Korean people will ultimately facilitate the healing process. But different circumstances, conflicting ideologies, and decades of mutual distrust will make unification the greatest challenge of the twenty-first century.

Kyongbok Palace and modern buildings, Seoul. One sees signs of the combination of the very old and the new throughout Korea. (Courtesy of Mary Connor)

163

SOUTH KOREA

The Family

For centuries Confucianism prescribed the basic rules for personal behavior and provided moral principles and rituals for family life. In spite of the radical changes of the twentieth century, this code remains basic to the life of every Korean. Today, as in the past, two Confucian principles are central to family life: the hierarchical order between the elder and the younger and the division between male and female. These standards continue to guide Korean society. While families are now smaller, the nuclear family of father, mother, and child is the norm in urban areas. The traditional view of family relationships and obligations continues to influence individual attitudes and behavior.

Even where parents and offspring live separately, intimate relationships are valued and sustained. In the traditional family, only the first-born son had the obligation to live with his parents. But now parents may live with their favorite son or even with a married daughter. Whether the parents live alone or with their children, the principle of maintaining the patrilineal family remains vital. The family register includes the names of paternal ancestors for over 500 years. Any two people coming from the same paternal ancestor (even though it might have been centuries ago) still may not marry. Ending a family line by failing to produce sons is considered unfilial and should be avoided. The popular preference for sons leads to high abortion rates for female fetuses, another indication of the strong influence of patriarchal ideology.

Every member of the family has strict guidelines and duties. Filial piety—children's obedience and respect toward their parents— remains a cardinal virtue. The code of behavior directs offspring to repay parental love and care. Although traditional relationships are changing, and obedience within the family is less strict and formalized, respect of the young for their elders remains strong and is expected.

In the Confucian tradition, the dominance of men was not questioned. The family continues to focus on the male. When a woman marries, she becomes a member of her husband's family; however, she is rarely considered a true member of the family because her blood is not from that family. The husband's principal role is to provide for the financial support of the family. The father's needs come before his family's, but not those of his parents.

A woman continues to be responsible for the home and family. She is expected to devote herself to being a good wife and mother. If she should work outside the home, it must never interfere with her domestic responsibilities. When her family lives in the home of her in-laws, she is obliged to serve her husband's parents. Aside from these responsibilities, a woman now has the power of the purse strings. Her husband gives her his salary and she gives him an allowance.

Traditionally, the relationship between a man and a woman was not necessarily close because the marriage was arranged. Recently, more women demand an active role in society, expect their husbands to be involved in household affairs, and desire a more romantic relationship. Korean men do not seem eager to move from the traditional male-oriented role.

Education continues to be highly valued and is considered the principal means of moving up the social ladder. Parents sacrifice their own interests for the education of their offspring. Since their parents have given them life, Korean children have traditionally believed they owe their parents everything. Sons and daughters work diligently for their families, sacrificing themselves and even their childhood for the sake of the family. If the family is poor, the eldest son will go to college, the other sons will complete middle school, and the daughters will complete primary school. The children's education reflects the gender division of the past.

The modern family continues the Confucian tradition of revering ancestors. Through the ritual services, offspring show filial piety, and the father talks about the behavior of the ancestors to teach moral values. Young couples in a rented house do not perform rituals for their ancestors, but once they own their residence, they do.

Modernization and industrialization produced great changes in the way of life of the Korean family and of society as a whole. The industrialization of the 1960s led to huge migrations of people from rural villages into urban areas. Prior to the Korean War, 80 percent of the village population lived in houses with straw roofs. Four decades later 80 percent are urban dwellers in huge high-rise apartment complexes. The process of this rapid change was difficult for most. The slower pace and supportive network of family and friends in the village were replaced by a fast pace of life, traffic jams, long commutes, and isolation from neighbors. People have had to learn to develop new networks of friends and to adapt to a highly competitive economic environment.

Korea continues to be a patriarchal and patrilineal society; however, there are significant changes in the role of the father in the contemporary family. The instrumental role carried out by the family head in the past has been taken over by the mother. In the past the father's authority was unconditional; now his authority rests on being a good provider. The filial obligation of children to their fathers is more flexible. The structure of the family has changed from being husband-dominated to wife-dominated, and from father-centered to child-centered.

One of the reasons for this major structural change is an extension of the high value Confucianism placed on education. In the traditional fixed-class structure, education was limited to the privileged yangban. In contemporary society it is available to everyone. Parents now sacrifice their own interests for their children's education in the belief that this will bring a higher level of prosperity for the next generation. Parents prefer to financially support their children's education as an investment in their future, rather than to give an inheritance.

The great emphasis on education and a strong motivation for achievement are directed towards the prosperity of the family and maintaining the family honor, an important Confucian principle. As in the past, the young continue to consider their moral responsibility to the family name. In the past, people sacrificed themselves for the reputation of their families and gained identity by worshipping their ancestors. Koreans today dedicate themselves to the reputation of their families and identify with the success of their children.

The process of modernization has had a powerful effect on many of the social structures and behavior patterns associated with family life. People are generally more materialistic, more women are working, children do not have as much supervision, and the divorce rate has risen. Only one percent belongs to the upper class. Most people work extremely hard for incredibly long hours in order to survive.

In another dimension of the culture, individuals may strive to reach their own potential but must remain ever mindful of the responsibility to family and group. However, a person's drive for wealth, power, and recognition can shatter notions of Confucian harmony. Koreans will take extraordinary risks to further their objectives. This tendency has contributed to social tension regarding disparity of income between the business elite and the laboring class.

In South Korea, the family has been extended to groupings based on common local origins, common school experiences, and common

Korean walls (Hahoe Village). The walls in Korea are very beautiful and distinctive. (Courtesy of Mary Connor)

places of work. People within such groups have a strong sense of shared identity and mutual responsibility. These associations function as an extended family and mutual aid society, whose members look out for one another through influence and connections.

Even though the culture is experiencing tensions and socioeconomic insecurities, the basic structure of the family and family values has been only slightly affected by the stresses of contemporary life. Confucian views still strongly condition attitudes and behavior. In a time of insecurity the Korean family will continue to be a sanctuary to the individual and the glue that binds the entire society together.

The Status of Women

Although rapid industrialization, modernization, and Western influences have had a great impact on the family as a whole, the most notable changes have occurred for women. They are now better educated and more able to participate in socioeconomic activities. But owing to persistent traditions, most women continue to suffer from inequality in their sexual relations, in the family, and in the workplace.

The ethical basis for the restrictions on women is rooted in tradition. Their behavior was clearly defined in Confucian texts. Their marriage was arranged and considered an alliance between families, the consummation of two ancestral lines. A woman was to obey her husband and sacrifice for the children. She needed to practice three submissions: first to her father, then to her husband, and finally to her sons. If she failed to carry out the prescribed behavior, heavy penalties were imposed. If a woman fulfilled her obligations, the male relatives protected and provided for her. Divorce was not possible for a woman; however, a man could divorce his wife for many reasons. A woman was to be in the private sphere of the home. Here she could exercise considerable authority and was the dominant figure in raising the children.

Women and the Family

The pattern of family life in Korea, at least in appearance, has followed that of Western countries. The size of families has steadily declined from 6.8 members in 1960 to 3.3 in 1995. In the past, three generations of a family lived under one roof. Now the form of families has become more diverse: single-person households; single-parent households due to the death of a spouse, divorce, or separation; and elderly couples living alone. The average period for women to have children has been shortened.

The structural changes in families affect both roles and expectations. As a result, the nature of family problems has changed, with new tensions emerging. Since more married women work, they want their husbands to assume a greater share of the household responsibilities. They desire greater warmth, kindness, and understanding from their spouses than might have been expected in the past. The overwhelming majority of married women who work endorse the idea of a woman's freedom to choose to work. However, the gender divisions and attitudes from the past persist in modern families. A professional woman of high status still must subject herself in private to the ancient limits that define her as her father's daughter, her husband's wife, and her son's mother. Although some may desire change, most women acquiesce to patriarchal traditions because notions of gender division are still respected within families.

Men spend much of their time outside the home because society and employers expect them to toil arduously. This obliges women to take exclusive charge of family affairs like housekeeping, child rearing, and maintaining relations with their parents-in-law. Men are pushed so hard that the number of deaths for middle-aged men in Korea is twice as high as deaths recorded in the United States or Europe. The traditional Confucian view of loyalty between male friends has added the factory and office to the military and government as networks of tightly bonded men.

Because of the changing conditions and the persistence of patriarchal traditions, the rate of divorce has increased from 5.8 percent in 1980 to 32.1 percent in 1998. Major reasons for divorce include adultery, personality conflicts, and friction between wives and their in-laws. Korea's rate is still lower than that of Western countries mainly because women find it more difficult to support themselves and because of the strong stigma of being a divorcée. Along with the increased divorce rate, domestic violence is known to be widespread. However, few victims take their problems to counselors or to the police. Not until 1989 did outraged women's groups finally pressure politicians into amending an archaic family law under which women could not inherit money nor have legal custody of their children.

Women in School

Educational opportunities for women have steadily expanded along with improved educational standards. The share of women with college and higher education backgrounds has steadily increased from 2.4 percent in 1975 to 13.1 percent in 1995. Despite the expansion of educational opportunities, gender inequality remains. In 1995 the share of men with college and higher education backgrounds as a percentage of the total male population was 26.6 percent, or twice as high as that of women. In 1998, 64.1 percent of all high school graduates attended four-year colleges, two-year professional colleges, or vocational schools. Although the gap remains between genders, women are making significant gains. In 1998, of those enrolled in higher education, 53.5 percent were male and 46.5 percent were female.

Gender inequality also exists in terms of college majors. In 1998 female students continued to be enrolled in fields traditionally considered women's areas. For example, 73.1 percent of all students at teachers' colleges were women. In the area of natural sciences, the percentage of women earning advanced degrees was very low. In engineering, female students accounted for only 5 percent of all B.S., 4 percent of M.S., and 2 percent of Ph.D. degrees. Discrimination and inequality are sustained through separate curricula for men and women, textbooks reflecting the gender division of work and traditional views of women, and attitudes of teachers.

Women in the Workplace

With educational and economic modernization, employment of women expanded. Since the 1960s, women's economic participation has grown from 26.8 percent to 49.5 percent in 1997. By 1998, 47.3 percent of all married women worked. Various factors led to this steady expansion of women in the workforce. Because of a labor shortage in the industrial sector, demand rose for women. Since women were also more educated, they desired to use their education in some economic activity and sought employment in line with their level of education. Additional factors for the increasing numbers of women in the workforce are the high cost of living, the decision to have fewer children, the presence of labor-saving devices in the home, and the general desire to live a more affluent life.

Although women's participation in economic activities has increased dramatically, the situation remains disappointing. Men dominate senior level, high-paying, executive positions. Women are confined primarily to unskilled tasks or so-called women's work, such as textile work, sewing, electronic assembly, and food processing. This mind-set about suitable employment has limited the choice of college majors and occupational interests. Many young women join the workforce between the ages of sixteen and twenty-two and are the backbone of the labor force that assembles microwave ovens, TV sets, and VCRs. They work to help the family until they get married.

The number of working women between the ages of 25 and 34 is low in all jobs. Seventy percent of all women in this age range quit their jobs when they get married, become pregnant, or take care of their children. Once they return to the labor market, they have less experience than their male counterparts and are hired at lower levels. Because of this phenomenon, employers hesitate to train their female employees in the belief that they will not stay.

Women with advanced educational backgrounds rarely find suitable opportunities to participate in economic activities. Those who advance into professional areas are engaged primarily in teaching or nursing. Of the total college graduates employed by the 50 largest companies in Korea in 1996, 87.9 percent were men and 12.1 percent women. Although the wage gap between the genders has declined, women receive approximately 62 percent of the income of men.

In the 1980s and 1990s a series of legal measures was adopted to promote the expansion of women's participation in economic activities. These measures supposedly provide for gender equality; however, equality in the real world is a different matter. One major problem for women in Korea is the fact that there is no support system for their household and child-rearing activities. It appears that men do not feel the need for such support because of the deep-rooted attitudes toward gender roles.

Women and Sexual Relations

In the realm of sexuality, there is considerable tension between traditional and contemporary thought. The area where women's traditional values are best displayed is attitudes toward chastity. Female virtues were tied to chastity in traditional Korea, and this is true today. If women are sexually assaulted, they do not report such incidents to the police out of fear of being seen as unchaste. Men still place such a high priority on virginity that sexually active unmarried women undergo considerable expense to repair their hymens. Women alone are expected to maintain their chastity while men's random sexual activities are tolerated. Consequently, prostitution and the sex industry are flourishing, while the denunciation of adultery is limited to women alone. Heterosexuality is considered normal, and homosexuality is severely condemned.

Although sexual violence was a hidden problem in the past, it has recently become a social issue. Beginning in the early 1990s instances of workplace sexual harassment and stalking were reported. Abortion has not been a topic of widespread debate as in the United States. Current practices reflect patriarchal ideology. Abortion is widely practiced. Married women abort because of the preference for sons, and unmarried women abort because of the social pressures related to chastity. Current practices also reflect patrilineal tradition. Because of the stigma of out-of-wedlock birth and the unacceptability of adopting outside one's bloodline, Korea remains the third top supplier of foreign adoptees. Since 1985, Koreans accounted for 30.2 percent of all children adopted from abroad.

Conclusion

Although there is no doubt that the contemporary family and Korea itself would collapse without them, women continue to be widely viewed as secondary and insignificant compared to men. The notion that men should work in the public sector and women stay in the private sector remains prevalent throughout society. The fact that the proportion of female legislators is the lowest among major Asian countries will inevitably inhibit reform.

Clearly, patriarchal attitudes and practices can only end when men join women to end them. Disappointment and anger can find a way to alter the culture and the institutions that perpetuate them. One hopes that this can come about without stigmatizing individual men whose behavior and attitudes reflect their own past oppression. Social change is fraught with difficulties, but women might find ways to maneuver to make it happen. Inevitably, men need to be convinced that change will bring an ultimately better world for both men and women.

SOUTH KOREA: AN EDUCATION SOCIETY

Historical Background

No nation has a higher degree of enthusiasm for education. Nowhere are children under more pressure to study. Education is universally regarded as the key to success. It is also considered the principal reason for the nation's rapid economic development. School also provides important social contacts for life. Graduates of the top universities can be confident of excellent employment opportunities and networks of influential people throughout their careers.

This emphasis on education is rooted in tradition. In the past education was the guarantee for acquiring respect and possible fame and fortune. Educational opportunities were limited to a small segment of society, the yangban class. Entry into government service was based on examinations after years of intense study of the Confucian classics. Scholarship, a position in government, and status were interrelated.

Education for the masses did not begin until the late nineteenth century. Western missionaries established schools that were open to all. They continued to function during the Japanese colonial period, although bound by discriminatory regulations. Despite these beginnings, less than 20 percent of the people ever attended any school by 1945, when Korea was liberated.

Educational development after 1945 was strongly influenced by the United States Army Military Government in Korea (USAMGIK), which ruled the country until 1948. It tried to develop an educational system based on democratic principles. During this formative period an anticommunist attitude prevailed. However, the traditional and Japanese influences remained strong, with their emphasis on discipline, respect for the state, and rote learning. Within a period of thirty years, Korea had one of the highest levels of education in the world, and literacy was almost 100 percent. In a period of fifty years the national math and science scores surpassed those of nearly every other nation in the world.

Contemporary Education

The current system of education had its start with the inauguration of the Republic of Korea in 1948 and has made astounding progress over the past four decades. Elementary and secondary education have registered over 95 percent enrollment, and higher education has become accessible to a larger portion of the population. The 1968 Charter of National Education declared that the purpose of education was "to help people to achieve a firm national identity and develop respect for history and tradition." The school system was outwardly very similar to that of the United States in providing a six-year primary education, three years of middle school, and three years of high school, followed by two to four more years of college or technical school. Twenty percent of the national budget, in additional to local government funding, is directed toward education. There are both private and public schools at all levels. Tuition fees in private schools are substantial.

The Ministry of Education's *1996 Background Report* lists the objectives of the educational system: "To improve basic abilities, skills, and attitudes; to develop language ability and civil morality needed to live in society; to increase the spirit of cooperation; to foster basic arithmetic skills and scientific observation skills; and to promote the understanding of healthy life and the harmonious development of body and mind." The Ministry closely supervises both public and private schools and determines curricula, textbooks, and instructional materials. The curriculum is essentially uniform throughout the country, with the notable exception that boys study technology and girls study domestic science.

In Seoul 36.5 percent of the high schools are coeducational, and the nationwide percentage is 52. Fees are charged in the middle and high schools, but 100 percent of the children attend middle school and 96.5 percent continue on to high school. The school year is 220 days, and

Daeil Foreign Language High School, Seoul. Daeil is considered one of the finest schools in Seoul. In Seoul 36.5 percent of the high schools are coeducational; however, boys and girls are still separated within individual classrooms by the arrangement of desks. The author spoke to this class about her U.S. school. (Courtesy of Mary Connor)

students attend school five and one half days per week. The calendar has two semesters; the first runs from March through July, and the second from September through February. There are summer and winter breaks; for high school students, however, ten optional half-days before and after each break are attended by nearly every student.

Parents, particularly mothers, organize their lives and schedules around the children's study routines and frequently move in order to live near a better school. Mothers who hover around a child's school are known as "helicopter moms." As a result of these meddlesome individuals, all mothers are generally banned from campuses until parent visitation day. After the school day, mothers make sure their children attend institutes for dance, music, martial arts, and varied academic classes.

The pressure to succeed begins in the primary grades and continues throughout the high school years. The primary school curriculum consists of nine principal subjects: moral education, Korean language, social studies, mathematics, science, physical education, music, fine arts, and practical arts. Upon completion of primary school, students advance to middle school for grades seven through nine. The curriculum consists of twelve basic or required subjects, electives, and extracurricular activities. It includes moral education, classical Chinese, vocational skills, and home economics. Upon successful completion of middle school education, all students desiring a high school education have to pass the state-administered qualifying examination. These tests are determining factors as to whether they will be on the college or vocational track.

High schools are classified into academic and vocational schools. In 1995 some 62 percent of students were enrolled in academic high schools and 38 percent in vocational high schools. The academic or college-bound courses of study include thirteen general and several specialized subjects. Students may study an additional language, such as Chinese, Japanese, French, or German; and in vocational schools they may study agriculture, engineering, or home economics. Since parents want their children to attend the top schools, students in some areas have been assigned to schools based on a lottery system and on middle school test scores. Many of the boys take ROTC, hoping to serve as officers when they fulfill their required military service.

College-bound students work so hard in high school that they see very little of their childhood. They arrive at 7:30 A.M. with boxed lunches and dinners. After a full day of classes that end in mid-afternoon, students continue their day with athletics, extracurricular activities, and study sessions until 5:00 P.M. After a box dinner the students will go to cram school or work with tutors until 9:00 P.M. They then come home to complete homework and are kept awake by coffee. After four or five hours of sleep, students wake for breakfast by 5:00 A.M., and their mothers have two boxed meals ready to begin another day.

The suicide problem comes and goes in Korea. The usual reason teens commit suicide is a failure to achieve good marks on the college entrance examination after taking it several times. Such students, feeling stress, pressure to succeed, and growing despondency commit suicide. Early in 2001 a suicide ring gained notoriety because one teenage student operated a Web site with instructions on various ways to commit suicide. Several teenagers apparently followed his instructions and committed suicide.

Even though Korea has many public and private colleges, mass education has created tremendous competition. In the past a college education guaranteed a good job. Now there are so many college graduates that underemployment and unemployment have become major problems. Neither a high school diploma nor a college diploma is necessarily good enough. The reason for the intensive study and tutorial help is the university entrance exam. Attending the best universities is the only guarantee to move into the best employment opportunities and professions.

The college examination is obviously critical to one's future. Only 15,000 of the approximately 875,000 taking the exam will be admitted to one of the top three universities. When students do not make it, they often spend the next year studying in private academies, hoping to better their score the next year. Mothers are known to go to Buddhist temples for 100 straight days to pray that their children will ace the most important test of their lives. Students study for months, getting little sleep, and parents shell out huge amounts of tutorial fees to have them coached. In 2001, it is estimated that the average family spent approximately $190 a month on tutoring. On the day of the exam, high school bands and cheering students meet test takers at school gates to cheer them on. Landings and takeoffs at the airport are banned during the listening comprehension portion of the test. Even the U.S. military will halt training on bases for nine hours to respect the national day of testing.

Until recently, graduating seniors could only apply to one college at a time. In the late 1990s the system was changed to be more like the one in the United States, where students can apply to several schools at once. This new system has made it more difficult for the college admissions officers, but a bit less traumatic for the students.

Once in college, students find that life is easier. The great majority will have time to relax, perhaps the only time in their adult lives that they will not feel pressured. Many breathe a sigh of relief and do as little work as possible. No matter what grades they receive, they will become members of the college's alumni group, and their place in the network of graduates is guaranteed. Campus life is very social, and most students enjoy it to the fullest. Another dimension of college life in South Korean colleges and universities is political and social activism. Although only a small proportion of college students are actively involved in planning and carrying out political demonstrations, they are more politically alert and active than their U.S. counterparts. Since the 1960s, students on the campuses have had the reputation of being the watchdogs of Korean society.

The Need for Educational Reforms

In spite of remarkable achievements in education, the Ministry of Education and the public at large are well aware that reform is still necessary. The emphasis on rote memorization of facts is not suited for remaining competitive in the global market. According to studies conducted by the Korean Educational Development Institute, three out of every ten students currently do not regard school as necessary to their lives, and in the near future possibly seven out of ten will share this view. When this author visited one of the best high schools in Seoul, a student candidly expressed her views. "When I finish at the university, I want to become a politician and reform the educational system."

This vocal young woman is part of a growing movement to bring reform to schools. Students resent the emphasis on and the attendant pressures of the college exam. The artistic but ill-disciplined student or the late bloomer may have nowhere to go. Education is what is in the textbooks and what might be on the exam, but it does not include preparation for life, critical thinking, or creativity.

Teachers complain that their workday is too long and express dissatisfaction about their pay. A teaching day is long. For most the day begins at 7:30 A.M. and ends at 5:00 P.M. The regular workload consists of five classes that meet four times each week, with an additional 20 classes that meet once a week. Many teachers see between 250 and 500 students in their classrooms every week. Teachers express frustration that it is not possible to know all of their students by name. Since teachers have so many pupils, they rarely assign written work. Language education is particularly flawed because the focus is on grammar and not conversation. In spite of the fact that the government passed a law that made it illegal for teachers to tutor, approximately 50 percent continue to do so.

An unhealthy result of the parents' desperation to get their children into a good university is the corruption that permeates the educational system from kindergarten upward. Parents routinely give teachers money or gifts so that they will not ignore their children. A government investigation revealed that there are parents who pay enormous sums of money to buy a place in a university.

The nation's most eminent institution of higher learning, Seoul National University, is not even ranked among the top 100 universities in the world. Over 90 percent of the university's faculty are alumni of that institution. Despite the fact that Korea has one of the world's highest Ph.D./population ratios, a survey revealed that professors published the least number of research papers in international academic journals of the twenty-nine member states of the Organization for Economic Cooperation and Development (OECD).

The Education Ministry has attempted to rectify the problems in the current educational system. One of the major objectives pointed to "the education of creative citizens in the knowledge-based society." The ministry's policies in 2000 were targeted at increasing the budget for key educational policy items, removing rote memorization from the center of education, and giving more weight to the development of individual students' creativity and ethical development. Additional plans were announced to reduce class size, revise procedures for evaluating students, and revamp the university curriculum. One of the major complaints of teachers was the fact that the ministry lowered the retirement age for high school teachers to sixty-two.

PHILOSOPHY AND RELIGION

In most countries religious affiliation has diminished with industrialization and urbanization. In South Korea, it is just the opposite. Despite rapid change and modernization, religion remains the nation's most influential nongovernmental force. The religious population has actually increased in each of the last four decades. Both traditional religions and Christianity, as well as numerous new spiritual movements, touch every aspect of society and exert a powerful impact in the daily lives of citizens.

Korea is one of the most religiously diverse countries in the world. Ancient religious practices and Confucian philosophy continue to have an enormous significance. It is also important to recognize that, like other Asians, Koreans are not exclusivist in their beliefs. Shamanism, Buddhism, Daoism, and Confucianism coexist with one another. Christianity is something of an exception. The combination of varied religious and philosophical beliefs together with a practical secular view of the world characterizes contemporary society.

According to a 1997 Gallup survey, nearly half of the population reported membership in a religious group. In spite of the high level of affiliation, only 48 percent of Koreans believe in God. Similar results were found in two previous polls. Unlike in the United States, where God is on the currency and in the legislature, Korea has no civic religion. A recent poll indicates that 95 percent of Americans believe in God.

The three major religious organizations support nationally broadcast cable television and radio networks. The Buddhist television network was the first of its kind in the world. Religious organizations publish more than 200 magazines and periodicals and operate daily newspapers of their own. In addition to managing numerous primary and secondary schools, religious organizations are affiliated with more than one out of every five colleges and universities in Korea. These groups also own land, hospitals, publishing houses, and prayer and rehabilitation centers.

The number of Koreans professing religious affiliation has increased significantly since the end of the war. From 1964 to 1994, the religious population jumped six times, while the total population expanded about one and one half times. This increase was particularly evident from the early 1960s to the end of the 1980s, the time of the most significant economic and urban development. Andrew Kim in "Religion in Contemporary Korea: A Sociological Survey" explains the sociohistorical factors that inspired such an increase in religious growth. He attributes this development to the painful legacy of Japanese colonial rule, the trauma of the Korean War, and the sense of isolation arising from rapid industrialization and urbanization. Churches provided a haven for refugees from the North and new urban dwellers who sought community and comfort.

Shamanism and Daoism

Shamanism, the oldest religion, continues to have a large number of believers. An estimated 2 to 3 million people regularly consult modern-day shamans whose places of business are on nearly every street corner. Seeing a psychologist is considered a sign of serious mental weakness, but it is perfectly acceptable to visit a fortune-teller.

Shamanism is centered on a priestess, a *mudang,* who makes contact with spirits through special techniques. An individual will hire a mudang to perform a ceremony, or *kut,* to communicate with the spirits. The ritual is regularly held for the launching of a new business or the dedication of a new building.

Decorations in restaurants, hotels, government offices, and even the presidential Blue House use many-paneled folding screens painted with themes whose basic symbolism and meaning can be grasped best through knowledge of Shamanism or its emphasis on longevity as a goal of life. Symbols of longevity (the crane and the turtle) and good luck (dragons, phoenixes, and unicorns) are found everywhere.

Another ancient religion, Daoism, failed to proliferate as an independent religion but has influenced Korean thought and society for centuries. Its syncretic belief in a multiplicity of gods was compatible with belief in the unseen spirits of nature. Daoism freely borrowed from Confucianism and Buddhism in its institutions, temples, ceremonies, and doctrines.

Daoism continues to manifest its influence on the people, such as their love for nature. It is also apparent in their search for blessings and longevity, two of its most prominent features. Everyday articles are adorned with symbols of prosperity and long life. The names of many mountains and valleys throughout the country indicate a strong influence of this religion. The influence of Daoism is most visible on the national flag with its yin/yang blue and red symbol representing the dualism of the universe.

Confucianism

Nothing has shaped Korean society as much as Confucianism. This philosophy was accepted so eagerly and in such a strict form that the Chinese regarded the Korean adherents as more Confucian than themselves. Today more than 200 shrines and numerous academies are scattered throughout the country. Although large numbers of people claim to be Buddhists, Christians, or Shamanists, everyone in Korea, to one degree or another, is Confucian. The ideals recommended by Confucius centuries ago continue to guide people in their social relations in the home, workplace, school, and government. The young are to respect their elders, children their parents, wives their husbands, daughters-in-law their mothers-in-law, students their teachers, employees their employers, and friends their friends. Everyone must pay respect to their ancestors. Leaders are to be moral. If they are not, as in the case in recent history, the leaders lose legitimacy.

Children learn before the age of ten that their lives are not their own, but belong to their family. Decisions are familial, not personal. The Confucian tradition influences one's choice of a marital partner because spouses may not have the same paternal ancestor. The decision of whom to marry is one that is made on the advice of the parents. Paternal grandparents are considered the real grandparents. The Confucian system guides people in the names they use to address family members and relatives. Three traditional family rituals (marriage, ancestor worship, and funerals), though somewhat changed, continue to be celebrated with a degree of ritual elaboration worthy of the past.

Pyongsan Sowon (Confucian Academy), near Andong. Young men studied at Confucian academies in preparation for the civil service. Daoist symbols are prominently featured on a wall of the academy. (Courtesy of Mary Connor)

Buddhism

Buddhism, which entered the peninsula in the fourth century, flourished throughout the Three Kingdoms period (57 B.C.E.–668 C.E.) and became the state religion during the Koryo dynasty (918–1392),

Pulguk-sa, near Kyongju. This temple was originally built in 528 C.E. and enlarged in 751 C.E.. The stone stairways and structures are original. Pulguk-sa, the most magnificent example of Silla architecture, was reconstructed along its original lines during the Park regime. (Courtesy of Mary Connor)

but it suffered a long period of repression during the Choson dynasty (1392–1910). Its spectacular revival is a major development in modern Korean history. Buddhism has almost nine million adherents.

Korean Buddhism, like that of China and Japan, is mainly of the Mahayana school, emphasizing the attainment of eternity through faith. The historical Buddha Shakyamuni taught that the fate of all living beings is to suffer throughout their lives. The attainment of Nirvana, or deliverance from life's suffering, is sought through the rejection of earthly desires and a progression through many reincarnations, which is followed by enlightenment. The three main foundations of the Buddhist faith are the Buddha himself, his teaching, and the community of monks whose conduct is guided by an Eightfold Path—a daily guide for righteous living and right thinking. Ordinary people are expected to be considerate and selfless toward others and to improve themselves according to the standards of righteous life but cannot expect to attain Nirvana within their lifetimes. Salvation is an individual matter, and the emphasis is on withdrawal more than on social action. This does not mean that Buddhism has no social conscience; love and charity toward all living things is a dominant part of the belief system.

Until very recently the majority of Koreans were Buddhist. The continuous influence of the West combined with the fact that the presidents of South Korea were Christian led to a temporary decline in the followers of Buddhism. Also, young people and those who

Rocks at Haein-sa Temple are piled on top of one another to signify wishes for good health and prosperity. (Courtesy of Mary Connor)

Sokka Pagoda, Pulguk-sa, near Kyongju. The pagoda is twenty-seven feet high and is regarded as the most elegant stone pagoda in Korea. A Buddhist text believed to have been printed before 751, the year the Sokka Pagoda was constructed, was recently discovered inside the pagoda and is regarded as the oldest Buddhist text printed with wood blocks in the world. (Courtesy of Mary Connor)

Haein-sa Temple, founded by two monks in the ninth century, is located in the mountains of Kayasan National Park and is one of the most beautiful and representative temples in all of Korea. The most famous attraction at the temple is the Tripitaka Koreana, *the most complete and important set of Buddhist teachings in the world. It was carved during the thirteenth century on 81,340 woodblocks. (Courtesy of Mary Connor)*

wanted to be more modern were inclined to join Christian churches. During the 1960s and 1970s the South Korean government supported the reconstruction of historic sites including many Buddhist temples. Many people began to reclaim the faith as something to honor and revere as opposed to something that was old-fashioned. As a result, membership in Buddhist congregations grew and is just about equal to that of Christian churches. Monks in some sects are permitted to marry. Buddha's birthday is a national holiday that includes parades, the lighting of lanterns, ritual, and festivities.

Buddhists recently became more involved in politics and society. After the tragedy in Kwangju in 1980, Buddhists adopted an activist role and were known to be overtly concerned with issues of poverty and justice. For the first time in modern history Buddhist monks could be seen demonstrating in the streets for democratic reforms. Buddhists have also opened meditation halls in condominium complexes and office buildings to provide places for urban followers to meet, meditate, and discuss Buddhist teachings.

Urban lay Buddhists have also modernized their music. They sing the words of their traditional rituals to well-known Christian hymns. In 1972 a Buddhist Bible was published. This Bible incorporates the most important and most popular sections of the immense canon in a book of a few hundred pages. Buddhists may be seen reading their Bible on subways and buses as Christians do.

There are now approximately forty Buddhist orders. Congregations are involved in charitable activities, education, and missionary work.

Korean wall, monk's quarters, and television aerial at Haein-sa. Monks live a very austere existence in the temple; however, the photographer took note of the television aerial. (Courtesy of Mary Connor)

There are more than 11,000 temples, over 26,000 monks, and Buddhist-run media outlets, including television programs, radio networks, and newspapers. The most famous Buddhist temples, such as Pulguk-sa and Haein-sa, are beautifully maintained, and tourists flock to these sites. It is common to see jolly young monks, with closely shaven heads and garbed in gray robes, laughing and enjoying the companionship of their associates in the streets and restaurants of Seoul.

Christianity

In spite of the fact that Korea is a country steeped in ancient beliefs, Christianity has become the dominant religion. It has been extraordinarily successful. Since the introduction of Catholic worship in the eighteenth century and the coming of Protestant missionaries in the late nineteenth century, Christianity has become the most popular religion, and its influence is seen everywhere. Women have been central to its growth. Until Christianity arrived, most people did not think of themselves as Buddhists rather than Confucians, or of Buddhism and Shamanism as being mutually exclusive. It has been primarily in response to people claiming to be Christian that others have taken religious labels for themselves. Together, Protestants and Catholics make up close to a third of the nation's population. They also appear to be among the most religious in terms of frequency of church attendance, praying, and scripture reading.

The fastest growing denomination in the 1990s was Roman Catholicism, with four million followers. It arrived in Korea in 1784 when a Confucian scholar named Yi Sunghun returned from Peking after being baptized by a French priest. Yi quickly converted other Confucian scholars to the new religion. In time it became a problem.

Authorities in Rome said that Catholics could not perform Confucian rituals because ancestor worship is a form of idolatry. When one of the converts refused to perform a Confucian ritual, he was sentenced to death and became Korea's first Christian martyr. The number of Catholics executed by the Choson dynasty government reached into the thousands by the end of the nineteenth century. Of that number, ninety-three Korean martyrs were singled out for particular piety and canonized by Pope John Paul II when he visited Korea in 1984. Numerous women were among those canonized. As a result of the Pope's visit, citizens could boast that South Korea had more officially recognized Catholic saints than any other nation outside of Western Europe.

The first Protestant missionaries arrived in 1884 and established Korea's first modern medical facilities and first modern schools. Horace Allen (1858–1932) a physician-missionary attached to the U.S. legation, opened the way for missionaries by saving the life of a member of the royal family after an attempted coup d'état. Allen opened the first hospital in Seoul in 1885. The next year Methodist missionaries opened two modern schools. One of the schools, the first to offer formal education for women, became Ehwa Womans University, now regarded as one of the best universities.

Protestant missionaries were allowed to proselytize and operate freely because the government felt their activities were helping the country to modernize. In 1898, in response to pressures from the West, the government acknowledged freedom of religion. Protestantism expanded rapidly for two reasons. One, its belief in the essential equality of all human beings was a revolutionary and appealing notion. And two, the nation was rapidly losing its independence to Japanese imperialism. As a result, many Christians became involved in nationalistic, anti-Japanese politics, such as the March First Movement, and demonstrated against the demands that they honor the emperor and the gods of Imperial Japan at Shinto shrines.

During occupation Christianity gathered strength and support from patriots who used church institutions as havens from Japanese oppression. When Korea was liberated from the Japanese and divided into a communist-controlled North and an anticommunist South, the church was presented with a new challenge: the loss of a substantial number of buildings along with much of its congregation. At that time more than one out of three Catholics and three out of every five Protestants lived north of the thirty-eighth parallel. Many Christians did escape from the North.

At the end of the Korean War churches grew rapidly. Since the early 1960s, when there were fewer than 1 million Protestants in South Korea, the number has more than doubled every decade. By 1997, there were approximately 100,000 ministers representing more than 160 Protestant denominations, making the Protestant Church of South Korea one of the most dynamic in the world. It was also the nation's largest denomination, with more than 9 million followers. Each Sunday 68 percent of Catholics and 74 percent of Korean Protestants attend church. By 1998, South Koreans supplied the third largest number of the world's missionaries. There are now approximately 60,000 Protestant churches and 1,100 Catholic churches in South Korea, making it the most Christianized non-Western country in the world, with the exception of the Philippines.

Five of the ten largest churches in the world are reportedly found in Seoul. The most conspicuous example is Youido Full Gospel Church, which has more than 700,000 members. The church's evangelical message has attracted huge audiences and influenced other churches to adopt it. Its threefold blessing is simply stated: Christ brings health, prosperity, and salvation. This theology of prosperity rests on the acceptance of the Holy Spirit: health, materialistic success in this world, and salvation in the next. The doctrine also supports the notion that illness, poverty, and misfortune are due to sin and the failure to live according to one's spiritual calling.

The "Newly Rising Religions"

Adding to the religious diversity of the nation are large numbers of independent churches, which comprise about 10 percent of all the churches in Korea, and dozens of new religious movements, including Ch'ondokyo, Taejong-gyo, Chungsan-gyo, Tongil-gyo (the Unification Church), and Won Buddhism. All of the major religious movements had their origins in very difficult times, such as when the country struggled against the West in the late nineteenth century and during Japanese occupation and the war. Most have small memberships and have a connection in some way to the Tonghak movement of the nineteenth century. These religions also share certain characteristics. They combine elements of Buddhism, Confucianism, Daoism, and Christianity with Shamanism to create a new belief. They promise the advent of a utopia following an apocalypse. Most stress the advent of a savior, who happens to be the founder of their particular sect, with the coming of a new world. Finally, most of these religions are nationalistic and express the belief that Korea is the chosen land and Koreans are God's chosen people.

This-Worldly Orientation of Korean Religions

In the past many people would have turned to Shamanism for the good things of the world. Today, instead, they turn to Christianity as a more appropriate, effective, and modern means to the same end. It is a well-known fact that the followers of Shamanism, and large numbers of Buddhists and Christians alike, have faith in the belief that Buddha, God, or spirits can grant them earthly wishes, such as health and wealth. Popular Buddhism does not focus on meditation or asceticism, but on prayers for granting wishes. Andrew Kim notes that Korean Christianity has also been "shamanized" to suit materialistic tendencies. Surveys support this strong, this-worldly inclination of making sense and providing security in people's lives.

This earthly tendency of many Buddhists and Christians, especially Protestants, is also reflected in the way they associate the offering with secular blessings. Buddhists give their offerings together with a list of prayer items to the temple. Both Catholics and Protestants contribute money to their churches whenever good fortune occurs, such as the birth of a son or when sons or daughters pass the university examination. According to the 1997 Gallup Korea survey, nearly 40 percent of the Protestant community indicated the belief that those who contribute money to the church will be blessed by more prosperity in return for their giving.

The Persistence of Confucianism

Before Korea became an economic success, many felt that Confucianism was one of the factors holding back development. It would be truer to say that industrialization here and in other Asian economies has been aided by Confucian values. The emphasis on harmony and respect for authority contributes positively to the effectiveness of business operations. The value of loyalty promotes the individual's and the company's interests. This commitment is one of the principal reasons that Koreans were willing to endure the longest workdays in the world for little pay from the mid-1960s to the mid-1980s. Additional Confucian values of sacrifice, cooperation, sincerity, and family as analogous to the company provided management with effective decision-making and labor control, both of which have been central to industrialization.

Current Religious Trends and the Issue of Reunification

One recent development has been the emergence of a large number of independent churches that are devoted to the end-of-the-world doctrine. There are more than 200 such groups with a membership of more than 100,000. Since Protestantism arrived, it has generally supported this doctrine. Certainly the advent of a new millennium and constant fear of nuclear war with North Korea have contributed to this development. Surveys support the belief that the majority of Christian Protestants believe in the literal Second Coming of Christ.

Religion could play an important role in the reunification process. It certainly serves as a potential unifying force since the Koreas share a common religious tradition. Confucian elements persist in the North and Shamanism undoubtedly has been a dominant belief for centuries. Buddhists and Christians from the South have provided food and needed services to the North; their assistance can provide a step toward ending decades of mistrust and helping to finally bring unity to the peninsula.

TRADITIONAL AND POPULAR CULTURE

In spite of the significant and rapid changes of the twentieth century, the traditional culture remains vibrant and resilient. Ethnic and linguistic unity, intense nationalism, the shared feelings of the bitter colonial experience, and the remarkable tenacity of the Korean people contribute to the persistence of ancient traditions.

The old and new coexist in both rural and urban landscapes and for all generations, though modified to fit changing times. However, radical alterations have come with constant foreign influences and globalization. Many fear that these external forces threaten their cul-

Hahoe Mask Dance Drama, Hahoe Village. The mask drama has been performed for centuries as a village ritual. Performances continue to delight modern-day audiences. (Courtesy of Mary Connor)

tural identity. Others are convinced that their culture will be reinvigorated by foreign elements.

Increased social mobility in recent years has influenced cultural preferences. The traditional arts of the aristocracy, their literature, history, poetry, and calligraphy, are no longer the dominate art forms. It is the folk art, painting, music, dance, and ceramics, done by poor or preliterate Koreans that is most evident and integral to cultural life today. Economic development since the 1960s enabled people to give more attention to the arts, both as creators and as consumers. And finally, the new technology of the Internet and the success of the film industry are increasing Korea's outreach in the world and its international stature.

With the 1988 Olympics, deregulation of travel abroad, and improvement of information and communication systems, people became increasingly aware of the importance of learning about different cultures and broadening their own experiences. In the 1990s performances or events that had been unthinkable ten years earlier, such as the Russian ballet and world-famous musicians and dance troupes, flourished in the Seoul Art Center and the National Theater.

Some of the finest Korean works of art were installed in stunning exhibitions at major museums worldwide, and the work of famous artists from around the world was shown in galleries and museums all over Korea. This led to the opening of Korean art galleries at the Metropolitan Museum of Art in New York in 1998 and the Los Angeles County Art Museum in 2000. Major exhibits were held at the British Museum and the Royal Ontario Museum. Naming the twenty-first century "The Century of Culture" showed that culture was becoming more central to Korean life.

Despite the continuous influence of Chinese culture over the centuries, Korean painting remained distinctive for its vigor, rhythm, and earthy qualities. Painters in the early periods were active in Japan and played an important part in the development of Japanese art. In the eighteenth and nineteenth centuries artists created a unique decorative style of folk painting that dealt with the everyday life of the masses. In the twentieth centuries artists experimented with Western media, borrowed certain oriental styles from Japan, and continued to develop the various styles of traditional painting. They tried impressionism, cubism, and abstract expressionism and worked with new materials, perspectives, and compositions to combine elements of traditional painting with modern painting. The 1980s witnessed the birth of "people's art" to protest against the military rule and injustices of the Chun regime.

Recent Korean art has received mixed reviews. Although critics comment that many works lack character and creativity, some artists have distinguished themselves both at home and abroad. Their artwork reveals traditional elements, cross-cultural expressions, and images of contemporary life. Probably the most well-known Korean artist is Nam-June Paik, the pioneer of what is known as video art and a major figure in avant-garde art. His video sculpture combines color television sets, interior frames and working parts of televisions, satellite dishes, neon tubing, wires, and laser disks. His art is described as being about liberation, meditation, and Eastern and Western values. Art critic Josef Woodard writes that Paik's art is for our time and beyond.

Literature of the twentieth century must be seen in the context of Japanese occupation, the Korean War, and the ideological conflicts between South and North Korea. Japanese occupation and the introduction of Western literary styles resulted in the growth of a literary movement whose ideas continue to dominate. This movement sought to bring literature to the masses. During occupation, poetry,

Hahoe Folk Village (Courtesy of Mary Connor)

short stories, and essays appeared that dealt with nationalistic themes and social and political concerns. Censorship by the Japanese government, however, led to imprisonment and execution, and for a time, the use of the Korean language was prohibited. Lacking publishing houses, novelists wrote for daily newspapers in serialized form, as they frequently do today.

It took many years for South Korean writers to recover from the turmoil and destruction of the war. Strict censorship initially prevented writers from dealing with the central issues dividing the people of North and South. As a result writers turned to topics relating to the Chosun dynasty and Japanese occupation. Under Presidents Park and Chun the government closed down literary magazines and blacklisted writers who appeared critical of their regimes. After liberalization began in the late 1980s a flood of literature about occupation, war, and reunification emerged from authors born after the war.

Much of this literature was somber and dealt with themes of alienation, frustration, and the dehumanizing aspects contemporary life. Poetry was nationalistic, dispirited, and filled with the emotion called han: living with great and sustained loss. The most celebrated poets of today are notable for their range of passion and themes revealing the Korean experience, love of nature, and empathy for other human beings. In recent years poets have also experimented and modernized traditional poem-songs *(sijo)* that were invented during the Koryo dynasty. Since the Asian economic crisis of the late 1990s, new topics, such as feminism, the information society, the environment, multimedia, popular culture, and sex, have appeared.

Ancient Chinese sources referred to the Koreans as "the people who loved singing and dancing." For centuries children grew up hearing the rhythmic sounds of percussion, a major element in folk music and an integral part of *nongak,* or (farmers' music) a form of rural entertainment performed by touring bands of musicians. Although the traditional music of the aristocratic class may still be well received, it is the music of the commoner that has experienced a revival and international recognition. In 1978, a musician named Kim Duk-soo started a percussion troupe, Samul nori, that revived and internationalized the farmers' bands of the past and has contributed to the world's appreciation of Korean musical traditions. The Samul nori form incorporates four percussion instruments: a small gong, a large gong, a barrel drum, and an hourglass-shaped drum. Traditional music and dance performances continue to attract large and enthusiastic audiences at Seoul's Chongdong Theater.

Another musical form of Korea's past that has experienced a great revival is the dramatic song called p'ansori. Originating in the folk traditions of the Choson dynasty, p'ansori was an epic performed by a single singer accompanied by a percussionist keeping rhythm on a drum and punctuating the singer's notes with contrapuntal sounds that interact with the emotionality of the vocalist. With seemingly no time constraints, the vocalist engages audiences for hours with a vocal range virtually unsurpassed in the music of any other culture. P'ansori is now known internationally as a result of two highly recognized films by the leading filmmaker, Im Kwon-taek. The 1993 film *Sop'yonje* was the first internationally recognized Korean film and incorporated the hauntingly beautiful sounds of p'ansori singing. Another example of the p'ansori genre is the story of a young woman named Ch'unhyang, one of the most beloved Korean folktales and an ideally suited story for p'ansori. It is a story of true love, long-suffering virtue, and triumph over evil. In recent times there have been several opera and film versions, the most recent directed by Im Kwon-taek and released in the United States in 2000. By far the form of classical music with the broadest appeal in Korea is the opera. In spite of the hardships caused by the Asian economic crisis, operas such as *Madame Butterfly* reaped large profits with all performances sold out.

Without question the most famous folk song is "Arirang," a lyric sung by a young woman whose lover is about to leave her to cross over the mountains through the Arirang Pass. The melody has touched the hearts of many generations of Koreans and continues to strike a chord with those that are still discovering the many textures and dimensions of the Korean culture.

Another popular art form from the folk tradition, and one that can be traced back as far as the Silla kingdom, may be found in the mask drama dance that was revived in the late twentieth century. The dramas, which were long, earthy, and satirical, brought diversion to the rural people from their arduous labor in the field. Visiting the mask drama at the Hahoe Village near Andong in southeastern Korea is highly recommended for all visitors.

Traditional dances (court, religious, and folk) continue to be performed domestically and abroad; however, it is folk dancing that is the most quintessentially Korean and the most popular. Evolved from Shamanistic ceremonies from thousands of years ago, folk dancing expresses inner emotions through outward gestures. The oldest and most popular is the *Farmer's Dance*. Accompanied by the sound of ear-splitting din of rhythmic gongs and drums, dancers spin and leap about madly as they travel from house to house driving away evil spirits.

Contemporary dance arrived during Japanese occupation. Through the difficult times of occupation and later the Korean War, young dancers struggled to reconcile Western dance techniques with the themes and emotions of the native dance. Though it is still considered a minor art form, the ballet was invigorated in 1984 by the formation of a private company, the Universal Ballet Company, which employed American teachers and often performed with foreign dancers. The year 1999 was considered "a golden year" for Korean ballet. Many dancers won awards in international competitions, and many domestic ballet performances attracted huge audiences.

A discussion of culture is incomplete without noting the largest surviving component of Korean classical culture—ceramics. Nearly 300,000 pieces exist in museums and private collections throughout the world. These works of art are some of the most prized and exquisite examples of ceramic work anywhere. Most famous of all are the celadon porcelains produced during the Koryo dynasty. The National Museum of Korea in Seoul houses some of the finest celadons of the Koryo period, and it also owns some exquisite examples of *punch'ong* ware of the Choson. While these porcelains symbolize the taste of the ruling aristocracy and the military, the remarkable achievements were created by the lowest classes. Not one of the artists' names is known today, but their innovations influenced Japan and beyond. Reproductions are available in art galleries and market-places throughout the country.

The film industry is currently one of the strongest elements of the Korean culture. The industry is optimistic that the visual media, including films, animation, and video, will be the major genre in the next generation. The number of young people drawn to the visual media is growing. A new generation of film directors has emerged, and Korea has hosted various film festivals. Films such as *Sop'yonje* and *Swiri,* have received international acclaim and broken box-office records. *Sop'yonje* (1993), by Korea's leading film director, Im Kwon-taek, was the first internationally recognized Korean film. *Swiri* a terrifying film about an attempt by North Korean comman-dos to bomb a soccer stadium where two leaders participating in a North-South summit are present, was seen by nearly 6 million Kore-ans and was also a huge success in Japan. The success of *Swiri* was made possible in part by the financial support of Samsung enter-tainment, which invested $2.9 million, three times the average pro-duction cost in Korea.

Female directors are no longer a novelty in the film industry. Byon Yong Ju's *Nazun Moksori (The Murmuring)* was chosen as one of the twenty-three best movies directed by a woman worldwide in the 1990s by the New York Women in Film and Television. *The Mur-muring* is a documentary about the lives of the surviving Korean women who were taken by the Japanese as "comfort women" during World War II.

The films, *Chorok Mulgogi (Green Fish)* and *Nappun Yonghwa (Bad Movie),* both directed by Chang Son-Wu, won the New Asia Award at the Vancouver International Film Festival and at the Tokyo International Film Festival, respectively. *Bad Movie* is about teenagers involved in drinking, drugs, and crime, children who live in the streets, and middle-aged alcoholics. The characters in the movie are not actors or actresses, but play themselves. When the film was released, its unconventional content, especially the explicit sex scenes, sparked considerable debate. Another film, *Arumdaun sijol (Spring in My Hometown),* won the Gold Award at the Eleventh Tokyo International Film Festival. The story, viewed through the main character's memory, is about a child growing up at a U.S. army base during the Korean War.

One of the big issues has been opening the Korean market to Japanese popular culture. In October 1998 the government agreed to permit the importation of Japanese films and videos. In September 1999 it vastly expanded the number of films that could be distributed, but Japanese animation was excluded. The area in which Japanese popular culture has the greatest impact is comic books. They are widely read, particularly by teenagers. Concerns are frequently expressed in Korea and in the Korean American community in the United States about the influence of Japanese pop culture on moral standards. Its influence is also significant in fashion trends, television programs, and pop songs.

The Youth Culture

Although the older generation suffered from occupation and war, the younger generation has only heard their stories of sacrifice, family separations, and hard times. For the most part the young refuse to accept their parents' or grandparents' frugal lifestyles, preferring individualism and consumerism to self-sacrifice. Unlike students in the 1980s, they are not interested in the political struggles of the past and are disenchanted by the corruption in government. Their interests are material, and their own lives seem more important than the welfare of society as a whole. Quick to respond to the latest craze and new ideas, they have grown up with MTV and the Internet. In the early 1990s, society censured them for their consumption and self-centeredness. They were called Orange-jok (the orange tribe) for the liberal lifestyle they pursued and because young women of this group could be enticed by oranges and expensive cars.

It is not surprising that the main cultural interest of the younger generation is not literature, but the visual media, such as animation, advertisements, videos, and films. They enjoy science fiction, magazines on contemporary culture, Japanese comic books, film noir, hiphop, reggae, soft rock, and ballads. The sound of their pop music is very emotional, and the melodies center around love and affections. The slower songs are known as ballads, and those that incorporate electric guitar and heavy drum sounds are known as rock ballads. In 1999 teens flocked to special performances by Michael Jackson, Mariah Carey, and Boys II Men. In the same year a summer concert in In'chon was so well attended that it was compared to Woodstock.

Although the older generation frets that the young are self-absorbed and indiscriminate in their acceptance of foreign culture,

many young Koreans cherish traditional culture, are wary of the bar-
rage of foreign elements, study hard, and plan to reform society. The
young are more educated and sophisticated than their elders. They
have traveled to a greater extent, have friends in foreign countries,
and are trained in international languages. The literary enthusiasts
utilize PC online communication services to introduce their work to
the public. BOP, a pocket-sized magazine, was put out entirely by
high school students who planned and edited the stories themselves.
This fad spread throughout Korea in the late 1990s.

The young gather in Taehang-no (University Street), the former
location of Seoul National University, which has the city's largest concentration of cafes, theaters, galleries, festivals, music halls, and
Internet cafes. In Taehang-no, one hears street performers play the
traditional musical arts of samul nori and nongak (farmer's music)
along with rock and roll, heavy metal, and hip-hop. The young may
be found packed in big pc-bang (Internet rooms), browsing the Internet at high speed, playing games, or downloading mp3s. Additional
entertainment can be found in *noraebangs* (karaoke rooms), video
rooms, and *oraksils* (video game arcades). A popular pastime, especially among those between the ages of eighteen and thirty, seems to
be drinking *soju,* a liquor like sake, but much more potent.

Sports and Recreation

The development of sports has been linked to the country's economic
situation and the hosting of the Summer Olympics in Seoul in 1988.
Since then there has been increased emphasis on physical fitness,
improved performance in international competition, and all kinds of
facilities from soccer stadiums to golf courses. Sports have become an
increasingly important part of everyday life. Spectator sports, such as
soccer, baseball, and basketball have become very popular. Every
town has a soccer team, and the whole country becomes excited
when Korea has a match with another country, especially Japan.
Female athletes excel in volleyball and table tennis and have won
international competitions. The sport that is most associated with
urban life is golf. Since land is so costly, golf is one of the most expensive sports in the country and is considered a prestige game played
primarily by wealthy businesspeople and government officials.

Traditional sports, such as Taekwondo, *ssirum* (wrestling), and
archery continue to be enjoyed. The martial art of Taekwondo, which
originated some 2,000 years ago, has become one of the most impor-

Cheju Island is a beautiful island that attracts honeymooners, Korean families, and foreign tourists. It is a place that Koreans hold very dear. (Courtesy of Mary Connor)

tant national pastimes and has spread throughout the world. At present there are over 144 countries that are members of the International Taekwondo Federation. Ssirum is similar to sumo wrestling and involves throwing one's opponent out of the ring.

When Koreans have some leisure time, they head for parks, the countryside, or the mountains. Although it may involve continuous traffic jams or long bus rides, it appears worth the effort because young and old genuinely love the out-of-doors. Their forms of recreation include picnicking, hiking, rafting, kayaking, windsurfing, and waterskiing. Going to the beach is becoming a new form of recreation. On weekends many families drive to other parts of the country to visit famous temples, historic sites, and their favorite scenic spots. The spectacular beauty of Cheju Island lures thousands of visitors each year, especially newlyweds.

NORTH KOREA

The spring of 1994 had a frightening resemblance to the summer of 1914, when World War I began. The Nuclear Crisis of 1994 remains a little-known event outside the Korean peninsula; however, the United States came the closest it had been to nuclear war since the Cuban Missile Crisis. The American public was unaware of the high stakes, and officials were mystified as to why the DPRK was behaving in such an irrational manner. Since that time, the risk of renewed war on the peninsula remains. Because the United States maintains a military presence and a strong commitment to the ROK, it makes sense to develop an intelligent view of what North Koreans think and

why. Space permits only a brief discussion of their political culture
and way of life.

The North Korean Perspective

Since 1945, North Korea has been a very isolated country. Its leaders
seldom travel outside the borders. Information is tightly controlled,
and the people spend their lives unaware of Western ideas or events
that have shaped the contemporary world. This detachment is not
new. For centuries, the country shunned foreigners and was known
as the Hermit Kingdom. A U.S. citizen, Commodore Robert Shufeldt,
forced the country to open its doors to the West in 1882. He proclaimed that finally he had accomplished "the feat of bringing the last
of the exclusive countries within the pale of Western Civilization."

To understand North Koreans, it is helpful to understand how they
perceive history. They look at their own experience as being shaped
by a Confucian ethic that respects authority, nurtures loyalty and
obedience, and encourages sacrifice for the family and the community as a whole. The Chinese acknowledged that the Koreans were
more Confucian than they were. And Koreans remember this fact
with considerable pride. As witnesses to China's humiliation by the
West and as victims of Japanese militarists, they grew to see themselves as superior. Some of this sentiment is reflected in the juche of
North Korea, which mistrusts the foreigner.

The leaders of North Korea between the 1940s and 1990s were
shaped by Japanese occupation. Educated in Japanese-controlled
schools, they learned the politics of Imperial Japan. The emperor
was god and his subjects were never to doubt him. Koreans, like all
Japanese subjects, were taught that they were an integral part of
the Japanese body politic. All were interconnected and functional
to the whole.

North Koreans view recent history quite differently than we do.
They know that the United States divided the peninsula without
consulting any Koreans. This is true, but it is relatively unknown to
most Americans. The people of North Korea believe that the United
States occupied South Korea to forge an alliance with the new post-
war Japanese government in order to dominate all of Asia. They
blame the U.S. support of Syngman Rhee for the permanent division
of Korea. When North Korea invaded the South in 1950, it was only
in response to the U.S.-organized international effort to oppose
reunification. The result was the loss of 2 million lives and the vir-

tual destruction of the country. The people believe that they essentially rebuilt the country with their own backbreaking labor and vow that they will never again be hurt in war or humiliated by foreign imperialists. They also accuse the United States of an irrational fear of communism that has kept the nation divided for more than half a century.

The Political Culture

The country's political culture is based on Confucian tradition, Marxism-Leninism, and juche. It explicitly rejected the Confucian heritage, yet the tradition persists. The personality cult of both Kim Il Sung and Kim Jong Il, the emphasis on the ruler's authority, the belief in filial piety, and the three-year period of mourning for the Supreme Leader all point to the continuity of the past. Kim Il Sung, with the initial guidance of the Soviet Union, effectively engineered a cultural revolution in attitudes and values according to Marxism-Leninism. Building on Confucian tradition, both Kims have taught that loyalty is the most essential of all human virtues.

Since the mid-1950s, the official ideology is no longer Marxism-Leninism, but Kim Il Sung's interpretation of communist thought called juche, which derives from North Korea's militant nationalism. Juche views Korea as a chosen land and embraces the idea that all civilization originated on the peninsula. As the juche philosophy evolved, Kim used varied terms to express views held for centuries: rejecting foreigners and foreign ideas and accepting all things Korean. The word *juche* means self-reliance and independence in politics, economics, defense, and ideology. A well-known tenet of juche is the people-centered view that man is the master of all things and can accomplish great things, given the necessary will and training. People are to be guided by a Great Leader—in this case, Kim Il Sung and his successor, Kim Jong Il.

Juche was also a declaration of political independence from Kim's communist supporters, the USSR and China. At a time when badly needed support from both the Soviet Union and China was diminishing, Kim Il Sung's writings began to emphasize self-reliance as a guiding principle. Other ideas include love and obedience for the Leader, loyalty to the party, commitment to the Three Revolutions (ideological, cultural, technological) for the transformation of the country, and devotion to practical service. Teachers use juche to create a state of mind based on correct thought that will lead to correct action, but it also means something inherently modern and Korean.

The veneration for the Great Leader grew over time. By the 1980s, when Kim Il Sung was in his seventies, Kim Jong Il began making juche part of a larger concept called Kimilsungism. By creating the concept of Kimilsungism, the Great Leader became a figure whom all Koreans could revere as a god. By the late 1980s there were at least 34,000 monuments to Kim, not including glass-covered benches where he once sat. He created an impenetrable and absolute state that no one can criticize. The most serious crime a person can commit is disloyalty to the Leader. Anyone caught treating pictures of the Kims with disrespect, such as letting them collect dust, is subject to disciplinary action. People are expected to inform on one another, even children on their parents, because if they do not report it and it becomes known, they will be implicated.

Kimilsungism and reverence for Kim Jong Il are seen in movies, pop songs, the fine arts, and literature. Documentaries promote loyalty and gratitude to Kim Il Sung. New pop songs in 1999 include such titles as "Here Comes General Kim Jong Il" and "Hymn of a Hero." In the same year over 700 paintings and 100 propaganda posters were produced, the majority of them hailing the achievements of Kim Il Sung or Kim Jong Il. The Workers' Party Publishing House also put out *Kim Jong Il, A Great Man Vol. 2* and *Kim Il Sung's Collected Works (Vol. 25–28).*

North Korean Society

The communists turned North Korea into a highly organized and regimented society, which criticized and then rejected traditional family ties. It destroyed the traditional class structure and established a classless society dominated by communist elites. At the same time, it abolished the traditional clan system, transferring the loyalty of children from their parents to the state, especially to Kim Il Sung, who became the father of all the people. Subsequently, North Korea created a collectivist spirit, which called for self-sacrifice, a rigidly organized life, and strict discipline in the interest of the whole. In practice, the collectivist spirit finds expression in loyalty to the Workers' Party and the glorification of Kim Il Sung.

Many other aspects of life under communism also worked to weaken family solidarity. The party controls where people live, work, and attend school, and also controls the choice of marital partner. To

P'yongyang traffic policewoman. (Photographed by Cheong Wa Dae, Presidential Residence of the Republic of Korea, Photographer's Press Pool)

revolutionize and reform women, they were freed from domestic work and placed in jobs outside the home. At one point about 80 percent of farmworkers and over 90 percent of the workers in light industry were women. This allowed more men to serve in the army.

It also created state-run nurseries and kindergartens where early indoctrination could begin.

In 1946 North Korea introduced laws mandating equality between the sexes, and in 1953 collectivizing farms, now called cooperatives. By these measures the traditional structure of the three-generation family was supposedly transformed into a two-generation family. Nevertheless, three-generation families continue to live together, in part because of a shortage of housing. The status of women has improved moderately. Filial piety and the continuation of the male line are still considered to be very important to family life, and there still is the tendency to prefer male to female children. Since private property no longer exists except for minor personal possessions, there is no inheritance. Social standing is still important, but the traditional status is reversed. Descendants of landlords and capitalists are officially discriminated against in terms of employment and education. Families of revolutionaries or outstanding workers are favored.

The state has played a decisive role in urbanization, where people need permits to travel, change jobs, and move. The capital city of P'yongyang now has more than 2.5 million people, and several other cities have populations of around one-half million. The agricultural population is still large. Income distribution is quite equitable, but the level of income is very low. In 1993, North Korea claimed that its average life expectancy was 77.5 years, but that number has been lowered to 59.8 years for men and 64.5 years for women because of malnutrition. Famine and related disease have claimed at least 1 million people.

There is an egalitarian sameness in the clothing of most people; however, party officials sport tailored suits and foreign watches and are driven in chauffeured Mercedes-Benz automobiles. The elite under the North Korean system seems to have the same entitlement of the old yangban class.

Education

The DPRK's educational and cultural policies seek to indoctrinate the people with socialistic thought so that they may develop the character of the Communist Man. Political study sessions begin in kindergarten and continue throughout life. They promote practical skills and instill loyalty to Kim Il Sung, Kim Jong Il, and the Korean Workers' Party (KWP). With these goals in mind, all schools are under the control of the government, and all teachers are members of the KWP. All education is free.

The current system is a result of numerous changes that occurred since 1945. The present eleven-year compulsory schooling was adopted in 1972. First, there is a one-year kindergarten class. It is followed by a four-year primary education (people's school) and a six-year course of study (higher middle school). Ideological instruction takes up more than half the day in elementary school and even more in the upper grades. Significant language reforms eliminated the use of Chinese characters in the written language, adopted Korean script in all printed material, and virtually eliminated the use of foreign words. Textbooks emphasize the history of the communist revolution, Kim Il Sung's achievements, and juche.

Post-secondary education is not compulsory. All of the colleges are technical and professional institutions. There are no liberal arts colleges or private schools. Students must work for their education. Many adult schools exist to educate workers and peasants.

The most prestigious and, until recently, the only comprehensive university is the Kim Il Sung University.

Religion

As in most communist countries, religion is officially discouraged. A limited number of the people still practice Buddhism, Christianity, and a Korean religion called Ch'ondokyo, but they have to belong to state-sponsored religious organizations that are closely monitored by the government. In the 1980s, after having no churches at all for decades, the government opened two churches in P'yongyang, one for Protestants and one for Catholics. There has been limited contact between North and South Korean Christians, primarily at international religious gatherings. Kim Dae-jung's Sunshine Policy could lead to some normalization of ties between Christian churches.

North Korean Defectors

The number of North Koreans escaping to and settling in the South began to increase noticeably in 1994, and by the end of 2000 the total number reached approximately 1,300 people. Before the 1990s, most political defectors fled their homeland for political reasons. Recently, however, refugees have cited hunger and discontent. Some escape alone. At times entire families have departed by boat or by traveling through China and Vietnam. Some are high-ranking officials and others are low-skilled workers. As long as food shortages and famine persist and enforcement is lax at the borders, it is likely that increasing numbers will attempt to flee.

Unfortunately, after living under political repression, escapees have found it very complicated and even painful to adjust to a freer environment and the market economic system. Notwithstanding a shared history, they suffer from feelings of isolation and alienation because of the difficulty of adapting to the South. This is largely attributed to the enmity engendered by the war and half a century of ideological confrontation between the two countries. If ways can be found to help these new refugees to adjust, it will help pave the way for eventual reunification.

References

Bok, Song. 2000. "Why Are So Many Men in Their 40s and 50s Dying?" in *Korea Focus* (November/December). Seoul: Korea Foundation.

Breen, Michael. 1998. *The Koreans: Who They Are, What They Want, Where Their Future Lies.* New York: St. Martin's Press.

Clark, Donald N. 1986. *Christianity in Modern Korea.* Lanham, MD: University Press of America.

————. 2000. *Culture and Customs of Korea.* Westport, CT: Greenwood Press.

Covell, Jon Carter. 1981. *Korea's Cultural Roots.* Seoul: Hollym Publishers.

Cumings, Bruce. 1997. *Korea's Place in the Sun: A Modern History.* New York: W. W. Norton.

Gibney, Frank. 1992. *Pacific Century: America and Asia in a Changing World.* New York: Kondansha International Ltd.

Handbook of Korea. 1993. Seoul: Korean Overseas Information Service.

Kim, Andrew. 2000. "Religion in Contemporary South Korea: A Sociological Survey." Lecture and unpublished paper presented at the Korean Studies Workshop at the University of Korea. (This source provided vital information for the section on contemporary religion.)

Kim, Byoung-Lo Philo. 1992. *Two Koreas in Development: A Comparative Study of Principles and Strategies of Capitalist and Communist Third World Development.* New Brunswick, NJ: Transaction Publishers.

Kim, Douglas. 2000. "Korea's 'Particular Institution,'" in *KoreAm* (May). Gardena, CA.

Kim, Elaine, and Chungmoo Choi, eds. 1998. *Dangerous Women: Gender and Korean Nationalism.* New York: Routledge Publishers.

Kim, Samuel S., ed. 2000. *Korea's Globalization.* Cambridge: Cambridge University Press.

Korean Institute of Curriculum & Evaluation, ed. 1999. "Korean Education for the New Millennium," Seoul: Ministry of Education.

————. 2000. "Curriculum, Assessment and College Scholastic Ability Test in the Republic of Korea." Seoul: Ministry of Education.

Lee, Kwang-kyu. 1997. *Korean Family and Kinship.* Seoul: Jipmoondang Publishing Company.

Lee, Sang Man. 2001. "Resettlement Training for North Korean Refugees," in *Korean Focus* (January/February). Seoul: The Korea Foundation.

Macdonald, Donald Stone. 1990. *The Koreans: Contemporary Politics and Society.* Boulder, CO: Westview Press.

Oberdorfer, Don. 1997. *The Two Koreas: A Contemporary History.* Reading, MA: Addison-Wesley.

Oh, Kongdan, ed. 2000. *Korea Briefing 1997–1999: Challenges and Change at the Turn of the Century.* New York: M. E. Sharpe, Inc.

Oh, Kongdan, and Ralph C. Hassig. 2000. *North Korea Through the Looking Glass.* Washington, DC: Brookings Institution Press.

Reitman, Valerie. "South Korea's Exam-Takers Have a Prayer," *Los Angeles Times.* 15 November 2000.

Roh, Jeong Seon, ed. 2000. *Korean Annual.* Seoul: Yonhap News Agency.

The Salad Bowl, "Things Korean I and II," http://www.thesaladbowl.com (cited July 26, 2001).

Shim, Young Hee. 2000. "Changing Status of Women in Korean Society," in *Korea Focus* (March/April). Seoul: Korea Foundation.

Suh, Dae-Sook, ed. 1994. *Korean Studies: New Pacific Currents.* "Korean Women's Labor Force Participation: Attitudes and Behavior" by Minja Kim Choe, Sae-Kwon Kong, and Karen Oppenheim Mason. Honolulu: University of Hawaii Press.

Sung, Kyung He. 2000. Director of International Research & Cooperation, Korean Institute of Curriculum & Evaluation. Lecture presented at Korean Studies Workshop at the University of Korea, June. Seoul, Korea.

Woodard, Josef. 2001. "A Slow Route through the Maelstrom: Nam June Paik, Video Art Pioneer at the Santa Barbara Museum of Art," in *Korean Culture* (Spring). Los Angeles: Korean Cultural Center of the Korean Consulate General in Los Angeles.

Zunsang, Han. 2001. "To Restore Student Confidence in Korea's School System," in *Korea Focus* (January/February). Seoul: Korea Foundation.

PART TWO
REFERENCE MATERIALS

Chronological Table

	Korea	China	Japan	Other Civilizations
B.C.E.	Paleolithic Age Neolithic Age			
5000		Bronze Age	Jomon Culture	Sumer and Egypt
2000	Tan'gun	Shang Dynasty Zhou Dynasty		
1000	Bronze Age	Iron Age		Greek Civilization Founding of Rome
500	Iron Age	Confucius		Buddha
300/200	Old Choson	Qin Conquest	Bronze Age	Alexander the Great
100	Three Kingdoms (traditional dates): Silla 57 B.C.E. – 935 C.E. Koguryo 37 B.C.E. – 668 C.E. Paekche 18 B.C.E. – 660 C.E. Confucianism established	Western Han Dynasty		Jesus Christ
C.E.	Kaya (42–564)	Xin Dynasty Eastern Han Dynasty		
200		Three Kingdoms Jin Dynasty	Iron Age	

	Korea	China	Japan	Other Civilizations
300	Buddhism recognized in Koguryo (372) Buddhism recognized in Paekche (384)			
400		Northern and Southern Dynasties		Fall of Rome (410)
500	Kaya absorbed by Silla (532–562) Buddhism recognized in Silla (ca. 535)	Sui Dynasties	Asuka Period Buddhism recognized in Japan (552)	
600	Parhae (698–926) Unified Silla (668–935)	Tang Dynasty	Nara Period	Mohammed
700	Oldest wood-block print (ca. 751)	Heian Period		
800				Charlemagne
900	Koryo (918–1392)	Song Dynasty		
1000				First Crusade
1100			Kamakura Period begins	
1200	Mongols invade Korea Movable type (1251)	Yuan Dynasty (1271)		
1300	Oldest Extant Movable Type Book (1377)	Yuan Dynasty ends (1368)	Marco Polo	

	Korea	China	Japan	Other Civilizations
1400	Choson (1392–1910) Han'gul (1446)	Ming Dynasty	Ashikaga Period	Gutenberg Columbus (1492)
1500	Hideyoshi Invasions		Momoyama	Martin Luther
1600	Manchu Invasion Sirhak scholars	Qing Dynasty	Tokugawa Period	Thirty Years' War
1700				American Revolution
1800	Western Learning Kanghwa Treaty (1876) Shufeldt Treaty (1882) Tonghak Rebellion (1894) Kabo Reforms (1894–1896) Independence Club (1896)	Opium War Taiping Rebellion Japan defeats China	Perry opens Japan Meiji Restoration	American Civil War
1900	Annexation by Japan (1910) March First Movement (1919) Division of Korea (1945) U.S./U.S.S.R. occupation (1945–1948) Republic of Korea (1948)	Boxer Rebellion Qing ends (1912) Twenty-One Demands Civil War China	Taft-Katsura Treaty (1905) Russo-Japanese War Rule of Korea Japan seizes Manchuria U.S. occupation of Japan	World War I Fourteen Points Great Depression World War II Cold War begins (1945)

Korea	China	Japan	Other Civilizations
Democratic People's Republic of Korea (1948)	People's Republic of China (1949)		Indo-China War
Korean War (1950–1953)			War in Vietnam
Miracle on the Han (1960s) Seoul Olympics (1988)			End Cold War (1989)
Death of Kim Il Sung (1994)	Asian Economic Crisis (1997)		
2000 June Summit (2000)			

Sources: Choi, Yong Jin, ed. 1999. *Korea: Lessons for High School Social Studies Courses.* New York: The Korea Society; Korean Overseas Information Service. 1993. *A Handbook of Korea.* Seoul: Samhwa Printing Co.; Murphey, Rhoads. 2001. *East Asia: A New History.* New York: Longman Press.

Significant People, Places, and Events

Ahn Chang-ho (1878–1939) Ahn is sometimes called Korea's number one patriot. Born in a village outside P'yongyang, he became one of the most prominent orators and energetic independence fighters. At sixteen he witnessed the Sino-Japanese War, grew incensed by his country's vulnerability to foreign powers, and spent the rest of his life trying to create a modern and independent Korea. At nineteen Ahn organized a chapter of the Independence Club in P'yongyang. From 1902 to 1906 he lived in the United States and dedicated himself to improving the lives of Koreans there. To promote Korean independence, he created the Hungsadan, which still publishes his written works. Upon his return to Korea, Ahn lifted the spirit of his people through his powerful oratory and raised funds for the independence movement. After the March 1, 1919, demonstrations, he fled to China and became one of the founders of the provisional Korean government in Shanghai. For a time he was also involved in anti-Japanese activities in Manchuria and was arrested in 1927. At a later date he was again arrested and imprisoned for four years. Upon release, he attempted to work for independence, but the Japanese restricted his activities. Ahn, also known by the pen name of Tosan, developed health problems and died at the early age of thirty-nine.

Ahn Sook-sun (1949–) In 1997, Ahn was designated a "living cultural treasure" for her extraordinary gifts as a musician. She grew up in a household of artists in North Cholla Province. Influenced by her mother's interest in traditional folk music, she learned to play the *kayagum* (12-stringed zither) and changgo (hourglass drum) and to perform the *tan'ga* (a short solo song) at an early age. When she was in elementary school, she participated in a changguk (a folk opera employing p'ansori singers). Wherever she performed, she was praised as a child prodigy. After years of special training from her uncle, she came to Seoul at the age of nineteen to study with one of the greatest music teachers in all of Korea. Since that time, she has mastered the musical styles of Korea's legendary musicians and dazzled audiences with her versatility, especially her improvised instrumental solos.

April Revolution (1960) By the spring of 1960 high school and university students were increasingly incensed by the fraud, corruption, and intimidation of the Rhee regime. When the body of a brutally murdered teenage demonstrator was found, 30,000 students marched on April 19 toward the presidential palace. Upon arrival, the police fired upon the unarmed students point-blank. As a result of these shootings, riots broke out in Seoul and other major cities. By day's end, 130 students had been killed and another 1,000 wounded in Seoul alone. Support for Rhee vanished. When 300 university professors began to demonstrate against him, even his own head of the Martial Law Command refused to fire on demonstrators. Rhee promptly resigned, and the First Republic was history. The April Revolution is also known as the Righteous Uprising of April 19th.

Catholic Persecutions (1801, 1839, 1846) One of the great attractions of Catholicism was its belief that all people are the children of God. For Korean women, Catholicism had particular appeal. The Rites Controversy was the specific issue that brought the Catholic challenge to the surface. A papal ruling in 1742 stated that Confucian ancestor worship and Christianity were incompatible. The government response to Rome was to adopt anti-Catholic edicts followed by the persecutions of Catholics. There were numerous martyrs, but the faithful were largely undeterred.

Ch'angdok-kung Palace (1405) This palace, one of the most impressive and important palaces in Korea, was built in 1405 by King T'aejong, the third ruler of the Choson dynasty, as a royal villa. Beginning with King Kwanghaegun, who moved the seat of government to Seoul in 1615, kings ruled the country from this palace for about 300 years. The palace has been listed as a World Heritage Site because it is an outstanding example of Far Eastern palace architecture and garden design. The buildings and gardens blend harmoniously with the natural setting. Since 1405, kings have continued to enlarge the grounds and add buildings. The palace was destroyed by fire several times but was rebuilt to retain the grandeur and dimensions of a Choson period royal palace.

Chong In-bo (1892–?) Scholar, patriot, and dedicated public servant, Chong is most remembered for being an accomplished historian. In his youth he loved to read and write poetry. After Japan annexed

Korea, Chong was involved in nationalist efforts as a professor at what became Yonsei University and Ehwa Womans University in Seoul. Throughout the occupation he continued to publish articles and books on Korean history. When it appeared that he would be arrested for his anti-Japanese writings, he left Seoul until liberation. In 1948 he served in the new government of South Korea and founded a national history college. When the Korean War broke out, Chong was kidnapped and taken to North Korea. Since that time, his fate has been unknown.

Chung, Myung-whun (1953–) Chung was born on January 22, 1953, in Seoul. He has become a world-renowned conductor. When he was seven, he gave his debut as a pianist. He studied at the Mannes School and then at Juilliard School in New York, where he received his diploma. At eighteen Chung conducted the Korean Symphony Orchestra. In 1978 Carlo Maria Giulini appointed him assistant for the Los Angeles Philharmonic Orchestra. In 1970, he won the *New York Times* competition for his piano performance. Since that time he has conducted in Germany, New York, and Paris.

Chung Chu-Yong (1915–2001) Known as the founder of the Hyundai Corporation, Chung Chu-Yong quit school, ran away from home at nineteen, worked in construction, acquired invaluable experience as a bookkeeper in a rice mill, and started the Hyundai Auto Repair Company in the 1940s. After establishing the Hyundai Construction Company (1947), he received major construction contracts during and after the Korean War. During the Park Chung Hee administration, he built dams, power stations, and major highways. In the early 1980s, Chung was the central figure behind Seoul winning the right to host the 1988 Olympic Games. At the age of eighty-two, he herded 500 head of cattle to North Korea through Panmunjom, heralding an appeasement with the North that ultimately led to the June 2000 Summit. After the Asian financial crisis, Kim Dae-jung pressured Hyundai and other chaebol to lower their debt/equity ratio below 200 percent and to dismantle family domination of management. In 2000, Chung and his two sons retired from active management of the company. After the restructuring, the family still had controlling interests in Hyundai Motors, Hyundai Electronics, Hyundai Construction, and Hyundai Securities. Chung once said, "Whenever there are difficulties, you grit your teeth and go on and this is how I have lived my life." By 2000, Hyundai encompassed fifty-two affiliated companies, and its combined revenues were about $150 billion. Chung Chu-Yong's autobiography is *Many Trials, But No Failures.*

Chun Doo Hwan (1931–) General, politician, and president of the Fifth Republic (1981–1988), Chun's authoritarian rule had a pivotal role in the direction of the government of the Republic of Korea. He grew up during Japanese occupation, entered the Korean Military Academy during the Korean War, spent one year training in American schools at Ft. Bragg and Ft. Benning, and received the U.S. Bronze Star for his military service in the Vietnam War. After President Park was assassinated, Chun seized power in the "12.12" Coup (December 12, 1979). After he arrested Kim Dae-jung in May 1980, massive demonstrations broke out in Kwangju followed by the arrival of tanks and machine guns that led to the tragic deaths of hundreds of civilians. The fallout from the massacre haunted Chun throughout his rule. After his presidency, he was convicted of military insurrection, treason, and the massacre of innocent citizens. He was initially sentenced to death for his crimes; however, the sentence was reduced to life in prison. In an act of reconciliation and forgiveness, Kim Dae-jung agreed to pardon the former president.

Demilitarized Zone (DMZ) Situated thirty miles northwest of Seoul, Panmunjom is the only location along the demilitarized zone (DMZ) where visitors are permitted. It is the location of the truce village where the armistice was negotiated at the end of the Korean War. Even though President Bill Clinton said that the DMZ was "the scariest place in the world," tourists flock to the site to see the truce village, learn the history of the DMZ, and gaze at North Korea. Unless they get special permission, no Korean nationals can visit this site.

General Sherman **Incident** (1866) In the early nineteenth century, Western nations tried to open Korea, known as the "hermit kingdom," to foreign trade. English, French, and Russian ships made fruitless efforts to open the doors of Korea. In 1866, an American trading ship, the *General Sherman,* sailed boldly up the Taedong River to P'yongyang, only to be set afire by a mob of local residents and soldiers. All twenty-four crewmen died. Five years later the U.S. government decided to try the same gunboat diplomacy that had proved successful in opening Japan. The Korean response was to open fire on U.S. ships. Although the United States managed to capture a few forts, the Korean government would not surrender. The U.S. fleet withdrew but would return again in 1882.

Haein-sa (802) This ninth century Buddhist temple is among Korea's most beautiful and representative. With its vast repository of Buddhist treasures it is located on Mount Kayasan, surrounded by mixed deciduous and coniferous trees. UNESCO has declared Haein-sa an international treasure. The most famous attraction is the *Tripitaka Koreana,* which is the most complete and important set of Buddhist teachings in the world. It was carved during the thirteenth century on 81,340 woodblocks. There are approximately 320 Chinese characters magnificently carved on each side of each block. The blocks are housed in two large buildings complete with a simple but effective ventilation system to prevent their deterioration. Approximately 220 monks and novices live within the temple compound.

Han Yongun (1879–1944) Han Yongun was a recognized poet, Buddhist monk, and independence fighter. In his youth he became a follower of the Tonghak movement. His father and brother were executed by the government for their involvement in the Tonghak rebellion. At sixteen he took refuge in a Buddhist temple, studied, and became a priest. He encouraged other monks to live among the poor to help improve their conditions. When Japan annexed Korea, he became a central figure in the independence movement. He signed the Declaration of Independence as a representative of the Buddhist community on March 1, 1919. As a result, he was arrested and imprisoned. In prison he was brutally beaten but managed to write letters and poetry, some of which are considered great masterpieces.

Hideyoshi Invasions (1592–1598) After Toyotomi Hideyoshi unified Japan, he planned to launch an invasion of Korea as a step to conquering the Ming empire. In 1592 the Japanese landed in Pusan and quickly moved north to Seoul, and then proceeded to take control of most of the country. Admiral Yi Sunsin and his famed turtle ships came to the rescue and began to destroy Hideyoshi's fleet. As a result, the Japanese lost their connection with their land armies, their supply routes were cut, and the grain-rich region of Cholla provinces remained safely under Korean control. Meanwhile, righteous armies of yangban, peasants, Buddhist monks, and slaves united and dealt severe blows to the Japanese military operations. Ming armies came to the rescue and helped to defeat the Japanese in bloody battles that led to the victory at Haengju in 1593, one of the most memorable triumphs against the invaders. After attempts were made to end the war, the Japanese launched a second campaign in 1597. This time, Admiral Yi trapped the Japanese fleet in a narrow channel and destroyed over three hundred ships. Hideyoshi died shortly thereafter; the Japanese forces withdrew and, for the next 250 years, adopted a policy of isolation.

Hong Nanp'a (1897–1941) A brilliant composer, violinist, and patriot, Nanp'a, as he is known, inspired people with his music during the difficult times of Japanese occupation. When he was thirteen, he was encouraged by a music teacher to study the violin, an instrument that was unfamiliar in Korea. As he traveled back and forth from home to his lessons, the Japanese police, who were also unfamiliar with the unusual shape of a violin case, frequently stopped him. He also studied music for a time in Tokyo. While in Japan, he became involved in the independence movement by distributing nationalist literature until the Japanese identified him. On his return to Korea, Nanp'a began to compose inspiring nationalist music. In 1920 he wrote one of his most famous songs, "Pongsonhwa," which became known as the song of the resistance. During the next sixteen years he taught and wrote music, became the vice-president of the future Korea Broadcasting System, and founded a philharmonic orchestra. In 1937 Nanp'a was arrested for his involvement in a nationalist organization, interrogated, and imprisoned for three months. He was never the same again and died several years later, leaving his wife and daughters behind.

Im Kwon-taek (1936–) Director Im Kwon-taek did not seem destined for a career in films. As a child he never saw a movie, and as a teen, he worked as a laborer. When he was hired in 1956 as a member of a film production crew, he performed manual labor. Four decades later, Im is internationally recognized as the most creative and gifted Korean film director. His nearly 100 films have won a host of prizes in Korea and the international film circuit. The *Chosun Daily,* Korea's oldest newspaper, cited three of his films—*Mandela, Kilsottum,* and *Sop'yonje*—as three of the top ten Korean films of all time. His latest film, *Ch'unhyang,* released in the United States in January 2001, narrates the most beloved of all Korean folk tales. In the film he combines the story of Ch'unhyang, a beautiful courtesan's daughter, with his passion for p'ansori, an ancient operatic form. His goal is to make films that reflect his life and those of the trouble-plagued Korean people.

Kabo Reforms The Kabo Reforms movement lasted from 1894 to 1896, a tumultuous two-year period when Japan dominated Korean politics as a result of its victory in the Sino-Japanese War. The officials who undertook the reforms had studied in either Japan or the United States and shared a common goal of modernizing Korea. They were committed to rejecting Chinese influence, establishing greater equality among the people, and fostering modern capitalism, values reflected in the reform measures they adopted. Measures dealt with terminating unequal foreign treaties with China, instilling national pride and patriotism, modernizing schools, abolishing the old governmental exam system, improving internal security through a new police system, and reforming the judicial and penal systems. After the Japanese destroyed the Tonghak armies in 1894 and murdered Queen Min in 1895, the king fled to the Russian legation and was temporarily out of range of Japanese control. Outraged by the brutality of the Japanese, the Koreans opposed the reforms, especially one that required men to cut their hair. The Kabo Reform movement collapsed.

Kim Chongsuk (1919–1948) Kim Chongsuk was a young communist who joined the guerrilla fighters in Manchuria during Japanese occupation. She is said to have cooked, sewed, and washed for the guerrillas and supposedly saved Kim Il Sung's life. She married Kim, who became the Supreme Leader of North Korea after World War II. In 1942, she bore him a son, Kim Jong Il, who became the leader of North Korea after his father's death in 1994. Long ignored as a partisan who fought with Kim, she ultimately became enshrined in the history of North Korea as a great patriot, dutiful wife, and devoted mother.

Kim Dae-jung (1924–) Kim Dae-jung was elected president of South Korea in 1998 during the most severe economic crisis to grip Korea and other parts of East and Southeast Asia in decades. Since his inauguration, he has worked to restore economic stability, restructure the chaebol, promote greater democracy, and improve relations with North Korea. In 2000 he was the honored recipient of the Nobel Peace Prize for his lifelong struggle for democracy and his crusade for reconciliation with North Korea. He attributes his achievements to his Catholic faith, love for his country, and the dream of reconciliation between the Koreas.

Born into a poor farm family of seven children on a small island in South Cholla Province, Kim grew up with his father's passion for books and philosophy, though without formal schooling until his family moved to the mainland. He was an excellent student and graduated at the top of his high school class, ultimately completing a master's degree in economics at Kyunghee University in Seoul. During the Korean War his future direction materialized as he saw "the suffering of the people caused by bad politics." He was captured briefly during the war but was one of the fortunate few who managed to escape. After the war, he made several attempts to win a seat in the National Assembly. He finally did in 1961, but Park Chung Hee staged a coup, took over the government, dissolved the assembly, and imprisoned him and other vocal opponents. After that time, Kim became one of the principal leaders of the political opposition. Because of his tenacious efforts to assume leadership in Korean politics, he faced death five times and endured six years of imprisonment and ten years in exile or house arrest. Not one to give up, he attempted to win the presidency in 1987 and 1992 but failed both times. After he forged a dramatic coalition with Kim Jong Pil, another opposition leader, he was elected president in 1997, at the height of the Asian economic crisis.

Kim Duk-soo (1951–) From the time he was five years old, Kim Duk-soo never considered being anything but a musician. At age five traditional music was the center of his world. He is now the most renowned traditional percussionist in Korea and a major figure in an international renaissance of modern percussion music. From the time Kim was thirteen, he performed in other countries and became aware of differing cultural and artistic traditions. Although he recognized that Korean percussion music was not well known, he believed that it had a unique beauty from the natural energy of Korean rhythms and the immense power of the traditional percussion instruments. With three other musicians, he took farmer band music and created a modern form known as samul nori, literally meaning "playing with four instruments." Owen Miller in the May 2001 issue of *Korea Now* writes that in the course of Kim's playing, "every possible permutation of rhythm seemed to be covered, every shade of sound from near inaudible softness to violent pounding, every tempo from painfully slow to heart attack—inducing speed." It is Kim's conviction that it is important to find new ways to absorb influences from other traditions and styles of music to develop a new creative culture that is both traditional and modern. He believes that when artists cling to past traditions, their art becomes lifeless, like something in a museum.

Kim Il Sung (1912–1994) Kim spent thirty-three years preparing for his political career and ruled North Korea for forty-nine years, longer than any other twentieth-century national leader. He overcame many hardships to reach and maintain the pinnacle of power, using both rewards and punishments to enforce his will. His absolute power was accepted by virtue of his long crusade against the Japanese, his belief in an independent and reunified Korea under socialism, and his charismatic personality. Endowed with boundless self-esteem, he fabricated his record, glorified his accomplishments, and built monument after monument to himself. Described as the personification of benevolence, he became known as the Great Leader and was truly loved and respected by the people.

When he was seven, his family moved from occupied Korea to Manchuria. When the Japanese took over Manchuria, Kim ended his formal education in the eighth grade and launched a political career. At seventeen, the Japanese imprisoned him for three months for organizing the Korean Communist Youth League. His military career began in his early twenties when he joined a group of guerrilla fighters called the Korean Revolutionary Army. In the early 1940s he fled to the Soviet Union. There Kim received military training, married Kim Chongsuk, and fathered his first son, Kim Jong Il. By the time the Japanese surrendered in August 1945, Kim was a captain in the Soviet army and a famous guerrilla fighter. In 1946, at the age of thirty-four, he was selected by the Soviets to chair the North Korean Interim People's Committee. Telephone poles and billboards were soon adorned with pictures and posters expressing how wise and far-sighted Kim was. By 1949 he had manipulated his way into the chairmanship of the Korean Workers' Party, a position he would hold until his death in 1994. Determined to reunify Korea by force, he started the Korean War with the reluctant support of Stalin and Mao Zedong. The entrance of 1 million Chinese into the war saved Kim from defeat. As soon as the armistice was signed in 1953, Kim began to eliminate all political opponents, took total control of the government, and proclaimed that he had defeated the Americans.

For the next forty years Kim Il Sung rebuilt North Korea and moved systematically and ruthlessly to increase his power. He was relentless in his efforts to construct a socialist society. He became adept at dealing with leaders of the communist world and obtaining financial support from China and the Soviet Union. Under his leadership the economy surpassed that of the South, and the standard of living improved enormously. By the 1960s his hold on the nation was absolute. In 1972, when he turned sixty years old, the veneration of Kim knew no bounds. The party journal said that Comrade Kim Il Sung, a genius of revolution and a great Marxist-Leninist, had lived his entire life for the people's freedom and happiness. In the same year he began to prepare his eldest son to succeed him; however, the formal announcement did not come until 1980. Until the day of his death by heart attack, he remained active. During his last years North Korea was beset with economic problems and increased political isolation. When he died, people genuinely mourned for him in the belief that the Great Leader had liberated them from the Japanese, won the Korean War, and revitalized the economy. In 1998 the position of president was abolished in order for Kim Il Sung to remain the eternal president.

Kim Jong Il (1942–) Kim used to be called Dear Leader, but since his father's death he has been more frequently referred to as the respected and beloved general, a designation more appropriate for his father than for him. Born in a Russian military camp, he was given the name of Yuri, which he kept until he was in high school. As a child he was known to be wild and constantly in trouble. After graduating from high school, he attended the Kim Il Sung University. Upon graduation in 1964 he was put in charge of his father's bodyguard, taking a position on the Korean Workers' Party Central Committee. In 1973 the thirty-one-year-old Kim was appointed to the Politburo and named director of the Organization and Guidance Department, the most powerful bureaucratic position in the party. It was clear that his father had chosen him to succeed. Kim Jong Il immediately began to consolidate his power by lavishing gifts on his supporters and eliminating all who opposed him. For most of the 1970s and 1980s he apparently ran most of the government operations. In 1992 he was appointed Supreme Commander of the Korean People's Army, in spite of the fact that he had never served. To consolidate his position, Kim had himself named chairman of the National Defense Commission. Between 1990 and 1998 the North Korean economy declined by approximately 55 percent and more than 1 million people starved to death. Kim Jong Il told his people to tighten their belts and eat two meals a day. By May 2001 international donors were feeding at least one-third of North Korea's 22 million people, but the government had not made any significant efforts to change economic policies or to reduce military expenditures, which were averaging 25 percent of the budget.

After his father's death in 1994, Kim Jong Il kept a low profile until the June Summit of 2000 with Kim Dae-jung. Prior to the summit, he never gave a public speech to a large audience nor traveled to any extent outside of North Korea. He was known to the world as a rogue dictator and described as being unpredictable, independent, arrogant, shy, disrespectful, impulsive, quick-tempered, and violent. At the June 2000 summit he surprised the world with his wit, charm, and social graces.

Kim has more control over the people than any other leader in the world. He maintains absolute power with military force and an elaborate surveillance system, and he has cut himself off from most contact with the world. His loyal supporters will not contradict him, yet his vision of what is best for the people is deeply flawed. Kongdan Oh, a North Korea specialist and staff member of the Institute for Defense Analysis, predicts in *North Korea through the Looking Glass* that Kim Jong Il will maintain his position for some time in spite of the fact that his "failed policies doom North Korea to international ostracism and poverty."

Kim Songsu (1891–1955) Kim was a well-known figure in the worlds of business, publishing, politics, and education. He is most famous for founding the *Dong-A Ilbo,* one of Korea's largest and most respected newspapers, and for being a major patron of Korea University. He was born to a family of some wealth and status, married at age twelve (a bit younger than the custom), became a father at age nineteen, and graduated from a Japanese university at age twenty-two. In 1919, he established a textile business using Korean funds and took great pride in hiring only Korean employees. He used his newspaper to keep the independence movement alive. The Japanese closed down the newspaper several times and closed it permanently in 1940 until liberation. Kim knew that the future of Korea rested on education. He helped to establish Korea University and hired an architect to design the main building after Duke University in North Carolina. A large statue of Kim stands in front of this building, and a beautiful auditorium is named after him. In the 1940s he helped to finance the Korea Democratic

Party (KDP), which supported Syngman Rhee in whose administration he served for a time before resigning over the arrest of opposition politicians. He died in 1955 after several years of poor health.

Kim Taegon (1821–1846) Kim Taegon, also called Father Kim, was the first Christian martyr of Korea. He studied theology and other subjects in Macao, fled to the Philippines during the Opium War, and, during a stay in China, became the first Korean to be an ordained Catholic priest. When he attempted to return to Korea with his fellow missionaries, he was imprisoned and later beheaded. The persecution of Catholics continued after his death. A large bronze statue of Kim stands next to the Han River in western Seoul and serves as a testimonial to Father Kim's faith.

Kim Whanki (1913–1974) Kim was a very famous artist. He grew up a free spirit, disliking authority and formality. He studied at the Nippon University in Japan and became involved in the avant-garde movement that was flourishing in Tokyo. In the 1930s he was particularly attracted to cubism, and his artwork became abstract and immersed with geometric shapes. He combined bright and warm colors with cool and dark colors to create a sense of vitality. By 1945 he was well on his way to developing a style that was distinctly Korean in its liveliness and love of tradition. He was particularly drawn to the artistic traditions of the Choson dynasty. His paintings were not drawn from nature, but combined stylized motifs from past works of art. From 1956 to 1959 he painted in Paris, but the experience had minimal impact on his style. He returned to Korea in 1965 and then traveled to New York, where he spent the remainder of his life. His work changed dramatically in his final years. The heavy texture of his earlier work disappeared, and his canvases became reminiscent of Oriental ink paintings. He began to create negative space by applications of thin paint or blank spaces on a raw canvas. Kim continued to develop this style, where the canvas seems like paper and the paint appears to be ink. Toward the end of his life his paintings became increasingly spiritual and conveyed the vitality and rhythmic quality characteristic of traditional Korean art.

Kim Woo-choong (1936–) Kim Woo-choong was one of Korea's most legendary, hardworking, and inspiring entrepreneurs. From almost nothing he built Daewoo, one of the largest and most successful companies in the history of South Korea. At age fourteen, Kim was forced to go to work to help the family survive during the Korean War. After the war he obtained a scholarship to attend Yonsei University, and by the time he was thirty, he founded Daewoo, which coincided with President Park's drive to develop an export economy. He was known to work fifteen hours a day, seven days a week. By 1978 Kim reached his goal of beating out Samsung Company by exporting over $705 million to become number one. Over the years he gave financial support to many foundations and scholarship funds. Until 1999, Kim was revered as a man who built a small textile business into Korea's second-largest industrial conglomerate. Since then, Kim has been charged with manipulating accounting books, stashing illegal funds, and securing illegal loans, whose amounts have yet to be identified. Prosecutors alleged that Kim and his associates organized what is considered Asia's biggest single financial fraud—false accounting that inflated the value of Daewoo's equity by $32 million. In July 2001 the Seoul District Court found nineteen former Daewoo Group executives guilty of distorting financial records and using falsified financial documents to obtain funds for their companies. The executives were fined $20 billion, and five of them were sentenced to jail. These are the largest fines ever levied by a Korean court. The prosecuting attorneys claimed that the ruling signified Kim Dae-jung's commitment to cleaning up the nation's corporate practices. Kim remained a fugitive, traveling between Europe and Africa to avoid charges including fraud and embezzlement.

Kim Young Sam (1927–) Kim Young Sam was inaugurated president of the Seventh Republic (1993–1998) and was the first duly elected civilian president in thirty-two years. He graduated from Seoul National University, served in the Korean War, and won his first election to the National Assembly at age twenty-seven. He became a vocal opponent of both the Park and Chun regimes, which caused him to be placed under house arrest and imprisoned. In 1987 he ran against Kim Dae-jung, Kim Jong Pil, and Roh Tae Woo for the presidency and lost. Undaunted he tried again in 1992 and became president in 1993. He encouraged political openness, deregulation of the economy, and globalization. He was instrumental in placing on trial former presidents Roh Tae Woo and Chun Doo Hwan on sedition charges; however, the Hanbo scandal and his son's conviction for bribery and tax evasion severely damaged his reputation. His popularity continued to decline as the onslaught of the Asian economic crisis hit South Korea.

King Sejong (1397–1450) King Sejong (r. 1419–1450), one of the greatest kings in Korean history, is famous for his commitment to improving the quality of life for his people and for the invention of the Korean written language, han'gul. In his youth he was passionate about learning, and this quest for knowledge motivated him for the rest of his life. He was fascinated by the world of science, especially astronomy. During his reign, constellations were charted, rain gauges were refined, and sundials and water clocks were developed. Handbooks to improve agricultural production and medicine were completed. He sought out talented people to serve, trained them in the art of good government according to the Confucian classics, and made sure that their talents were utilized. His main goal was to find ways to improve literacy. King Sejong considered his greatest accomplishment the creation of han'gul, a phonetic writing system that was easier to learn than the complicated Chinese writing system. Great political achievements included the defeat of the Japanese pirates who menaced the coasts and the extension of the northern border of Korea to the Yalu River.

Korean American Treaty (1882) The first treaty of friendship and commerce between the United States and Korea was signed in 1882 in what is now called Inch'on. A Chinese statesman and Commodore Robert Shufeldt, the American negotiator, worked out the terms of the treaty, the first signed with a Western power. It was an unequal treaty typical of the age of imperialism. Korea understood one of the clauses to mean that the United States would come to its aid in any circumstance, which was not true. This treaty was followed by similar agreements with European nations.

Korean War (1950–1953) On June 25, 1950, in an attempt to reunify the country, a large military force of the Democratic People's Republic (North Korea) with Soviet-made heavy tanks crossed the thirty-eighth parallel and launched a well planned attack on South Korea. The attack prompted U.S. President Harry S Truman to send American troops—without a declaration of war—to stop the communist aggression, which he believed was masterminded by the Soviet Union. When the United Nations Security Council voted to defend South Korea, the Soviet representative was not present to veto the resolution because the Soviets were boycotting the United Nations to protest its refusal to grant membership to the People's Republic of China. The first American soldiers could not stop the North Korean advance, and within weeks, the South Koreans and Americans were pushed back to a small area around Pusan. Truman reconsidered the American objective of containment and advocated the goal of reunification of Korea by force. In September 1950, General MacArthur executed a daring amphibious landing at Inch'on, moved inland, and liberated Seoul. The UN forces then moved beyond the thirty-eighth parallel and advanced to the Yalu River, the border between North Korea and China. Suddenly 150,000 Chinese soldiers crossed the river, forced the UN soldiers into quick retreat, invaded South Korea, and retook Seoul. In early 1951 the UN counterattacked. When the front stabilized, the United States and Moscow were receptive to negotiations; however, MacArthur called for an attack on communist China. Truman promptly fired him for insubordination. In July armistice talks began; however, the fighting continued for two more years. One of the most contentious issues was the fate of thousands of POWs. After the death of Stalin in 1953, a settlement was reached. An armistice was signed on July 27, 1953, and a four-mile-wide demilitarized zone (DMZ) was established across the peninsula. There has never been a formal end to the conflict. Marking the fifty-first anniversary of the outbreak of the Korean War, Kim Dae-jung, on June 25, 2001, said that his country and North Korea should sign a formal peace treaty.

Kwangju Uprising (May 1980) On December 12, 1979, in what is now called the "12.12" coup, Major General Chun Doo Hwan took control over the military of the Republic of South Korea. In response to the Yusin Constitution (which removed restrictions on the term of office of a president) and Chun's declaration of martial law, students and citizens took to the streets of Kwangju. With the arrival of the army, hundreds if not thousands of citizens were killed. During the Kwangju demonstrations, citizens appealed in vain to the U.S. embassy to intervene. The United States took no action, and many South Koreans concluded that it supported Chun. The tragic developments led to increased opposition to the Chun regime and anti-American sentiments. Kwangju has become a symbol of the aspirations of the South Korean people for democracy.

Kyongju For almost 1,000 years Kyongju was the capital of the Silla dynasty. Today the city is an outdoor museum that includes tombs of the royalty, temples, shrines, palaces, gardens, and castles. In the forested mountains surrounding the city there are thousands of

Buddhist shrines, temples, rock carvings, pagodas, and statues. Historic sites that are particularly recommended for tourists are Ch'omsongdae (an ancient stone observatory built in the 7th century), Punhwangsa Pagoda (built by Queen Sondak in the 7th century), Pulguk-sa (the finest example of Silla architecture and constructed in the 8th century), and Sokkuram grotto (8th century). Kyongju exemplifies the brilliance of the golden age of Silla culture. In 1979 the United Nations Educational, Scientific, and Cultural Organization (UNESCO) recognized the city as one of the world's ten historic sites.

Lee Taeyong (1914–1998) Lee Taeyong, an advocate for women's rights, became the first female lawyer in South Korea. She graduated from Ehwa Womans University in 1936, married an influential politician, became a devoted wife and mother, and crusaded for more legal rights for women. She created the Legal Aid Center, the first institution in South Korea that focused specifically on resolving women's problems, such as domestic violence and conflicts with in-laws. In order to improve a woman's legal rights, Lee successfully lobbied the government to create a family court to hear cases involving domestic abuse and divorce. Her efforts led to the passage of a family law that provided rights of inheritance and child custody, an essential step to guarantee greater equality for women. She died at the age of eighty-four.

March First Movement (March 1, 1919) Japan firmly established rule over Korea in 1910. President Woodrow Wilson's famous Fourteen Points (1918) raised the hopes of people throughout the world when he championed the concept of national autonomy and self-determination. The leaders of the Korean independence movement adopted a plan to have a nationwide demonstration on March 1, 1919, expressing the desire of the Korean people to be free and independent of Japan. Thirty-three Korean nationalists signed the Declaration of Independence, which was proclaimed at rallies throughout the country. The response of the Japanese was immediate and brutal. More than 500 demonstrators were killed, approximately 26,000 were arrested, and thousands of homes and churches were burned. Yu Kwansun, a teenage protester, was arrested and tortured, and died in prison. It was not until August 15, 1945, that the hopes of the March First Movement were realized.

Mongol Invasions The Mongols invaded Korea in 1231 during the Koryo Dynasty (918–1392). When they invaded, the court moved to

Kanghwa Island. Over the next twenty-five years, the Mongols invaded the country six more times, slaughtered the Koryo Dynasty's peasant troops, took more than 200,000 captives, and destroyed great cultural relics, such as the Tripitaka woodblocks that had been produced 200 years earlier. Eventually peace was established, but the Koryo prince was forced to acknowledge the suzerainty of the Mongol dynasty (Yuan) in China. The kings were forced to marry princesses of the Yuan dynasty and to assist in the invasion attempts against Japan. By the mid-fourteenth century the Yuan dynasty was in decline; however, the Mongols left bitter memories.

Nuclear Crisis of 1994 In June 1994 the United States nearly went to war with North Korea to stop its nuclear weapons program. The International Atomic Energy Agency (IAEA), having failed to gain full access to the North's nuclear sites to determine whether it had reprocessed plutonium, turned the matter over to the United Nations Security Council. The United States was hoping to get enough votes to impose economic sanctions on P'yongyang, which North Korea regarded as a declaration of war. President Clinton dispatched substantial reinforcements to South Korea. As tensions continued to rise, the U.S. Command moved ahead with military preparations, and Seoul engaged in the largest civil defense exercise in many years. Former president Jimmy Carter then played a historic role on the peninsula. Acting as a private citizen, he crossed the DMZ with his wife to meet Kim Il Sung. Their meeting paved the way for an agreement that became the October Framework. It promised P'yongyang that in return for freezing its graphite reactors and returning to full inspections under the Nuclear Non-Proliferation Treaty, a consortium of nations would supply light-water reactors to help solve the North's energy problems. Less than three weeks later Kim Il Sung died. Seven years later, North Korea remained a nuclear threat, although not as great a threat as it would have been had the framework not been negotiated.

Pang Chong Hwan (1899–1931) Pang Chong Hwan, known as Sop'a, was an independence fighter, children's advocate, and founder of Children's Day, which is celebrated on May 5. During Japanese occupation Sop'a helped to publish an independence newspaper. Because of this involvement, he was arrested and tortured. When he refused to confess, he was released. He then returned to publishing the nationalist newspaper. In the 1920s he started a youth association to encourage the young to participate in sports and the arts and founded Korea's first children's magazine. In order to attract attention to the needs of children, he founded Children's Day, a much-celebrated holiday in South Korea. He died at the young age of thirty-two of a heart attack.

Park Chung Hee (1917–1979) Park Chung Hee was the third president of the Republic of Korea. Park, whose father had fought with the Tonghak rebels, was raised in poverty. He trained at officer's school in Japan during occupation and graduated from the Korean Military Academy during U.S. occupation. On May 16, 1961, Major General Park Chung Hee in a military coup seized control of the government of President Chang Myon and established military rule that lasted for the next thirty-two years. His term as president was marked by extraordinary economic development, but it also included political and social repression. He was assassinated in 1979 by one of his own men, the head of the Korean Central Intelligence Agency.

Rhee, Syngman (1875–1965) Syngman Rhee, patriot and first president of the Republic of Korea, led his country during some of the most turbulent years of its modern history. Prior to the presidency he was active in the Independence Club, imprisoned and tortured for his revolutionary activities against the pro-Japanese government, and elected president of the Korean government in exile. At the age of seventy-three, he was elected president of the First Republic (1948–1960). During the difficult years of the Korean War, Rhee became increasingly autocratic, and thousands of leftists were executed without trial. After being reelected several times, he became increasingly unpopular because of his oppressive tactics and ruthless suppression of the opposition. When it appeared to the public that the 1960 election was rigged, there were massive demonstrations that demanded his resignation. He resigned on April 27, 1960, and went into exile in Hawaii, where he died five years later.

Roh Tae Woo (1932–) Roh Tae Woo, president of South Korea (1988–1993), grew up during the final and most harsh years of Japanese occupation. A close friend of future president Chun Doo Hwan, he became the head of South Korea's elite First Division during the Vietnam War. He supported Chun's military coup after the assassination of President Park in 1979 and served in varied cabinet posts. Growing opposition to repressive rule led to popular demands for democracy, and the public considered Chun's choice of Roh as his replacement, just one more military dictator. But Roh surprised everyone by announcing his support for democratic reforms. In 1988, in the first peaceful transition of power in modern Korean history, he won a free election and began a five-year term as president. He took steps toward reconciliation with North Korea, established formal diplomatic relations with Moscow and Beijing, and allowed for more press freedoms. Since the constitution prevented him from running for a second term, he supported Kim Young Sam for president. In 1995 Roh was charged with accepting $654 million in secret political donations. In 1996 he was tried, along with Chun, convicted, and sentenced to serve twenty-two and one-half years in prison. President Kim Young Sam pardoned him in 1997.

Samyongdang (1544–1610) At thirteen, Samyongdang decided to study Buddhism and become a monk. In his thirties he was widely admired within the Son sect (Zen). When Hideyoshi invaded Korea in 1592, Samyongdang organized a Buddhist army and successfully repulsed the invaders; however, the Japanese managed to take many prisoners of war. The warrior monk turned special envoy to Japan to negotiate their release. His efforts were very successful, and within a year, over 3,000 prisoners were released. Later he moved to the Haein-sa Buddhist Temple to restore his health but died within the year. There is a monument in his memory at this spot, one of the most famous and beautiful temples in all of Korea.

Queen Sondak (r. 632–647) Queen Sondak was one of the most influential queens in Korean history. In a period of more than 1,000 years, only two other queens achieved as much authority and influence. Known as a kind, respectful, wise, and farsighted leader, she ruled at a time when there was intense rivalry between Silla and the kingdoms of Koguryo and Paekche. By initiating a policy with Tang China, the queen paved the way for the eventual unification of Korea. She not only concerned herself with the defense and security of Silla and her throne but also with improving conditions of her people and supporting cultural advancement. The famed Buddhist temples of Hwangnyong-sa (a nine-story wooden pagoda) and Ch'omsongdae (one of the oldest astronomical observatories in the world) were built under her direction.

Russo-Japanese War (1904–1905) Tension built up between Russia and Japan after the former made inroads into Manchuria and acquired leases on Port Arthur and Dairen. Japan decided to go to war and, contrary to world expectations, won a series of quick victories, forcing Russia to sue for peace. The Treaty of Portsmouth ended the war and established international recognition of Japan's supremacy in Korea.

Seoul Olympics (1988) For most of the world the 1988 Olympics was a great athletic event, but for the people of South Korea, it was the Republic's coming out party, a chance to show the world that it was strong, highly industrialized, and prosperous. The South hoped that the Olympics would stimulate its economic growth and improve its global stature. The North resented Seoul's hosting of this great event. North Korean athletes did not participate in the games, which were not broadcast there.

Sirhak Movement (Practical Learning) During the seventeenth century, as economic and political problems grew more severe, a group of Confucian scholars advocated reforms and started the Sirhak movement. They challenged the abstract theories of the neo-Confucian scholars and recommended the adoption of practical solutions to solve the political, economic, and social problems. They resented the monopoly of power held by the yangban and their own exclusion from important government positions. To reform the condition of agriculture, the Sirhak thinkers advocated an agricultural economy based on the independent, self-employed farmer. The movement also incorporated ideas to improve the penal code. Some Sirhak thinkers from Seoul took issue with the emphasis on agricultural reform and promoted the gradual expansion of commercial and manufacturing to improve the standard of living of Choson society. Their writings included a severe indictment of the yangban class. They recommended the radical idea that government functionaries should be educated professionals drawn from all walks of life. This movement, which promoted the rights of man and social equality, continued to grow throughout the eighteenth century and ultimately had a profound impact on the reform and progressive movements of the late nineteenth.

Shin Saimdang (1504–1551) One of the most famous and respected women of Korean history, Shin Saimdang is admired for being the ideal mother, wife, and daughter. She was also a respected painter, embroiderer, and poet. Her son, Yi I (Yulgok), is one of the most celebrated Confucian scholars.

Sino-Japanese War (1894–1895) At the time of the largest peasant uprising in Korean history, the Tonghak Rebellion, the Korean government asked China for help. After China sent in troops, Japan decided that only a war with China would remove Chinese influence in Korea. The combined forces of China and Japan defeated the Tonghak. China then proposed that both forces leave Korea, but Japan was determined to pursue its expansionist ambitions. The war began with the sudden seizure of the royal residence, Kyongbok Palace. Japanese troops fought the Chinese on land and sea and quickly won in impressive victories. A total victory culminated in the Shimonoseki Treaty, which recognized Korea's full independence from China and ceded Taiwan and the Liaotung Peninsula (part of Manchuria) to Japan.

Sydney Olympics (2000) On September 15, 2000, more than 110,000 fans at the Olympic Opening Ceremonies cheered as the athletes from North and South Korea marched together for the first time, waving a unification flag and holding hands before a standing ovation in Sydney, Australia. The marchers wore identical uniforms with a badge bearing a blue map of the Korean peninsula. Despite the joint march, the Koreas competed in the Games as two different entities under their own flags and names. South Korea won eight gold, nine silver, and eleven bronze medals to finish twelfth in the overall medal standings. It dominated archery and Taekwondo and came in second-best among Asian countries, beaten only by China. North Korea had its worst Olympics ever, finishing with a silver and three bronze medals for sixtieth place.

Taft-Katsura Agreement (1905) In this treaty between the United States and Japan, President Theodore Roosevelt gave approval for Japan's supremacy over Korea with the understanding that Japan would recognize U.S. hegemony over the Philippines. Horace Allen, the U.S. minister in Seoul, tried to prevent Japan from taking Korea, but Roosevelt would not listen.

The Tonghak Movement (Eastern Learning) The Tonghak movement was introduced to Korea in the mid-nineteenth century, outlived its founder, Ch'oe Cheu, and influenced the course of modern Korean history. The movement, which was both religious and social, drew support from impoverished peasants who were attracted to its egalitarian ideas. Its goal was to fight against corrupt government, social injustice, the privileged yangban, and Catholicism. Its founder, whose desire was to rescue the suffering masses both spiritually and physically, combined what he believed to be the best elements of Confucianism, Buddhism, and Daoism in order to oppose Western Learning (Catholicism) with Eastern Learning; however, his doctrine actually included some elements of Catholicism and Shamanism. The movement supported the belief that God and humans are one in spirit and that everyone is equal regardless of class. The government grew alarmed that Tonghak objectives would soon be achieved. Subsequently, Ch'oe Cheu was arrested and executed for sowing discord in society and misleading the people. For a time the movement weakened, but the leadership of Ch'oe's successor, Ch'oe Sihyong, brought it new vitality. In the 1890s it steadily grew as economic and political conditions worsened under the powerful Queen Min. Protests escalated and exploded in a full-scale uprising, the Tonghak Revolution of 1894, the largest peasant uprising in Korean history. When the government called for the support of Chinese troops to suppress the rebellion, the Japanese decided to challenge China, and the result was the Sino-Japanese War. Tragically, the movement that Ch'oe founded to rid Korea of foreign influence paved the way for Japanese control over the entire peninsula.

Treaty of Kanghwa (1876) In 1876 Japan sent General Kuroda Kiyotaka with a sizable force of warships to demand that Korea enter treaty negotiations. Although a majority of Choson's high officials did not want to deal with Japan, the king was persuaded to sign the Treaty of Kanghwa, Korea's first modern treaty. Signed under pressure, it contained provisions typical of an unequal treaty. The most important article proclaimed that Korea was an independent nation. Japan's objective was to pave the way for its aggression because China for centuries had claimed suzerainty over Korea.

Wang Kon (877–943) Wang Kon, known posthumously as T'aejo, unified the later Three Kingdoms after a period of intense warfare on the peninsula and established the Koryo dynasty (918–1392) with Kaesong as its capital. He named the dynasty Koryo, a shortened form of the name Koguryo, meaning "high mountains and sparkling waters." Once he had defeated his enemies, he was particularly adept in placating them by giving them land and government positions and allowing them to marry women of the former Silla royal family. Before his death he drafted ten injunctions for his successors to observe.

Western Learning (Catholicism) Jesuit missionaries in Ming China introduced Catholicism to a visiting Korean scholar in the early seventeenth century. The Sirhak thinkers were the first group to take an intellectual interest in Catholicism, or Western Learning as they called it; however, they were not inclined to adopt it. Support for Western Learning grew after Yi Sunghun (1756–1801), a scholar baptized by a Jesuit priest in Peking in 1783, returned to Korea with many religious books to establish Catholicism in Korea. The number of converts grew rapidly in spite of the opposition of the government and the yangban class. What Sirhak converts seemed to have found in Catholicism was a means to struggle against the social and political inequalities of the Choson dynasty. Catholicism brought renewed hope and the promise of creating a heavenly kingdom on earth. The government began to fight back by persecuting Catholics after 1791; however, it could not eradicate Western Learning's deep roots.

Wonhyo (617–686) Wonhyo was one of the most respected Buddhists of the Silla period. As a teacher and one of the most prolific writers of his time, he greatly influenced many young people. He wrote some 180 volumes on a wide range of topics in an attempt to synthesize the various Buddhist sects in China and Korea. The principal focus of his life was to bring Buddhist faith and practices to commoners. He stressed that all people can be reborn in the "Pure Land," or Western Paradise, where the Buddha dwells if they have a sincere heart. At one point he fell in love with a widowed princess and fathered a son, Sol Ch'ong, who became one of the great sages of Korea. Wonhyo had broken his vow of celibacy, so he no longer wore a Buddhist robe but wore ordinary clothes as he traveled the countryside.

Yi Hwang or T'oegye (1501–1570) Yi Hwang, whose pen name was T'oegye, was Korea's foremost Confucian scholar. His portrait appears on the 1,000-won banknote. His writings contributed to the spread of neo-Confucianism in Japan during the Tokugawa period and are known throughout the world. At the age of twelve he began his quest to understand philosophy. His motto was "Sincerity and Reverence." In 1515 he established the Tosan Sowon Confucian Institute in Andong, where he studied and lectured. For several hundred years the institute was the most highly regarded school for those who aspired to be civil servants. The buildings have been converted to a museum containing nearly 5,000 of his works.

Yi I (1536–1584) Yi I (pen name Yulgok) is one of the most famous sages and Confucian philosophers. He is widely respected for his interpretations of previous Confucian scholars and his own views on Confucianism. With the assistance of his educated and devoted mother (see Sin Saimdang), Yi I completed the basic studies in the classics by the age of seven, composed poetry at eight, and passed the literary civil service exams when he was thirteen. He continued his education by studying the Buddhist scriptures and the Daoist classics. When he was twenty-nine, he passed the civil service examination. Rising to the highest levels of government, he served as governor, vice director of the Royal Academy, minister of justice, and minister of defense. Two years before his early death at age forty-eight, he completed one of his most important works, *A Key to Annihilating Ignorance (Kyongmong Yogyol)*.

Yi Sunsin (1545–1598) One of the greatest military heroes in Korean history, Admiral Yi Sunsin and his famous turtle boats defeated the Japanese in 1592. The great conqueror, Toyotomi Hideyoshi, planned to conquer the world starting with Korea. With only twelve ships in his fleet, the admiral was able to destroy over three hundred of the enemy's ships. As the Japanese retreated, Yi Sunsin was killed by a stray bullet.

Yu Kwansun (1904–1920) Considered by many to be Korea's Joan of Arc, Yu Kwansun, at the age of sixteen, became one of the most famous independence fighters. After she helped plan the March 1, 1919, demonstration against Japanese occupation, she continued to organize protests, was arrested and tortured, and died along with an estimated 7,500 Koreans who participated in demonstrations that swept the country. Since her death, she has become an important symbol of the patriotic spirit of Korean youth. In her lifetime she represented something that was new, but common now: the participation of women in political activism.

Yusin (Revitalizing Reforms) (1972–1979) In 1972 President Park announced what is known as the Yusin system, which began the Fourth Republic. Citing domestic and international insecurity, Park proclaimed martial law and carried out what some call a "coup in office." The Yusin Constitution made it possible for Park to remain in office indefinitely through well-controlled electoral procedures, to dismiss the cabinet and the prime minister, and to dominate the

National Assembly. Through this system, he transformed the presidency into a legal dictatorship. All political parties were dissolved, and restrictions were placed on free speech and the press. By the end of 1972, Park was more firmly entrenched than ever. Although his control appeared total, the price was high. It ultimately led to civil unrest, betrayal, and death by assassination.

Korean Language, Food, and Etiquette

Many people think that their own language is easy, while all foreign languages are difficult. Actually Korean is among the easier languages to learn, much easier than English. The language of the Korean people is simple to repeat because each syllable has equal value. The vowel sounds are distinct and regular. There are few stressed syllables. Neither is there any sharp discrimination of gender in the personal pronoun. Verbs have no special distinction for third person, singular or plural. There are ten vowels, eleven vowel blends, and fourteen consonants. These sounds could be memorized in an hour or two and recognized in listening to a person speak Korean on audiotape. With practice on a few simple phrases, an English-speaking person could make herself understood quite readily.

Of course, building a vocabulary in another language is a long process that requires hours and hours of repetition. One must combine the vowel sounds with the consonant sounds. Here again practice makes perfect. Like the opera singer, we can do our *ba, be, bi, bo, bu, na, ne, ni, no, nu,* etc. Because they learn their own language piecemeal, on an as-needed basis, children do not have to go through this systematic preparation. And neither would foreign adult learners, if they had to survive in a totally Korean-language world. That is the saturation approach to learning a language.

For the methodical late learner, matters are made much easier by the creation of a written system for reproducing Korean sounds. This system is called han'gul and was invented in 1446 under Sejong, one of the wisest kings of the Choson Dynasty. Before the invention of han'gul, only a few of the elite could read and write Korean, and they had to use Chinese characters, which were totally foreign. This approach was difficult because it took an enormous amount of time to memorize thousands of Chinese characters, each representing a spoken word. Thus most people remained illiterate.

Using a regular phonetic system of writing eventually produced widespread literacy. Commoners could now read and understand their language without actually hearing a sound. Literacy allows any visual learners the opportunity to see the sounds they hear, in this way reinforcing the learning process. An added feature of han'gul is

241

that written characters over a store without display windows let the shopper know what is inside without actually having to enter.

The Korean language is distantly related to Mongolian (Altaic) and Japanese. Once there were two forms of the language: the Puyo in the North and the Han in the South. In the seventh century, the unified kingdom of Silla brought about one language. In the tenth century the Kaesong dialect became standard. It is not at all related to Chinese, except for the fact that Chinese characters were used to represent different words. All spoken languages are living and thus change. With globalization certain common words, especially those connected with air travel and computers, are creeping into vocabularies all over the world.

THE WRITTEN LANGUAGE

The vocabulary of the modern Korean language is made up of about 40 percent indigenous words and 60 percent loan words, the vast majority of which are Chinese. One result is a dual system of native and Sino-Korean numerals. Another is that more formal or academic works are written in mixed script, using Chinese characters *(han-cha)* and han'gul. In order to read the daily newspaper, the average person must know at least 1,800 hancha. College students must know twice as many. In recent years it has become less common to write Sino-Korean characters in newspapers, books, periodicals, and academic journals in South Korea. Many people express concern that the origins and meaning of the Chinese characters will ultimately be lost. North Korea abolished the use of hancha for purely nationalistic reasons.

Although han'gul is described as a simple and scientific alphabet, learning how to use it is difficult. The formation of words is very different from that of the Western alphabet. Writing syllables is such that they resemble a Chinese character. For example, the syllable *han* in the word *han'gul* is formed by an *h* in the top left corner, an *a* in the top right corner, and an *n* at the bottom, the whole syllabic group forming what looks like a Chinese character. It is possible to create over 2,350 characters in this way. Spaces between written words are often deleted, causing considerable difficulty for those who are attempting to learn the written language. Another challenge is the fact that the pronunciation of Korean words has changed over time. Many words are not pronounced as they are spelled. Korean adjectives have conjugations like verbs.

The order of words in a clause or sentence is subject, object, and verb; qualifying elements precede the objects qualified; dependent clauses precede independent clauses. Culturally the language reflects a rigidly hierarchical social structure. Words must be chosen carefully depending upon whether you are addressing a child, relative, adult, employer, or colleague. In preference to actual names, titles are often used in daily life.

An additional problem is that the official romanized spelling has changed over the years. In fact, the Ministry of Culture and Tourism

---

The Korean Alphabet (Han'gǔl 한글)

Consonants

Letter	Pronunciation	Letter	Pronunciation
ㄱ	k/g	ㅋ	k'
ㄴ	n	ㅌ	t'
ㄷ	t/d	ㅍ	p'
ㄹ	r/l	ㅎ	h
ㅁ	m	ㄲ	kk
ㅅ	s	ㄸ	tt
ㅂ	p/b	ㅆ	ss
ㅇ	ng	ㅉ	tch
ㅈ	ch/j	ㅃ	pp
ㅊ	ch'		

The sound of the consonants ㄱ, ㄴ, ㄹ, ㅂ, and ㅈ may be either voiced (e.g., g, b, j) unvoiced (e.g., k, p, ch) depending on the sounds preceding and succeeding it. Written consonant sounds often change depending on the sounds before and after it. The consonant ㅇ acts as a place marker for sound clusters that begin with a vowel sound. See below for some examples.

Vowels

Basic Vowels	Pronunciation	Diphthongs	Pronunciation
ㅏ	a as in father	ㅐ	ae as in ankle
ㅑ	ya as in yard	ㅒ	yae as in yea
ㅓ	ǒ as the o in son	ㅔ	e as in egg
ㅕ	yǒ as in young	ㅖ	ye as in yellow
ㅗ	o as in oak	ㅘ	wa as in water
ㅛ	yo as in yo-yo	ㅙ	wae as in weather
ㅜ	u as in blue	ㅚ	woe as in way
ㅠ	yu as in you	ㅝ	wǒ as in won
ㅡ	ǔ as the u in pull	ㅞ	we as in weight
ㅣ	i as in India	ㅟ	wi as in we
		ㅢ	ǔi = u in pull + i in police; often pronounced as "i" or "e"

Examples

Each written word in Korean is formed from syllabic components. The first consonant is always placed to the left or above the vowel or diphthong and may be followed by another consonant or consonant cluster. Syllables are read top to bottom or left to right to down. The combination of the letters "si" (시) is always pronounced "shi."

Han'gŭl	Transliteration/Pronunciation	Meaning
산	san	mountain
불	pul	fire
신앙	sinang (pronounced "shinang")	faith, belief
태도	t'aedo	attitude
행복	haengbok	happiness
합리	hap-ri=> hamni	rationality
학문	hak-mun=> hangmun	learning, scholarship
외국사람	woeguk saram	foreigner

---

announced a new system of romanization in 2000. This replaces the one that has been widely used in Korea and abroad since 1984. One can also find several different romanizations of words, making place names especially problematic. The letters *ch* and *j, b* and *p, d* and *t,* and *s* and *sh* are often used interchangeably. Examples include the different spellings of the famous temple, *Bulguksa* and *Pulsuksa,* and the city, *Inch'on* and *Incheon.* It is wise to be aware of these discrepancies and to know enough han'gul to be able to arrive at your intended destination and not somewhere else.

THE SPOKEN LANGUAGE

Koreans will appreciate the effort you make to speak their language. If you mispronounce a word, they will be courteous but will probably correct you. Any investment you make will bring substantial advantages, whether you are visiting or conducting business. For anyone intending to spend a substantial amount of time in Korea, learning han'gul is a must.

Think of words as being composed of syllables, each syllable taking one beat. Each syllable must be pronounced clearly and with the same amount of stress. Each syllable must be equal in length. When you pronounce the consonants *pp, tt, kk,* and *tch,* give them an especially strong emphasis. The *s* sounds very weak. The Korean sound *ss* is tense and sounds like a very emphatic English *s.* There are many more rules, but these suggestions will give you a start. There is considerable information in most travel guides and over the Internet.

The following phrases are divided by syllable and are very useful Korean expressions:

How are you? The following is appropriate any time of the day and also means good morning, good afternoon, and good evening.
an-nyng ha-sim-ni-kka 안녕하십니까?
an-nyŏng ha-se-yo 안녕하세요?

I am fine, thanks.
ye, choh-sŭm-ni-da 예, 좋습니다
ye, chal chi-naem-ni-da 예, 잘지냅니다

Hello (When on the telephone)
ye-bo se-yo 여보세요

Nice to meet you. (When meeting someone for the first time)
man-na-so pan-gap-sŭm-ni-da 만나서 반갑습니다

My name is Mr. Smith.
che i-rŭm-ŭn Sŭmisŭ im-ni-da 제 이름은 스미스 입니다

Welcome (Please come in)
ŏ-sŏ o-sip-si-o 어서 오십시오

Goodbye (Said by host, or person staying behind)
an-nyŏng-hi ka-sip-si-o 안녕히 가십시오

Goodbye (Said by guest, or person leaving)
an-nyŏng-hi ka-sip-si-o 안녕히 계십시오

Thank you
kam-sa ham-ni-da 감사합니다

You are welcome
ch'ŏn-man e-yo 천만에요

I am sorry
mi-an ham-ni-da 미안합니다
choe-song ham-ni-da 죄송합니다

Excuse me
sil-lye ham-ni-da 실례합니다

Just a moment (informal)
cham-kkan man-yo 잠깐만요

I like Korea
han-gug-ŭl choh-a-ham-ni-da 한국을 좋아합니다

Yes
  ne 네
  ye 예

No
  a-ni-o 아니오

I like it
  choh-a-ham-ni-da 좋아합니다
  choh-a-hae-yo 좋아해요

I am hungry
  pae ko-p'a-yo 배 고파요

I am thirsty
  mogi mal-la-yo 목이 말라요

Bathroom
  hwa-jang-sil 화장실
  (Outside of Seoul you may encounter single-sex bathrooms.)

FOOD

Traditional dietary customs are evident in everyday foods, those eaten on special occasions, and those that are preserved for later use. Although many Koreans are receptive to foreign food trends, their indigenous dietary culture reflects ancient tradition. They take unusual pride in preserving the recipes and cooking methods of their ancestors. Food plays an essential role in traditional rites of passage. Dietary customs reveal the importance of Confucian values, family and community traditions, and the veneration of nature. The ancient ritual of drinking and singing after a meal persists. These customs serve as a foundation for the nutritious and distinctive flavor combinations particular to Korean cuisine.

Aside from the impact of tradition, food is particularly significant to the older generation. Those old enough to remember the Korean War and its aftermath vividly remember the hard times when people were starving. There is also a preoccupation about health. Mothers and grandmothers spend considerable time making sure that family members, especially the children, get the nutrition they need. Even though the standard of living has improved remarkably, the older generation continues to value food as if it were rationed. Children grow up hearing *"mogo, mogo,"* meaning "Eat! Eat!" Koreans insist that their guests eat more than they want. This insistence is based on the host's desire to appear generous and concerned about the visitor's health.

Korean food is particularly appealing to foreigners because of the wide range of selections, delicious flavors, and nutritional value. Rice remains the staple of the diet and an essential part of every meal, including breakfast. The variety one experiences in eating Korean food is provided by side dishes. The food is known for its distinct aromas and peppery tastes. Chili and pepper are used in abundance, with garlic and sesame (seeds, oil, and paste), to produce strong, dominant flavors. Beef, seafood, and beans are the main ingredients used by the cook, supplemented by eggplant, great amounts of cabbage, radish, and cucumber.

Everyday food is relatively simple, but a banquet to celebrate a wedding, a sixtieth birthday, the autumn festival, or a similar occasion is as lavish as possible. Important occasions may offer as many as thirty dishes that include salads and an assortment of different kinds of kimchee.

Common Korean Dishes

Rice A discussion of food must start with rice, the basic food of the people. In fact, the Korean expression for "Have you had breakfast?" is "Have you eaten rice today?" A simple meal can be made of a bowl of rice and a few flavorful side dishes, such as kimchee or soup. Koreans grow two main varieties. One is *tapkok,* rice that grows in lowland paddies everywhere. It is slightly sticky when served. The other main variety is upland rice, usually dried and milled for flour and beer brewing. In the past, rice meant wealth and was a tangible way for farming people to estimate their worth. In hard times rice was equated with life itself.

Kimchee People who know little about Korea know that kimchee is the national dish. It has been part of the diet for centuries, and cooks boast that there are over two hundred variations, depending on region, season, and personal preference. It is the ubiquitous side dish and is made with a uniquely pungent mixture of fermented vegetables, usually cabbages and radishes. Koreans are passionate about kimchee and have been heard to say that it nourishes the soul as much as the body. Students who live abroad have experienced withdrawal symptoms without it. Every autumn there is a ritual in every household. It is the time when cabbage is particularly sweet and tender and the best time for making kimchee. The cabbage is cut up, salted and seasoned with chili, pepper, and garlic, and packed into large stone jars to ferment. Modern life is causing centuries-long habits to change. Kimchee can be found ready-made in chilled supermarket compartments. But the tradition is central to eating habits. A family of four eats about twenty heads of cabbage in the form of kimchee during an average winter.

Soup In addition to rice and kimchee, every meal includes soup, the only liquid given with the meal. The variety of soups is very broad and can range from bland vegetable soup to an incredibly powerful stew made with tofu and red pepper paste. People love a bowl of hot soup particularly during the cold winter months. Meats, fish, and vegetables are the primary ingredients. *Kalbi-tang,* rich beef soup, is one of the favorites. *Mandu-guk* is meat dumpling soup that resembles Chinese wonton soup, but the Korean dumplings are much bigger than the Chinese ones. The dumplings are filled with beef, pork, garlic, green onions, and vegetables.

Beans Koreans are also very fond of beans, an important source of protein in their diet. Mung beans are cooked whole or ground into a flour to make a popular snack, *pindaettok,* crunchy fried pancakes seasoned with chopped kimchee. Soybeans are cooked whole or used to make bean curd. *Toenjang* is fermented bean paste used as a soup base and is also a condiment mixed with red pepper paste. A red bean, *p'at,* the same as Japanese *azuki,* is used in many desserts.

Noodles Noodles are made from either buckwheat or regular wheat flour. The most popular are the brownish buckwheat noodles served in soups based on beef, poultry, or anchovy stock. *Mokkuksu* is the simplest of all noodle dishes and is cooked in either beef or chicken stock and served with kimchee. *Kalguksu* is a hot and filling dish. The noodles are made from buckwheat and potato flour seasoned with a pepper paste. *Mullaengmyon* is cold noodle soup perfect for hot summer days. Diners particularly love *chapch'ae,* a noodle dish with mixed vegetables. If one has not eaten Korean food, trying chapch'ae is a good place to start.

Seafood Seafood is plentiful and diverse. Abalone, crabs, crayfish, scallops, clams, and shrimp are used frequently. Octopus is stewed with strong seasonings into a delicious dish that is a particular favorite of fishermen. Kelp and seaweed provide extra nutrients and fresh-from-the-sea taste.

Pulgogi One of the most popular dishes is *pulgogi*, broiled beef strips and ribs of beef that exemplify an age-old tradition of cooking on an iron hot plate at the table. Meats of all kinds, including mutton, pork, poultry, and seafood are cooked in this way. One marinates the meat well in advance in a spicy mixture that includes soy sauce, sesame oil, garlic, ginger, pepper (or chili), toasted sesame seeds, and green onions. White rice, bowls of several *namul* (vegetable) dishes, and kimchee complete the gamut of flavors that make pulgogi appreciated around the world.

Kalbi kui *Kalbi* is another well-known dish that is cooked in the same way as pulgogi, but it uses short ribs instead of beef slices. The beef short ribs are marinated in a mixture of green onions, garlic, sugar, sesame oil, and soy sauce.

Pibimpap If you are visiting Korea, *pibimpap* is a must. A very simple but popular dish, pibimpap is a bowl of piping hot rice served in a stoneware bowl with a variety of vegetables, cooked and raw, arranged on top.

Kujol-p'an This is an interesting dish of pancakes that may include a choice of nine different fillings, such as shredded black mushrooms, grated carrots or radishes, diced green onions, eggs, chopped kimchee, sautéed beef, and ground toasted sesame seeds.

Sinsullo *Sinsullo,* a very popular dish, is a hot pot of meats, vegetables, and nuts simmered together and eaten with a tart vinegar and soy sauce dip.

Desserts Seasonal fruit or rice cakes are usually served at the end of the meal. Sweets and desserts are generally eaten as snacks, not during main meals.

Common Beverages

Alcoholic The local wines are potent and vie with the strong flavors of the food. The lowliest wine for everyday consumption is *makkoli.* It is an unfiltered rice wine, sour in taste, and milky white. The quality varies by age and place, but it is very basic to village life. *Takchu* is a wheat-based wine that is low in alcohol and made from grain husks. *Yakchu* is another popular wine, but it is of a finer quality than takchu and has a higher alcohol content. *Chongjong,* also called ch'ongju, is a rice wine that is served warm like Japanese sake. Soju, the most potent of all and something like vodka, is one of the most popular drinks. The most common form of soju is made from sweet potato starch and has an alcohol content of around 20 percent. Premium soju (called Andong soju) is made from rice mash and has a higher alcohol content that runs between 20 and 35 percent and is considered more flavorful. Koreans also enjoy beer, both domestic and imported.

Nonalcoholic People drink rice or barley water after meals. The traditional teas are ginseng, ginger, and cinnamon. There is also a special tea called *ssanghwa-tang,* containing such fruits as jujubes, chestnuts and pine nuts, and honey water.

ETIQUETTE

How Not to Succeed in Korea

Walk on the right side of the sidewalk. Walk through someone's home with your shoes on. Call a Korean by his given (first) name. Refer to the wife of Mr. Kim as Mrs. Kim. Introduce yourself to a prominent person. Speak to a younger person before an elderly person. Make constant eye contact when in conversation. Invite someone to lunch Dutch treat. Pour your own water first. Bring up serious topics of conversation during a meal.

These behaviors are natural to Americans but a mistake in Korea. Koreans are very forgiving of the blunders made by foreigners; however, by avoiding these behaviors a visitor will show sensitivity and respect. Most Korean customs have much longer histories than American ones and have served Koreans well for thousands of years.

How to Behave Well and Succeed Harmoniously in Korea

Hierarchy By Confucian standards age is one of the most important factors to consider. Elderly persons in Korea receive special treatment and are given more consideration than anyone else. When encountering a group of people, the elderly are to be acknowledged first. No one should ever question the wisdom of an elderly person. Respect is not limited to the elderly alone. Throughout one's life one is to defer to someone who is older.

Humility A valued quality is humility. Americans value aggressive behavior, especially in business. Although modesty is valued in the West, the culture allows one to express pride in accomplishments. Koreans are demure about their accomplishments and allow others to give them praise. Modesty is considered a sign of good manners and breeding.

Although Westerners acknowledge a compliment with a "thank you," Koreans consider this too bold and often will deny the compliment. Rejecting praise is a sign of humility.

Maintaining Harmonious Relations Confucian principles continue to provide guidelines for conduct between individuals. Koreans wish to avoid conflict. If there are difficulties between two people, they prefer a third party to act as an intermediary to avoid open confrontation; this allows both parties to save face. If a visitor encounters problems, he should be flexible. A Korean will likely concede changes to maintain harmony.

Americans respect people who admit they do not know something. For Koreans it is much more complicated. To admit that one does not know something can cause a person to lose face. As a result, Koreans may not admit ignorance or uncertainty and may well try to answer even though they know they could be wrong.

Koreans are very proud of their heritage and their country and are very eager to ask visitors about their impressions; however, negative comments will not be well received. If one must say something negative, intersperse the negative with positive comments. It is best not to criticize anything Korean.

In many aspects of interpersonal communication, one must be sensitive to another's feelings to avoid giving pain. If a person is invited to a drinking party, he is expected to drink. If he says "no," it will ruin the general atmosphere of the party. It is considered bad form even when one does not drink alcoholic beverages. However, there are some possible acceptable excuses. A person can say that he is taking traditional Korean medicine and cannot drink, or he can say that his religion discourages drinking. With experience one can gradually learn how to say "no" without giving offense.

One must also be aware that a "yes" answer does not mean that a Korean agrees or intends to comply. It simply means that the person understands the situation or that he will do his best to comply. The word "no" is seldom expressed. It is expressed indirectly. For example, a banker will not say "no" to a person wanting a loan, but he will make the terms so difficult that the person will reject the offer. If a Korean says "yes" but does not comply, he did not mean to deceive you. It simply means that it was not possible to carry out the action.

Kibun To understand interpersonal relations, behavior, and thought, it is important to know the concept of *kibun*. There is no exact equivalent in the English language. Kibun (feelings, mood, or state of mind) is of prime importance. In essence it is the person's inner sense, his very being. This invisible part of a person can be damaged by loss of face, disrespect, or unhappiness. All cultures value how people feel emotionally, but few cultures place as high a value on this as Koreans do. They are expert at sensing another person's emotional state and very helpful in getting one out of a bad mood by simple gestures. Kibun enters every aspect of life. Often Americans need to prove themselves right, but to the Korean harmonious relations are more important than efficiency, honesty, or truth. To foreigners, Koreans may seem too sensitive. For example, a Korean's kibun is damaged when someone does not show him proper respect by bowing soon enough or low enough, not using honorific words, or by handing him something with the left hand. These are rules of etiquette known by every Korean. Although they may seem unimportant or foolish to the foreign visitor, they should be respected and observed.

Nunch'i Another concept that is related to kibun is *nunch'i*. The concept of nunch'i relates to one's ability to assess nonverbal communication. In a society where being in harmony with others is vital, judging another person's state of mind is critical. If a person develops this ability, he will know when to ask delicate questions or to ask the boss for a favor. In Korea communication requires people to focus on nonverbal behavior that provides clues to another's mood or inner feelings. What is most important is genuine friendship. Developing skills in assessing verbal and nonverbal communication is recognized as a means of developing good friendships, maintaining harmony in the home, and negotiating successfully in business relations. Korean Americans are apt to announce how they feel, but Koreans are taught to control their emotions and to disguise their feelings. Therefore, determining the particular mood of a Korean may be a challenge, but it is a skill that could bring great satisfaction and reward in improved communication and international understanding.

Introductions Introductions are very important in Korea. Essentially, an introduction will affect how two people relate to each other in the future. Introducing a person of low status to a person of high status is not common. It is also unusual for Koreans to introduce themselves to someone with whom they have no connection. A third party will introduce two people to one another. When the two people meet, a formal ritual follows. Each announces that it is the first time to see the other person. They will then face each other directly, bow, and say their names followed by *"man-na-so pan-gap-sum-ni-da"* ("We meet for the first time" or "I am glad to meet you"). Foreigners are not expected to bow, but the foreigner who does will likely win respect. Following the bow, business cards are exchanged using both hands. Both people will glance briefly at the card to note the name and position, but then it is carefully tucked away. Business cards help clarify status in relations. Knowing a person's status is critical, since the proper language level to be used depends on the position of each person.

Forms of Address Names are very personal. Westerners like to develop relationships by addressing another person by his or her given name. In Korea the first name means the family name, such as Park or Kim. If you call someone directly by their given name in Korea, it is an insult in most social circumstances. Refer to individuals as Mr. Kim or Miss Park. Position names or titles are very common, such as Librarian Kim, Reverend Park, or Director Lee. It is important to know that Korean women keep their family name when they marry; therefore, do not call Mr. Kim's wife, "Mrs. Kim," but refer to her as "the wife of Mr. Kim."

Clothes Confucius reportedly said that clothes distinguished a cultured man from a barbarian. Although notions of appropriate clothing are becoming more relaxed, Koreans take personal appearances seriously. Foreign businesspeople are well advised to ensure that their appearance reflects the image they want to project. It is best to dress well and conservatively at all times. Avoid jeans, T-shirts, and shorts unless you are told it is acceptable to wear them.

Gift Giving Gift giving is an important dimension of the culture. Koreans love to give gifts. If a visitor does not bring a gift, it is impolite. The gift should be simple and personal. If it is extravagant, it will create a sense of obligation. The best gifts are ones that leave the recipient in good spirits and wanting to voluntarily reciprocate. In the world of business and government elaborate gifts are often given. Westerners may consider it unethical, but until recently it has not been frowned upon. If someone offers a gift, it is the custom to decline it at least twice.

Punctuality Koreans are fairly relaxed about time and may be five to twenty minutes late for appointments. It is not uncommon for meetings, movies, and other public events to begin a little bit late. If one is invited to a function, it is perfectly acceptable to be ten to fifteen minutes late; however, being more than thirty minutes late is considered rude.

Humor A visitor should avoid jokes, puns, and sarcasm. Keep it simple, observe the appropriateness of your remark, and be sensitive to any comment that could be misinterpreted. Also, avoid using Korean slang and Japanese loan words. Do not compare Korea with Japan.

Gestures Some gestures in Korea will confuse the visitor. The Korean gesture for "come here" is similar to the Western "goodbye." Koreans always use the right hand when giving an object to a person of higher status. To show the most respect, both hands hold the object as it is given or received. When passing objects to people of lower status, either hand is acceptable, but using both hands is inappropriate. When Koreans are happy, they smile and laugh as other people do. However, Koreans may also smile when they are ashamed or uncomfortable.

Shopping When shopping in Korea, it is perfectly acceptable to bargain in individually owned stores and booths. It can take more time, but it can become thoroughly enjoyable for most people. Department stores and chain supermarkets usually have fixed prices. When a shopper has done her research and knows a good price when she sees it, she will strengthen her negotiating power and ultimate satisfaction. Although bargaining is an old practice, many simply compare prices at different stores and purchase an item wherever the price is lowest. It has been said that a Korean gentleman does not bargain.

Personal Space The Korean concept of space is sometimes a source of frustration and misunderstanding among foreigners. If someone bumps into you it America, you expect an apology. Americans are more territorial and often claim space, albeit temporarily. Koreans live in one of the most densely populated countries in the world. For example, approximately 1,234 Koreans live in one square mile as opposed to approximately 73 Americans per square mile. Koreans are accustomed to congestion on streets, subways, buses, and marketplaces. Customarily they do not apologize for coming too close to another person because they have not violated a rule of their culture.

Eating and Drinking When invited to a Korean home, expect to be served a meal. A low table will be set, and people will sit on cushions. The whole meal will be served at one time, with rice and soup beside individual plates and all side dishes will be spread out on the table. The hostess will usually say, "We do not have much to eat, but please eat a lot." This is indicative of Korean hospitality: that even the biggest feast is not good enough for their guests. Everyone waits to eat until the most elderly person begins.

One needs to be sensitive about conversation during dinner. If you are a daughter-in-law eating with a stern mother-in-law or if you are a Korean citizen and your host is the president of the Republic of Korea, unnecessary conversation is not appreciated. If you are an American having dinner with Korean friends, you should speak. If you do not, it will give the impression that you are dissatisfied with the hospitality of the host.

Koreans eat mainly with chopsticks but rice and soup should be eaten with a spoon. During the meal, leave your spoon and chopsticks, when not in use, on top of your bowl. When you have finished eating, put them beside your plate. The hostess will encourage guests to eat more than they want, but this is an expression of concern. Since there is usually too much food, no one expects the guests to eat it all. It is the custom to decline the offer of more food. If you decline three times, your message will be clear to the host. The host will not ask you again if you want more food. It is not the Korean custom to praise the cook for the delicious food; however, if guests say that the food is good, it will definitely be appreciated. There are two particularly unacceptable behaviors at the meal table. Never eat with your fingers. Never blow your nose at the table.

When drinking or dining out in Korea, the rule is simple. The person who suggests going out pays. It is considered very impolite to go

Dutch treat. Usually people argue over who pays, but inevitably it is the person who initiated the get together. The American custom of Dutch treat is very unsettling to Koreans.

For men, drinking after hours is a common and necessary occurrence in Korea. It is considered essential for developing a sense of trust and building close relationships. In Korea drinking to excess is expected, essential for bonding with other men and forging the proper relations conducive to business. Because of the influence of the West, it is important to realize that not all Koreans behave in the manner described.

There are some simple, but very essential, customs that any visitor should observe. It is important to observe certain table manners. When drinking, offer to pour for the others at the table, starting with the eldest member of the party. To show respect, both hands should be used when pouring and when accepting a drink. The eldest family member sits at the table first, and the others must not take up their chopsticks or spoon until he or she begins eating. When using the chopsticks, the spoon must not be placed back on the table until one is finished eating. When using the chopsticks, the spoon is placed in the rice or soup bowl or leaned against its edge. No one is excused from the table before the eldest is finished.

Organizations

GOVERNMENT ORGANIZATIONS

Embassy of Korea
2450 Massachusetts Ave., N.W.
Washington, DC 20008
Telephone: (202) 939-5600
Fax: (202) 797-0595
E-mail: (general) usa@mofat.go.kr
Internet: http://www.koreaemb.org/

Consulates General of Korea
Atlanta
229 Peachtree St., Suite 500
International Tower
Atlanta, GA 30303
Telephone: (404) 522-1611
Fax: (404) 521-3169
E-mail: kcgatlan@ix.netcom.com
info@consulatekorea-atl.org

Boston
One Gateway Center 2nd Floor
Newton, MA 02458
Telephone: (617) 641-2830
Fax: (617) 641-2831
E-mail: jeonghakp@aol.com
Internet: http://www.mofat.go.kr/boston.htm

Chicago
NBC Tower Suite 2700
455 North Cityfront Plaza Dr.
Chicago, IL 60611
Telephone: (312) 822-9485
Fax: (312) 822-9849
E-mail: koconchi@amrs.com
Internet: http://www.mofat.go.kr/chicago

Honolulu
2756 Pali Highway
Honolulu, HI 96817
Telephone: (808) 595-6109
Fax: (808) 595-3046
E-mail: korea@hits.net

Houston
1990 Post Oak Blvd. #1250
Houston, TX 77056
Telephone: (713) 961-0186
Fax: (713) 961-3340
E-mail: kbshon73@mofat.go.kr

Los Angeles
3243 Wilshire Blvd.
Los Angeles, CA 90010
Telephone: (213) 385-9300
Fax: (213) 385-1849
E-mail: lac@anet.net

New York
335 E. 45th St.
New York, NY 10017
Telephone: (212) 752-1700
Fax: (212) 888-6320
E-mail: info@koreanconsulate.org
Internet: http://www.koreanconsulate.org/

San Francisco
3500 Clay Street
San Francisco, CA 94118
Telephone: (415) 921-2251
Fax: (415) 921-5946
E-mail: gslee87@mofat.go.kr

Seattle
2033 Sixth Avenue #1125
Seattle, WA 98121
Telephone: (206) 441-1011
Fax: (206) 441-7912
E-mail: shhong86@mofat.go.kr

Washington, D.C.
Consulate of the Embassy
2230 Massachusetts Ave., NW
Washington, DC 20008
Telephone: (202) 939-5661
Fax: (202) 342-1597

Hagatna (Guam)
125 C Tun Jose Camacho St.
Tamuning, Guam 96931
Telephone: (671) 647-6488
Fax: (671) 649-1336

BUSINESS AND ECONOMIC ORGANIZATIONS

American Chamber of Commerce in Korea
#4501, Trade Center
159-1 Samsung-dong
Kangnam-Ku, Seoul 135-731
Telephone: (82-2-564-2040)
Fax: (82-2-564-2050)
E-mail: info@amchamkorea.org
Internet: http://www.amchamkorea.org

"Established in 1953, the American Chamber of Commerce
(AMCHAM Korea) seeks to promote the development of commerce
between the United States and Korea. AMCHAM's Korea membership
includes nearly 2,000 individual members and over 900 companies."
The Web site features an array of informative resources related to
business and investment in Korea. The chamber offers seminars and
regular briefings on conducting business in Korea.

Convention and Exhibition Center
135-731 Kangnam-gu
Muyok Center COEX
Seoul
Telephone: (82-2-6000-0114)
Fax: (82-2-6000-1301)

COEX, located in the Korean World Trade Center, stages trade fairs
and exhibitions. It is the largest such venue in Asia and includes
exhibition facilities and trade expo halls. The facility fully supports

businesses with other services such as secretarial and translation, telecommunication, postal, and stationary support facilities.

Federation of Korean Industries
28-1 Youidodong
Yongdingp'o-gu, Seoul
Telephone: (82-2-3771-0114)
Fax: (82-2-3775-0745)

"FKI is a private, nonprofit organization of Korea's leading business and industrial associations."

Korean-American Association
450 Kongduk-dong
Mapo-gu, Seoul 121-720
Telephone: (82-2-776-5320)
Fax: (82-2-707-7101)

The objective of the Korean-American Association is to promote friendship and understanding between peoples of the Republic of Korea and the United States and to strengthen economic, social, and cultural relations between the two countries. Established in 1962, it is a nonprofit, non-governmental organization with binational membership. The association offers seminars and musical concerts, holds exhibitions, arranges tours to visit U.S. military bases in Korea, and organizes American-Korean associations in cities in the United States.

Korean-American Business Institute
7Fl., Sunkiss Venture Bldg., 628-14
Yeoksam-Dong
Kangnam-Ku, Seoul
Telephone: (82-2-753-7750)
Fax: (82-2-561-6921)
E-mail: kabifj@unitel.co.kr

The Korean-American Business Institute (KABI) was founded in 1974 and aimed to provide consultation, research, government and industry relations, management training and service support toward the advancement of mutual understanding and cooperation in the field of international business. It has contributed to the strengthening of business ties with the United States and foreign countries.

Korea's Chamber of Commerce and Industry
45, 4-ga Namdaemunno
Jung-gu, Seoul
Telephone: (82-2-316-3114)
Fax: (82-2-771-3267)
Internet: http://www.kcci.or.kr

KCCI is a national federation of leading Korean business people "devoted to the development of commerce and industry, the promotion and protection of the interests of those engaged in business, and the strengthening of international economic relations."

Korea International Trade Association
Trade Tower, Room #4603
World Trade Center
Kangnam-gu
Seoul 135-729
Telephone: (82-2-6000-5346)
Fax: (82-2-6000-5181)
Internet: http://www.wtca.org,
http://www.wtc-seoul.com

The World Trade Centers Association (WTCA) is the world's largest nonprofit and nonpolitical association serving to develop and facilitate international trade.

Korea's Foreign Trade Association
159-1, Samsung-dong
Kangnam-gu, Seoul
Telephone: (82-2-551-5114)
Fax: (82-2-551-5100)

Korea's Foreign Trade Association (KFTA), a parent organization and owner of the Korea World Trade Center and Korea Exhibition Center (KOEX), is a private nonprofit organization composed of licensed traders in Korea.

Korea Trade-Investment Promotion Agency
300-9, Yomgok-dong, Seocho-gu
Seocho P.O. Box 101, Seoul
Telephone: (82-2-3460-7114)
Fax: (82-2-3460-7777)

E-mail: net-mgr@kotra.or.kr
Internet: www.kotra.co.kr

The Korea Trade-Investment Promotion Agency (KOTRA) is located in the Trade Tower of the World Trade Center in Seoul. It is a non-profit, state-run agency dedicated to promoting the country's external trade. KOTRA manages nine trade centers in the United States and over 100 trade centers throughout the world. In April 2001 KOTRA published an English guidebook for foreign investors on making investments in North Korea.

UNITED STATES KOREA TRADE CENTERS

Atlanta
Five Concourse Parkway N.E. Suite 2181
Atlanta, GA 30328
Telephone: (770) 508-0808
Fax: (770) 508-0801
E-mail: kotra@mindspring.com

Chicago
111 East Wacker Drive, Suite 2229
Chicago, IL 60601
Telephone: (312) 644-4323
Fax: (312) 644-4879
E-mail: info@kotrachicago.com

Dallas
12720 Hillcrest Rd., Suite 390
Dallas, TX 75230-2040
Telephone: (972) 934-8644
Fax: (972) 239-4191
E-mail: ktcdfw@swbell.net

Detroit
2000 Town Center Suite 1840
Southfield, MI 48075
Telephone: (248) 355-4911
Fax: (248) 355-9002
E-mail: ktcdtt@aol.com

Los Angeles
4801 Wilshire Blvd., Suite 104
Los Angeles, CA 90010
Telephone: (323) 954-9500
Fax: (323) 954-1707
E-mail: lakt@yahoo.com

Miami
One Biscayne Tower, Suite 1620
Miami, FL 33131
Telephone: (305) 374-4648
Fax: (305) 375-9332
E-mail: ktcmiami@aol.com

New York
460 Park Ave., Suite 402
New York, NY 10022
Telephone: (212) 826-0900
Fax: (212) 888-4930
E-mail: kotrany@ix.netcom.com

San Francisco
690 Market Street, Suite 903
San Francisco, CA 94104
Telephone: (415) 434-8400
Fax: (415) 434-8450
E-mail: ktcsf@aol.com

Washington, D.C.
1129 20th St. NW, Suite 410
Washington, DC 20036
Telephone: (202) 857-7919
Fax: (202) 857-7923
E-mail: dcktc@bellatlantic.net

CULTURE/EDUCATION/ EXCHANGE ORGANIZATIONS

Asia Society
725 Park Ave.
New York, NY 10021
Telephone: (212) 288-6400

Fax: (212) 517-8315
Internet: http://www.asiasociety.org

"The Asia Society is America's leading institution dedicated to fostering understanding of Asia and communication between Americans and the peoples of Asia and the Pacific. A national, nonprofit, nonpartisan educational organization, the Society provides a forum for building awareness of the more than thirty countries broadly defined as the Asia-Pacific region. Through art exhibitions, and performances, films, lectures, seminars, and conferences, publications and assistance to the media, and materials and programs for students and teachers, the Asia Society presents the uniqueness and diversity of Asia to the American people."

Council for International Exchange of Scholars
3007 Tilden Street NW Suite 5L
Washington, DC 20008-3009
Telephone: (202) 686-4000
Fax: (202) 362-3442
E-mail: jmcpeek@iie.org

The Council for International Exchange of Scholars (CIES) is a division of the Institute of International Education (IIE) based in New York City. IIE is a private, nonprofit organization, which assists the Department of State in administering Fulbright grants for graduate study. College graduates, graduate students, and Ph.D. candidates in Korean Studies may apply for Fulbright grants.

Korean Culture and Information Centers

The following organizations serve as resources for information on Korea and Korea-U.S. relations. They organize and support cultural and academic activities.

Korean Cultural Center of Los Angeles
5505 Wilshire Blvd.
Los Angeles, CA 90036
Telephone: (323) 936-7141
Fax: (323) 936-5712
Internet: http://www.kccla.org

The Korean Cultural Center actively serves the Los Angeles area by providing information on Korea. The center contains an extensive library of more than 15,000 volumes in both English and Korean and a video collection. The library furnishes information on the arts, history, language, philosophy, and contemporary affairs. Galleries exhibit traditional and modern art. Additional activities include a film night, cultural performances, workshops, and Korean language classes. The center publishes *Korean Culture,* a quarterly magazine that covers many aspects of Korean life.

Korean Cultural Service of New York
460 Park Avenue, 6th floor
New York, NY 10022
Telephone: (212) 759-9550
Fax: (212) 688-8640
Internet: http://www.koreanculture.org

The Korean Cultural Service promotes mutual understanding between Korea and the United States through its cultural and academic activities. The service provides information on Korea and Korea-U.S. relations and guidance to students who wish to participate in exchange programs. The service has an extensive library of more than 10,000 books, periodicals, CD-ROMs, and videotapes. Its gallery serves as a public forum for art exhibitions that promote cultural exchange. Activities include performances of traditional and modern music, drama, dance, and other performing arts. The service also offers lectures and seminars by selected experts and instructors.

Korean Cultural Service of Washington, D.C.
2370 Massachusetts Avenue, N.W.
Washington, DC 20008
Telephone: (202) 797-6343
Fax: (202) 387-0413
E-mail: korinfo@koreaemb.org
Internet: http://www.koreaemb.org

The Korean Cultural Service of Washington, D.C. aims to promote awareness of Korean culture within the American community. By offering cultural and educational events such as monthly film nights, Korean language and culture classes, art exhibitions, lectures, and book readings, the KCS helps to facilitate mutual understanding between Korea and the United States. The service also offers a variety of media resources. It houses two libraries, a Korean-language library and an English-language library, both collections containing a wide range of resource materials pertaining to Korea. The KCS has an extensive collection of educational and entertainment films and videos. Most are available either in English or with English subtitles. Korean language and culture classes are offered throughout the year. Teacher workshops provide educators an opportunity to learn how to implement Korean lessons into their curriculum.

Korea Foundation
Seocho P.O. Box 227
Diplomatic Center Building
1376-1, Seocho 2-dong
Seocho-gu, Seoul 137-072
Telephone: (82-2-3463-5600-1)
Fax: (82-2-3463-6075-6)
Internet: www.kf.or.kr

"The mission of the Korea Foundation is to contribute to better understanding of Korea in the international community and to promote international friendship by carrying out various exchange activities between the Republic of Korea and foreign countries." The Foundation supports fellowships for Korean studies and Korean-language training. To obtain information on the fellowships, contact the Fellowship Program Team at the following address: fellowship@kf.or.kr

Korean Information Service
Government Information Agency
82-1 Sejongno
Jongno-gu, Seoul
Telephone: (82-2-398-1910)
Fax: (82-2-398-1882)
Internet: http://www.korea.net/kois/

Some of the major functions currently performed by the Korean Information Service (KOIS) are to operate and administer Internet sites (Korea.net), assist international news media covering Korea, organize international forums, exchange journalists, academics, and opinion leaders, carry out projects to introduce Korea and Korean culture, publish foreign-language books, disseminate overseas books, films, and videotapes helpful for understanding Korea, and to operate cultural centers abroad.

Korean National Commission for UNESCO
Youth Unit
P.O. Box Central 64
Seoul, Korea
Telephone: (82-2-755-9068)
Fax: (82-2-755-9069)
E-mail: iyc@unesco.or.kr

Young adults between the ages of 18–27 are eligible to participate in the International Youth Camp (IYC), which is an annual project of the Korean National Commission for UNESCO. "Over the years, IYC has enriched the lives of the nearly 3,100 young people worldwide who have been participants in the program. Through involvement in an interesting and challenging program of workshops, tours, projects, and discussions on international issues, IYC participants have enjoyed opportunities for self-development, physical conditioning, and intellectual stimulation. Living and working together, the participants have gained a better understanding of themselves, each other, and the world around them. The IYC will continue this long-term effort to promote international understanding and cooperation, to inspire its participants to respect human dignity and to encourage the development of an enlightened work ethic. The Korea youth camps involve students in human rights projects, environment programs, and the preservation of ancient cultural sites."

Korea Society
950 Third Avenue, 8th Floor
New York, NY 10022
Telephone: (212) 759-7525
Fax: (212) 759-7530
Internet: http://www.koreasociety.org

The Korea Society is a private, nonprofit, nonpartisan organization dedicated solely to the promotion of greater awareness, understanding, and cooperation between the people of the United States and Korea. In pursuit of its mission, the society arranges programs that facilitate discussion, exchanges, and research on topics of vital interest to both countries in the areas of public policy, business, education, intercultural relations, and the arts. The Korea Society, in cooperation with the Korea Foundation, offers fellowships for social studies and language-arts educators, including K–12 classroom teachers, and professors or instructors in schools of education.

Lesson plans created by the fellowship recipients are available.

The Korea Society also nominates five American delegates for the UNESCO youth camp each summer and pays camp participation fees. The Korea Society supports Project Bridge, a year-long program of intercultural youth leadership activities for Los Angeles and New York high school students. The program includes a two-week education study tour of Korea every April. The participation of the Los Angeles delegation is arranged in collaboration with the Pacific Century Institute (PCI) in Woodland Hills, California. The Korea Society also provides additional opportunities to travel to Korea. Each year awards are given to both American students and teachers whose essays are selected in a Korea Society contest. The winners are eligible to receive all-expense-paid trips to and from Korea. There are additional monetary awards for those who enter.

Overseas Koreans Foundation
6th Floor, Diplomatic Center
1376-1 Seocho-2 dong
Seocho-gu, Seoul 137-072
Telephone: (82-2-3463-6265)
Fax: (82-2-3463-3999)
E-mail: hongjh@okf.or.kr
Internet: http://www.okf.or.kr

The Overseas Koreans Foundation (OKF) hosts an annual Summer Cultural Training Program. In the past several decades there have been over 200,000 Korean children sent overseas for adoption. Since the 1980s, many adult adoptees have been returning to Korea to search for their birth families; to seek connection to their cultural heritage, language, and identity; and to work and live. OKF wishes to develop positive links between adoptees and Korean society and increase international awareness regarding issues of Korean adoption. The program focuses on Korea's rich cultural heritage and provides adoptees abroad the opportunity to explore their motherland and gain a better understanding of Korea through language study, cultural training, and touring. OKF covers all expenses except airfare.

Pacific Basin Institute
Pomona College
333 N. College Way
Claremont, CA 91711
Telephone: (909) 607-8035
Fax: (909) 607-7468
E-mail: pbi@pomona.edu
Internet: http://pomona.edu/pbi

A nonprofit corporation established in 1979, the Pacific Basin Institute (PBI) is dedicated to improving communication among the peoples of the Pacific Basin and increasing understanding about the cultures, politics, and economics of Asia/Pacific nations. The Pacific Basin archive of film and documentary video materials was greatly expanded by the footage used for PBI's award-winning television series, *The Pacific Century*. PBI sponsors a continuing series of conferences, symposiums, and lectures featuring scholars, authors, and public figures. An on-going publication program of translations from Asian languages is designed to offer modern works of Pacific Basin authors. PBI is updating footage for a new release of *The Pacific Century* series, including segments on Korea and China.

Pacific Century Institute
Headquarters
6200 Canoga Avenue, Suite #410
Woodland Hills, CA 91367-2450
Telephone: (818) 227-6620
Fax: (818) 704-4336
E-mail: pci_la@yahoo.com

Regional Office
c/o Kenneth J. Tuggle
Brown, Todd & Heyburn
400 W. Market St., 32nd Floor
Louisville, KY 40202-3363
Telephone: (502) 568-0269
Fax: (502) 581-1087

East Asian Office
c/o Chung-in Moon
78-9 Yonhee 2-dong
Seodaemun-ku, Seoul

Telephone: (82-2-322-0911)
Fax: (82-2-365-5524)
E-mail: cimoon@yonsei.ac.kr

The Pacific Century Institute (PCI) is a multinational organization working with a broad spectrum of individuals and groups to foster positive change around the Pacific Rim. Boasting an international board of advisors, the Pacific Century Institute is designed to serve as a catalyst for improving understanding and developing greater communication among peoples of the Pacific Rim nations. Focusing on government officials, scholars, and business people, PCI uses a multifaceted approach to working with the concerns of the Pacific Rim. It supports seminars, conferences, research, scholarships, and a social concern program. The institute works with the Korea Society in New York to support the Project Bridge program, a year-long program of intercultural youth-leadership activities for Los Angeles and New York high school students. The program includes a two-week education study tour of Korea every April.

TOURISM ORGANIZATIONS

Korea National Tourism Organization
10, Da-dong
Jung-gu, Seoul 100-180
Telephone: (82-2-7299-487)
Fax: (82-2-319-0086)
Internet: http://www.knto.or.kr/
E-mail: kntotic@www.knto.or.kr

The function of the Korea National Tourism Organization (KNTO) is to promote and facilitate tourism. First-hand information and free brochures are provided to assist with pre-trip planning. While in Korea, travelers should seek the assistance of the KNTO Tourist Information Center, which provides numerous in-country services, including the services of a team of guides that can provide on-site translation and interpretation. To obtain information on the guide service, check http://www.goodwillguide.com/english.

Los Angeles
4801 Wilshire Blvd., Suite 103
Los Angeles, CA 90010
Telephone: (323) 643-0025

Fax: (323) 643-0028
E-mail: kntola@mail.wcis.com

New York
One Executive Drive, Suite 100
Fort Lee, NJ 07024
Telephone: (201) 585-0909
Fax: (201) 585-9041
E-mail: kntony@ring3.net

Chicago
737 North Michigan Ave., Suite 910
Chicago, Il 60611
Telephone: (312) 981-1717
Fax: (312) 981-1721
E-mail: kntocg@idt.net

KOREAN-AMERICAN ORGANIZATIONS

Also Known As
P.O. Box 6037
FDR Station
New York, NY 10150
Telephone: (888) 467-2183
E-mail: jlieberthal@mail.alsoknownas.org
Internet: http://www.alsoknownas.org

Also Known As (AKA) primarily services the New York Metropolitan area, but it has a national outreach program to provide information to adoptees and their families anywhere in the United States. In the New York area, AKA offers language, heritage, and mentorship programs. The organization can also provide information on summer camps for adoptees. The Internet site will link to the Also Known As office in Washington, D.C.

Korean American Coalition, Headquarters
3727 W. 6th St., Suite 515
Los Angeles, CA 90020
Telephone: (213) 365-5999
Fax: (213) 380-7990
E-mail: kacla1983@aol.com

The Korean American Coalition (KAC) has offices in Los Angeles and Washington, D.C., three chapters in California (San Francisco, Sacramento, and Garden Grove), and affiliates in Anchorage and Honolulu. "Founded in 1983, KAC's mission is to advocate the civic, civil rights, leadership, legislative, and political interests of the Korean American community. KAC is a nonprofit, nonpartisan membership organization."

Washington, D.C.
P.O. Box 7325
Ben Franklin Station
Washington, DC 20044
Telephone: (202) 296-6401
Fax: (202) 296-6407
E-mail: kacdc.org

Korean American Librarians and Information Professionals Association
Choonhee Rhim, President
East Los Angeles College Library
1301 Avenida Cesar Chavez
Monterey Park, CA 91754
Telephone: (213) 265-8625
Fax: (213) 265-8759
E-mail: rhimcl@laccd.cc.ca.us
Internet: http://kalipa.apanet.org/

The Korean American Librarians and Information Professionals Association (KALIPA) was founded in 1983 to exchange professional knowledge among Korean American librarians and information professionals in the United States. It works to promote cooperative library programs between Korea and the United States and cooperates with other organizations that share similar concerns and interests. To encourage more Korean Americans to become librarians, KALIPA awards scholarships to Korean American students studying library and information science.

Korean Camps
There are over twenty summer camps for Korean adoptee children throughout the United States. The camps offer opportunities for children to learn about their heritage and issues related to adoption. Young people between the ages of four and eighteen participate in

such activities as learning the language, dance, drama, Taekwondo, cooking, and art. Some camps offer family retreats. At this time there is no national association.

Colorado Heritage Camp (303) 388-3930
Iowans for International Adoption (641) 423-4224
Camp Pride (Illinois) (847) 367-7862
Hands Around the World (Illinois) (847) 255-8309
Camp Sae Jong (Michigan) (248) 851-7314
Family for International Children Heritage Camp (Michigan)
   (616) 532-2937
Korean Culture Camp (Michigan) (810) 229-4111
Camp Moon-Hwa (Minnesota) (507) 282-2399
Camp Choson (Minnesota) (715) 381-2728
Kamp Kimchee (Minnesota) (218) 764-2692
Korean Culture Camp (Minnesota) (612) 470-5496
Camp Moo Gung Hwa (North Carolina) (919) 596-5112
Holt Heritage Camp (Nebraska) (541) 687-2202
Camp Friendship (New Jersey) (732) 287-5349
Camp Sejong (New Jersey) (201) 784-1081
Camp Mu Ji Gae Korean Culture Day Camp (New York)
   (518) 426-2606
AFSA's Y2K Korean Culture Camp (Ohio) (440) 779-1533
Holt Heritage Camp (Oregon) (541) 687-2202
Dillon Korea Heritage (Oklahoma) (918) 748-4600 x206
Korean American Pride Camp (Utah) (801) 280-6559

National Korean American Service and Education Consortium, Inc.
National Office
50-16 Parsons Blvd., #100
Flushing, NY 11355
Telephone: (718) 445-3939
Fax: (718) 445-0032
E-mail: nakasec@nakasec.org
Internet: http://www.nakasec.org

"The National Korean American Service and Education Consortium, Inc. (NAKASEC) seeks to empower the Korean American community through education and advocacy. NAKASEC was founded in 1994 by five Korean American community organizations located across the United States NAKASEC's program areas include education, civil rights and immigrant rights advocacy, civic participation, research, leadership, coalition-building, and culture. NAKASEC programs focus on serving those with less resources and access, such as women, youth, seniors, low-income residents and recent immigrants."

Women's Organization Reaching Koreans
P.O. Box 125
Vergudo City, CA 91046

"Women's Organization Reaching Koreans (WORK) is a nonprofit, education, and advocacy organization dedicated to promoting sociopolitical issues and addressing injustices of concern to Korean American women. Through coalition building with other organizations concerned with gender, race, and class, WORK is committed to raising consciousness, promoting activism, and creating a space where Korean American women's voices can be heard."

Annotated Bibliography of Recommended Works on Korea

The books below are organized by categories according to the chronology of the narrative section of this book. Considerable thought has been given to include the most highly regarded, current, and readable sources. For additional resources consult the references at the end of each chapter.

In the following sections certain books are mentioned more than once. This is to assist people with interests in certain areas, such as Korea's economy, and students who are seeking a particular focus.

Periodicals, literature, Internet sites, CD-ROMS, and films are listed after the book resources.

BOOK RESOURCES

Geography and History

Cumings, Bruce. *Korea's Place in the Sun: A Modern History.* New York: W. W. Norton. 1997. 527 pp. An engaging and informative history that emphasizes the twentieth century. The author devotes a chapter to America's Koreans.

Eckert, Carter et al. *Korea Old and New: A History.* Seoul: Ilchokak Publishers. 1990. 454 pp. (available in paperback). This source is one of the most widely consulted and acclaimed books about Korea. It is a basic text in Korean Studies courses.

Hart-Landsberg, Martin. *Korea: Division, Reunification, and U.S. Foreign Policy.* New York: Monthly Review Press. 1998. 266 pp. (available in paperback). An excellent introduction to the causes and consequences of the Korean War. The author evaluates U.S. foreign policy and sees reunification as the optimal solution for Korea.

Kim, Yung-Chung, ed. *Women of Korea: A History from Ancient Times to 1945.* Seoul: Ehwa Womans University Press. 1976. 327 pp.

This is one of the most thorough studies to date of the status, role, and activities of Korean women through the country's long history.

Korean Overseas Information Service. *A Handbook of Korea.* Seoul: Samhwa Printing Co. 1998. 592 pp. (This book is often given free of charge to educators at Korean Consulates). The handbook is updated every few years. It is a very comprehensive resource that covers history, geography, language, religion, customs, the arts, government, education, and foreign relations.

Lee, Ki-baik. *A New History of Korea.* Seoul: Ilchokak Publishers. 1984. 474 pp. Lee's book is considered one of the most detailed, scholarly, and reliable sources available.

Lee, Peter H., ed. *Sourcebook of Korean Civilization.* Vol. I. New York: Columbia University Press. 1993. 750 pp. This book is the most comprehensive English-language anthology of primary source material on Korean civilization ever assembled. It incorporates documents related to economic, political, social, and cultural developments in Korea from early times to the sixteenth century.

Lee, Peter H., ed. *Sourcebook of Korean Civilization.* Vol. II. New York: Columbia University Press. 1996. 574 pp. This volume includes primary source materials related to economic, political, social, and cultural developments in Korea from the seventeenth century to 1945.

Macdonald, Donald Stone. *The Koreans: Contemporary Politics and Society.* Boulder, CO: Westview Press. 1990. 320 pp. A very readable, accurate, and balanced account of contemporary Korea. It covers Korean society and culture, economic and political development in North and South Korea, foreign relations, and the challenges of reunification.

Nahm, Andrew. *A Panorama of 5000 Years: A Korean History.* Seoul: Hollym. 1987. 128 pp. This is a reliable, concise introduction to Korean history and culture. It includes beautiful illustrations.

Oberdorfer, Don. *The Two Koreas: A Contemporary History.* Reading, MA: Addison-Wesley. 1997. 472 pp. An extremely well written, balanced account of historical and political developments on the peninsula since 1945. Particularly engaging is Oberdorfer's account of how close the United States came to war with North Korea in 1994.

Oh, Kongdan, ed. *Korea Briefing, 1997–1999: Challenges and Change at the Turn of the Century.* New York: M. E. Sharpe, Inc. 2000. 243 pp. (available in paperback). Korean experts examine the economic, political, diplomatic, and cultural developments of the late twentieth century.

Oh, Kongdan, and Ralph C. Hassig. *North Korea through the Looking Glass.* Washington, DC: Brookings Institution Press. 2000. 256 pp. (available in paperback). This book will become basic reading for those interested in why North Korea has survived in spite of the fall of the globalist socialist system. It is a fascinating as well as disturbing account of a mystifying nation. It provides insight into the extraordinary challenges of reunification.

Saccone, Richard. *Fifty Famous People Who Helped Shape Korea.* Seoul: Hollym Corporation. 1993. 242 pp. Saccone's book is the only English-language edition that focuses extensively on bibliographical information on Korean monarchs, politicians, military figures, philosophers, religious figures, businesspeople, scholars, artists, writers, composers, publishers, and patriots. It was an invaluable resource for this author in the Significant People, Places, and Events section.

Suh, Dae-Sook. *Kim Il Sung: The North Korean Leader.* New York: Columbia University Press. 1998. 437 pp. (available in paperback). Suh's book is considered one of the most definitive sources on Kim Il Sung and his impact on the history and politics of North Korea.

Economy

Eckert, Carter et al. *Korea Old and New: A History.* Seoul: Ilchokak Publishers. 1990. 454 pp. (available in paperback). This resource provides a very clear explanation of the economic development of South Korea from 1945 to 1990.

Kim, Byoung-Lo Philo. *Two Koreas in Development: A Comparative Study of Principles and Strategies of Capitalist and Communist Third World Development.* New Brunswick, NJ: Transaction Publishers. 1992. 210 pp. Kim describes the economic, political, and social development of both North and South Korea since 1945. A chapter is devoted to economic development.

Oh, Kongdan, and Ralph C. Hassig. *North Korea through the Looking Glass.* Washington, DC: Brookings Institution Press. 2000. 256 pp. (available in paperback). The authors provide a detailed examination of the North Korean economy in the 1990s.

Song, Byung-Nak. *The Rise of the Korean Economy.* New York: Oxford University Press. 1997. 306 pp. (available in paperback). A detailed, lucid account of South Korea's economic development from an impoverished Third World country to one of the most industrialized nations in the world. Song's book is of particular value to students of Asian economics, as well as to professional people with an interest in understanding Korea's growth.

Political Development

Eckert, Carter et al. *Korea Old and New: A History.* Seoul: Ilchokak Publishers. 1990. 454 pp. (available in paperback). An invaluable resource for understanding the political development of Korea from early times to the 1990s. It is particularly strong in its coverage of political developments from the colonial period to modern times.

Kim, Byoung-Lo Philo. *Two Koreas in Development: A Comparative Study of Principles and Strategies of Capitalist and Communist Third World Development.* New Brunswick, NJ: Transaction Publishers. 1992. 210 pp. The book provides comparisons of the economic, political, and social development of both North and South Korea since 1945. One chapter is devoted to political development.

Oh, John Kie-chian. *Korean Politics: The Quest for Democratization and Economic Development.* Ithaca, NY: Cornell University Press. 1999. 257 pp. This is one of the finest books available on the evolution of democracy in South Korea. The author enlightens the reader about the impact of tradition on contemporary politics. It is an invaluable and engaging resource.

Oh, Kongdan, and Ralph C. Hassig. *North Korea through the Looking Glass.* Washington, DC: Brookings Institution Press. 2000. 256 pp. (available in paperback). A very informative but disturbing commen-

tary of the ideology, leadership, politics, and foreign policy of North
Korea in the 1990s.

Culture and Society

Arts of Korea. New York: Metropolitan Museum of Art. 1988. The cat-
alogue was published in conjunction with the opening of the Korean
Art gallery at the Metropolitan Museum of Art. Includes essays on
Korean history, ceramics, sculpture, and painting.

Breen, Michael. *The Koreans: Who They Are, What They Want, Where
Their Future Lies.* New York: Saint Martin's Press. 1998. 276 pp. An
informative, personal account of Korea and the Korean people today.

Clark, Donald N. *Christianity in Modern Korea.* Lanham, MD: University Press of America. 1986. 55 pp. This is considered one of the
most highly regarded books on Christianity in Korea and its role from
the late eighteenth century to recent times.

Clark, Donald N. *Culture and Customs of Korea.* Westport, CT:
Greenwood Press. 2000. 204 pp. An excellent introduction to the
Korean people and their religion, arts, literature, daily life, and customs. It includes a concise history of Korea and information on life
in North Korea today.

Covell, Jon Carter. *Korea's Colorful Heritage.* Seoul: Hollym Corporation. 1985. 128 pp. The author, a highly regarded art historian, provides background on varied elements of Korean culture, especially
the arts and religion. It includes beautiful illustrations.

Hur, Sonja Vegdahl, and Ben Seunghwa Hur. *Culture Shock! A Guide
to Customs and Etiquette.* Portland, OR: Graphic Arts Center Publishing Co. 1997. 247 pp. This is a very helpful guide for understanding Korean culture and customs. It is essential reading for businesspeople and travelers.

Kim, Joungwon, ed. *Koreana: Korean Cultural Heritage: Traditional
Lifestyles.* Seoul: Samsung Moonhwa Press. 1997. 264 pp. This is the
fourth volume in a series created by the Korea Foundation to foster
a better understanding of Korean studies abroad. It examines such
aspects as clothing, food, housing, family systems, rites of passage,

regional traditions, and folk culture. A wealth of beautiful photographs augments the text, bringing traditional culture alive.

Koo, John H., and Andrew C. Nahm, eds. *An Introduction to Korean History and Culture.* Elizabeth, NJ: Hollym Corporation. 1997. 475 pp. An ideal introduction to Korean culture.

Lee, O-Young. *Things Korean.* Rutland, VT: Charles E. Tuttle Company. 1994. 145 pp. O-Young Lee, a former Korean minister of culture, provides a useful guide of traditional culture with over 100 memorable photographs and illustrations. The Korean enthusiast will treasure this book.

Saccone, Richard. *The Business of Korean Culture.* Seoul: Hollym Corporation. 1994. An extraordinarily helpful and interesting guide to customs and etiquette.

Yi, Kun Moon. *The National Museum of Korea.* Seoul: National Museum of Korea. 1998. 282 pp. The catalogue includes a clearly written text and photographs of Korean art from early times through the Choson dynasty.

PERIODICALS

Education about Asia. Published three times a year. This eighty-page illustrated magazine includes articles, book reviews, and lessons about Korea. For subscriptions: Association for Asian Studies, 1021 E. Huron St., Ann Arbor, MI 48104-9876.

Korea Focus: On Current Topics. Published bimonthly by the Korea Foundation. This publication provides timely articles on recent events and current issues. An invaluable resource for keeping up-to-date with developments in Korea. The Foundation's Web site (http://www.kf.or.kr) provides the full text of *Korea Focus* articles. For subscriptions: Korea Foundation, Seocho P.O. Box 227, Seoul, Korea.

Korea Journal. The Korea Journal publishes scholarly papers, book reviews or book notes, and translations of Korean literary works including short stories, poetry, and drama. Published quarterly by the Korean National Commission for UNESCO. Articles include information on ancient, traditional, and contemporary Korea. For further information: e-mail kj@mail.unesco.or.kr.

Korea Observer. A quarterly journal published by the Institute of Korean Studies, a private non-profit research institute, founded in 1968, for the purpose of encouraging Korean studies, especially in the fields of the humanities and the social sciences, and for promoting cultural exchanges with other nations. e-mail: INST68@chollian.net

KoreAm Journal. The journal is published monthly nationwide to provide a forum for English-speaking Korean Americans. It includes feature stories, poetry, fiction, artwork, and photographs. E-mail: koream@koreamjournal.com. www.koreamjournal.com

Korean Culture. Published quarterly by the Korean Cultural Center of the Korean Consulate General in Los Angeles. The journal offers articles on a wide range of subjects pertaining to the traditional and contemporary culture of Korea. Korean Cultural Center, 5505 Wilshire Blvd., Los Angeles, CA 90036-3892. Web site: http://www.kccla.org.

Koreana: Korean Art and Culture. Published quarterly by the Korea Foundation. This magazine includes articles on Korea's past and present, people, travel, the Internet, events, and exhibits. Beautiful photographs of Korea are included in every issue. The Foundation provides on-line access to abstracts of *Koreana* articles and their accompanying photos at: http://www.kf.or.kr/koreafocus. For subscriptions: The Korea Foundation, C.P.O. Box 2147, Seoul, Korea.

Korean Studies. A semiannual journal published by the University of Hawaii Center for Korean Studies. This publication "seeks to further scholarship on Korea by providing a forum for discourse on timely subjects, and addresses a variety of scholarly topics through interdisciplinary and multicultural articles, book reviews, and essays in the humanities and social sciences." *Korean Studies* is now available in the Project MUSE electronic database. Web site: http://muse.jhu. edu/journals/ks/.

RECOMMENDED LITERATURE

Buck, Pearl S. *The Living Reed.* Wakefield, RI: Moyer Bell. 1996. 478 pp. The famous author of *The Good Earth* also wrote a fine novel about Korea. The *Living Reed* is a poignant story based on factual material from the 1860s to the division of Korea in 1945. There are memorable accounts of the experiences of families during the Japanese colonial period.

Choi, Sook Nyul. *The Year of Impossible Goodbyes*. Boston: Houghton Mifflin Company. 1993. 169 pp. (available in paperback). A moving story about what happens to the members of a family who lived in North Korea in 1945, their joy at the end of the war, the beginning of Soviet occupation, and their courageous flight to the South.

Kim, Richard E. *Lost Names: Scenes from a Korean Boyhood*. Berkeley: University of California Press. 1988. 198 pp. (available in paperback). Richard Kim creates vivid scenes from childhood at the height of Japanese occupation. It is a memorable story of courage and endurance.

Lee, Helie. *In the Absence of Sun*. New York: Harmony Books. 450 pp. Release date April 2002. The author recounts her American family's risky attempt to rescue her uncle from North Korea, the most isolated and tyrannical regime in the world. Her book is the sequel to *Still Life with Rice*.

Lee, Helie. *Still Life with Rice*. New York: Scribners. 1996. 320 pp. (available in both hardcover and paperback). While focusing on the remarkable life of her grandmother, Helie Lee provides memorable images of Japanese and Soviet occupation and civil war. The book is not only a tribute to her grandmother's will to survive, but to the courage of the Korean people.

Potok, Chaim. *I Am the Clay*. New York: Ballantine Books. 1992. 241 pp. (available in paperback). The acclaimed author of *The Chosen* and veteran of the Korean War writes a very moving short story of the experience of a family during the war.

INTERNET

Information on Korea is available on numerous Web sites. This list includes some of the most helpful sources.

http://www.bok.or.kr The Bank of Korea (financial information) http://www.bluehouse.go.kr/english The Blue House/President of the Republic of Korea

http://www.chosun.com Chosun Ilbo, a major newspaper

http://www.han.com/gateway.html Gateway to Korea includes links to news, travel, business, arts and entertainment, research, universities, organizations, and Internet sites.

http://www.knto.or.kr The Korean National Tourism Organization

http://www.kois.go.kr The Korea Overseas Culture and Information Service. It is a window to Korea and one of the most comprehensive sites.

http://www.koreaherald.co.kr The Korea Herald Newspaper

http://korea.insights.co.kr It includes all sorts of information from history to culture, philosophy, and religion—in such media as text, images, and audio.

http://korea.net A portal site created by the Korea Information Service to provide information about Korea in English. It contains links to 11,000 English sites from Korea and other countries. It provides news (http://news.korea.net) and provides other services such as BBS, Chat, Clubs, and Games.

http://www.koreanwar.org The Korean War

http://www.koreatimes.co.kr Korea Times Newspaper

http://www.mct.go.kr Ministry of Culture and Tourism

http://www.moca.go.kr National Museum of Contemporary Arts

http://www.museum.go.kr The National Museum of Korea

http://nk.chosun.com/english Information about North Korea

http://www.nso.go.kr National Statistics Office

http://www.ocp.go.kr The Office of Cultural Properties

http://www.skas.org/ The Society of Korean-American Scholars includes an online directory of Korean-American Web sites.

http://www.state.govt The U.S. Department of State provides extensive up-to-date information on both North and South Korea.

http://www.thesaladbowl.com/mjpark/index.html *Things Korean I and II* was created by a student who studied and traveled in South Korea in 2001. There are many photographs accompanied by an engaging commentary.

http://www.2.hawaii.edu/~asiaref/korea/internet.htm The University of Hawaii lists extensive Internet resources on Korea.

WEB SITES FOR LEARNING KOREAN

There is an online course for learning the Korean language. It is accessible anywhere at anytime. It was developed by the Korean Language Education Center of Seoul National University. Since Korean is now an SAT subject exam, the study of Korean has become very popular among Korean-American students. KoreanTutor manages each subscriber's progress and provides a study guide based on a student's strengths and weaknesses. Additional information is available at sjchoi@koreantutor.com.

Additional Web sites to assist with learning Korean are as follows:
http://languagelab.bh.indiana.edu/korean.html
http://www.interedu.go.kr
http://www.Korean.sogang.ac.kr
http://catcode.com/kintro/

CD-ROMS

Facts About Korea 2001. 2001. Seoul: Korean Information Service (KOIS). *Facts About Korea* contains hundreds of pages of information and multimedia material on Korea.

Korea Folk Art Festival. 1995. Seoul: Ministry of Culture and Sports. Multimedia introduction to the rich world of Korean folk arts—farmer's music (nongak), folk drama, folk games, and folk songs—based on the Korea Folk Art Festivals held in the 1990s.

Korean Culture: The First Twenty Years. 2001. Los Angeles: Korean Cultural Center. Contains pictures, quick-time videos, and sounds introducing Korean culture and, more importantly, all of the articles and artwork contained in the first twenty years of *Korean Culture* magazine (1980–1999), which is widely used in classrooms throughout the West, where reliable information on Korean civilization remains scarce.

Korean through English. 1995. Seoul: Ministry of Cultural and Sports. Contains three interactive textbooks to help students coming from an English-speaking background learn to read, write, and speak in the Korean language.

Touch the Spirit. 1995. Seoul: Korean National Tourism Organization. Contains photos, quick-time movies, and sounds introducing Korea's scenic spots and great vacation getaways. It also contains materials and contact information to help plan a vacation or trip to Korea.

A Window on Korea. 1994. Seoul: Korean Overseas Information Service (KOIS). Contains pictures, text, music, and video introducing Korean history, society, customs, and economy with a navigable text.

A Window on Korea 2. 1998. Seoul: Korean Overseas Information Service (KOIS). Contains a comprehensive overview of Korea, with over 500 pages of detailed navigable text and a searchable index. Photos, quick-time movies, and sounds are integrated for a multimedia experience. Links to Internet homepages are provided for quick access to updated information.

FILMS/VIDEOS

Videos for the classroom are available through the Korea Society, Consulates General, and Korean Cultural Centers. To purchase or rent videos on Korea, check the Web site of Films for the Humanities and Sciences (www.films.com), Filmakers Library (www.filmakers.com), First Run Icarus Films (www.echony.com/~frif), and the Social Studies School Service (www.socialstudies.com).

To obtain information on how to acquire a specific video or advice about media resources, contact the Asian Educational Media Service (http://www.aems.uiuc.edu). The service publishes a newsletter.

Few feature films with English subtitles are available. The following two films are exceptional and very appreciated by American audiences.

Ch'unhyang. Im Kwon-taek's film based on one of Korea's most famous folk tales. Beautiful cinematography, traditional costumes, and the hauntingly beautiful sounds of p'ansori. Released in 2001. English subtitles. Available through Amazon.com. (Search for Chunhyang).

Sop'yonje. Im Kwon-taek's award winning film. A memorable film that touches one's heart and introduces the audience to the sounds of p'ansori. Set in Korea in the 1950s and 1960s. English subtitles. Available through Korean Cultural Centers and the Korean Embassy in Washington, D.C.

A film *(P'yongyang Diaries)* on North Korea is available for rent or purchase from First Run Icarus Films. *P'yongyang Diaries* is a remarkable film simply for the fact of being made. It provides a much-needed counterbalance to the available print and film resources, which are almost entirely devoted to South Korea.

Index

About the Author

Mary E. Connor is the senior member of the history department at Westridge School in Pasadena, California. She received the Korea Society Fellowship to study and travel in South Korea during the summer of 2000. She is on the curriculum committee for the National Council for Social Studies.